Endorsements for *Beat the Odds*

*"**Beat the Odds** is the playbook every manager should read to be sure of winning beyond the next few quarters."*

—**Lee Iacocca**

"Hurray! A business book wh ... rs/entrepreneurs but anyone involved in buildi ... ness. One of the most important points you sh ... dds is the critical importance of creating fluid mechanisms and ideas that will shape the future of your organisation. Unlike so many other management authors, Rudzki's ideas are authentic."

—**Anita Roddick**, Founder, The Body Shop

"If you've ever wondered why some companies seem to go on and on like stars in the sky and other companies seem to shine brightly like meteors, only to disappear too quickly, this book is for you. If you are working for a company and you want it to be a star and not a meteor, you should read this book.

"The author has distilled his vast experience into easy-to-understand principles that can make a positive difference in how today's companies perform. Real examples from the corporate world make a convincing case."

—**John A. Jordan, Jr.**, Retired Senior Vice President,
Bethlehem Steel Corporation

*"**Beat the Odds** is both insightful and enjoyable to read. Bob Rudzki writes from a different perspective in a manner that is very readable. His crisp message on the nine principles for success, which are profiled with excellent current real-life case examples, provides clear direction for managers on how to ensure their companies win. **Beat the Odds** is a book you must use when developing your company's strategy and ensuring its tactical execution."*

—**Avner Schneur**, Founder, President and CEO, Emptoris, Inc.

*"**Beat the Odds** introduces a logical framework for predicting whether companies are likely to sustain success not just in the short term, but for decades to come. The book brings real examples forward and challenges common beliefs about organizations. It is a great read for anyone trying to understand long-term company performance."*

—**Martin Barkman**, Senior Vice President,
Commercial Operations, SmartOps Corporation

"*Beat the Odds* provides a practical roadmap for executives in companies of all sizes seeking to improve their management effectiveness. The author's sound advice and illustrative examples capture the lessons learned from decades of personal experience spanning a variety of industries. This book is an easy, insightful, and eminently worthwhile read."

—**Leonard Sherman**, Ph.D.,
Senior Lecturer, Northeastern University,
Former President, Accenture Procurement Solutions

"*Beat the Odds* is a valuable handbook for anyone interested in ensuring the viability of his/her organization. Following its principles will increase the reader's effectiveness in today's complex and challenging business environments. Bob Rudzki knows what he is talking about, combines solid research with years of experience, and presents the practical application of theory to real-world stories of success and failure.

"*This is a must-read book that will deepen your understanding of the opportunities before you, and guide you to making a big difference in the long-term success and sustainability of your organization.*"

—**Carol Weber**, Principal, the Cahill-Weber Group
and Visiting Professor, Darden Graduate School of Business,
University of Virginia

"*The 'building blocks of organizational success' identified by Rudzki aren't new concepts, but the clear-headed explanation of their ordering and interrelationships reflects a seasoned insight. My 40 years' experience in industry and leadership positions resonates with his perspective.* ***Beat the Odds*** *provides a framework to help the serious manager find sustainable success and avoid getting lost in the forest of fads.*"

—**Thomas J. Wonsiewicz**, President, Lane Enterprises, Inc.

"*Beat the Odds* illustrates that the long-term viability of a corporation is more than just about strategy and metrics, it's about core business principles and continuous diagnosis. Bob Rudzki's nine principles for long-term organizational health and success are something that every leader who thinks about the future should read and follow."

—**John M. Anderson**, Vice President and Partner, A.T. Kearney, Inc.

Beat the Odds

Avoid Corporate Death and Build a Resilient Enterprise

Beat the Odds

Avoid Corporate Death and Build a Resilient Enterprise

Robert A. Rudzki

ISBN-10: 1-932159-68-1
ISBN-13: 978-1-932159-68-4

Printed and bound in the U.S.A. Printed on acid-free paper
10 9 8 7 6 5 4 3 2 1

Library of Congress Cataloging-in-Publication Data

Rudzki, Robert A., 1953-
Beat the odds : avoid corporate death and build a resilient enterprise / by Robert A. Rudzki.
p. cm.
Includes bibliographical references and index.
ISBN-10: 1-932159-68-1 (softcover : alk. paper)
ISBN-13: 978-1-932159-68-4 (softcover : alk. paper)
1. Industrial management. 2. Success in business. 3. Business failures—Prevention. I. Title.
HD31.R7965 2007
658.4—dc22 2006038380

Direct all inquiries to J. Ross Publishing, Inc., 5765 N. Andrews Way, Fort Lauderdale, FL 33309.

Phone: (954) 727-9333
Fax: (561) 892-0700
Web: www.jrosspub.com

DEDICATION

This book is dedicated to my father, Eugene M. Rudzki, who beat the odds in many ways.

My father:

- *Survived the invasion of Poland, 1939, and the battle to defend Warsaw*
- *Survived wounds incurred while seeking to reach Allied lines and survived capture by the Soviets*
- *Survived a Soviet concentration camp*
- *Survived the Italian campaign and the battle of Monte Casino in World War II (decorated officer of the Polish 2nd Army fighting alongside the British)*
- *Survived a journey from Italy to England, where he continued his engineering studies and also learned English, then to Canada, and finally to the United States, to establish his family in the land of opportunity*
- *Survived corporate life and politics in American business*

Dad faced tremendous odds during his lifetime and beat them all. And, while not a survivor of his final battle, the battle with cancer, my father demonstrated how to beat the odds—once again—and win the war against cancer by maintaining good humor and a spiritual perspective.

TABLE OF CONTENTS

About the Author .... **xi**

Acknowledgments .... **xiii**

Part I. Understanding the Reasons Underlying Success and Failure

Chapter 1. Introduction 3

Chapter 2. Why Nine Principles? (Aren't There Enough Business Books Already?) 9

Part II. The Building Blocks of Success: Nine Principles for Organizational Fitness and Success

Chapter 3. Principle 1: Establish a Purpose 17

Chapter 4. Principle 2: Live and Defend Your Core Values 27

Chapter 5. Principle 3: Create the Future 35

Chapter 6. Principle 4: Articulate an Inspiring Vision—and Lead! 43

Chapter 7. Principle 5: Develop the Right Strategy, Business Models, and Competencies 55

Chapter 8. Principle 6: Align and Energize the Organization 69

Chapter 9. Principle 7: Measure Only What You Want to Achieve 77

Chapter 10. Principle 8: Decide! Act! Get on with It! 87

Chapter 11. Principle 9: When in Doubt, Apply Common Sense 97

Chapter 12. Implications for the Organization and for Individuals 103

Part III. Profiles of Success: Three That Are Beating the Odds

Chapter 13. Six Generations and Still Strumming: Martin Guitar 109

Chapter 14. Starting Off on the Right Foot: LANXESS Corporation 125
Chapter 15. Retooling the Management Tool Kit: ITT Corporation 137

Part IV: Next Steps
Chapter 16. The Path to Ensuring Long-Term Health 155
Chapter 17. Reader Exercises Illustrating the Nine Principles 163

Epilogue: Making a Difference Starts Here...177

Appendix A. Assessment and Diagnosis Templates 179

Appendix B. Quotable Quotes 215

Source Notes 229

Index 235

ABOUT THE AUTHOR

Robert A. Rudzki is a former corporate senior executive who is now President of Greybeard Advisors LLC, a firm that helps enterprises improve their near-term financial performance and long-term business viability (**www.GreybeardAdvisors.com**). He is also a director of a security software company and an advisory board member of several companies. In the course of his 30-year career, Rudzki has held a wide range of executive management positions in finance, accounting, procurement and logistics, and business development, and has had P & L responsibility overseeing a group of successful services businesses. As a result of his career assignments, he has had the unique opportunity to interact with hundreds of executives and companies, and to study first-hand their efforts at achieving success, or triggering failure. During his corporate career, he was Senior Vice President at Bayer Corp., where he led a nationally recognized transformation effort that contributed to substantial performance improvements. Before Bayer, he was a senior executive at Bethlehem Steel Corp., where his initiatives led to the steelmaker's recognition as one of *Purchasing* magazine's Best Places to Work and to a top-quartile ranking in a best practices survey of 160 global corporations. Rudzki is coauthor of the best-selling supply management book *Straight to the Bottom Line™: An Executive's Roadmap to World-Class Supply Management* and is also a regular speaker at professional conferences and senior management summits. He can be reached at: **rudzki@GreybeardAdvisors.com**.

ACKNOWLEDGMENTS

This book is about the mortality of organizations (which numerous studies have suggested is a statistical inevitability) and how you can delay or entirely avoid that fate. In an interesting parallel, recent developments in human medical science suggest that human mortality may be on the verge of a breakthrough. Some scientists, including Ray Kurzweil, believe that medical science will advance so much in the next few decades that, for all practical purposes, human death can be avoided.[1]

In spite of these intriguing trends and dramatic projections, there comes a time in one's life when you realize that perhaps you should share your accumulated learnings and perspectives with others, before running up against your own limits of mortality, whatever they may be. Doing so can take many forms: participating in civic and nonprofit organizations, tutoring, mentoring, presenting ideas at professional conferences, writing articles, even writing a book. Each of these endeavors offers professional and personal satisfaction. Each requires a support base to be successful.

My network of support for this book was very straightforward. My parents, Eugene and Fiorina Rudzki, through their mastery of English as a second language and their insistence that their children excel in communication skills and all subjects, ensured that the basic tools were present for professional success. They offered enthusiastic support for this project as it progressed over the years, just as they did for all of my professional activities.

My wife, Nancy Eleanor, a great partner in so many things, proved to be a valuable partner on this project as well. She provided insightful reactions to how the initial manuscript was organized and offered candid editorial suggestions during the redrafting. My son Alexander, as a youngster during the early stages of this project, was the expert behind creating many of the graphics included in the manuscript. Later, as a successful entrepreneur during high school and college, he made additional suggestions for the near-final manuscript. And my younger children, Edward and Elizabeth, offered support in their own special ways.

I owe special thanks to a group of deeply talented people who reviewed the evolving framework and the emerging manuscript and offered constructive feedback that improved the content and the clarity. They were not just readers; they represented key perspectives: senior executives of large corporations, CEOs of midsize companies, senior partners in consulting and legal firms (who, by their very role of interacting with senior management, see a lot of good and bad in business), senior bank officers, retired military officers, executive directors of nonprofit organizations, and leadership and organizational development consultants. I would in particular like to acknowledge the following for their valuable input: Bryan Anderson, Ben Boylston, Eleanor Boylston, Mike Daniel, Randy Dearth, Donna Bodek Goss, Jack Jordan, Bruce Klassen, Melissa Plotsky, Tom O'Neill, Rohan Paul, Don Robertson, Len Sherman, and Tom Wonsiewicz. I also acknowledge the thoughtful early editorial suggestions by my sister-in-law Susanna Boylston.

I want to highlight the important role of professional writer and editor John Kerr, of Ergo Editorial Services, Inc. (Stow, Massachusetts), who I enlisted to interview and investigate the three remarkable organizations that are profiled in Part III. John's critical and unbiased perspective was essential not only to writing three case study chapters, but he provided a final litmus test of the validity and usefulness of the *Beat the Odds* framework. John also provided valuable recommendations for improving the rest of the manuscript as it approached the delivery date to the publisher. Any shortfalls in follow-through rest solely with me.

The largest group of "contributors" to acknowledge is composed of the many executives and companies that I had the good fortune to interact with over the years. Representing former colleagues, peers in other organizations, suppliers, customers, financial institutions, start-up companies, even non-profit organizations, this extensive pool of organizations and their employees became my de facto research pool. I've used some of their specific experiences and stories in various parts of the text, disguised in some cases for reasons that will be obvious as you read on. Their real-life successes and failures, and the lessons learned, became the practical spark that ignited my professional interest in identifying, developing, testing, and—ultimately—sharing the fundamental framework and diagnostic tools explained in this book.

—R. A. Rudzki

Part I

UNDERSTANDING THE REASONS UNDERLYING SUCCESS AND FAILURE

1

INTRODUCTION

Why do senior executives dutifully submit to annual physical exams but don't take the same kind of preemptive approach to the organizations they run? Why do they undergo an array of tests to gather facts and uncover subtle issues before they emerge into full-fledged personal health problems, yet they "wing it" when it comes to the organization's diagnosis?

It's a very significant concern, and one that has bothered me over the years. Corporations are living organisms too, and their basic design allows them to outlast their human founders. But many corporations have the seeds of terminal illness deep within them today. Left unidentified or unaddressed, those malignant cells can bring down a corporation long before its founders reach retirement.

The numbers bear this out. In the United States alone, there have been more than 600,000 outright business failures (bankruptcies) in the past 10 years.[1] An often-referenced source, an internal study of long-lived corporations by Royal Dutch/Shell, noted that only a handful of corporations have survived and prospered for more than a century.[2] Bethlehem Steel, once an icon of American business, almost reached its ninety-ninth birthday, then had no more. (Interestingly, General Motors' troubles appeared to be peaking as GM achieved its ninety-ninth birthday in early 2006.)

In another study, 1,008 companies were studied for the period 1962 to 1998. Only 160 of them survived this 36-year span.[3] The inescapable conclusion is that there are factors at work that limit a corporation's life expectancy to less than 50 years.

Beat the Odds sets out to offer a framework for diagnosis—one that if acted upon positively and decisively can help ensure that an organization enjoys robust good health over a long life. Three factors drove me to research and write the book. First, as a senior officer at a longtime North American manufacturing corporation that eventually collapsed, I often noted the absence of, and inattention to, many of the principles laid out in this book. Worse, I observed the presence of many destructive behaviors that acted like cancerous cells on the overall health of the organization.

Second, I knew that the stakes for businesses are becoming higher. Globalization creates threats and opportunities, for both revenues and cost structure. Ditto with the increased transparency of information. Shorter product life cycles have turned the competitive battle into one of innovation and speed. At the same time, managers must now manage not only across their organizations but across the "extended enterprise," including their key suppliers. And earnings growth has become an excruciating challenge. As documented by consulting firm Bain & Company, "profitable growth is becoming increasingly elusive and more fleeting for most companies, and . . . this is likely to be even more true during the coming decade."[4]

My third motivator is perhaps the most pressing. It's not so much that many executives—including those who religiously read the business best sellers—still don't "get it." It's that there are still too many examples of dysfunctional companies—symptomatic of executives who refuse to get it. Clearly there is still a message to be sent.

Preeminent business thinker Peter F. Drucker once noted that there are only three things certain in business: confusion, friction, and malperformance. One hypothesis underlying this book is that the problem described by Drucker is actually compounded by the aggressively dysfunctional behavior of leaders and managers. If you were to view their individual and collective actions with a clinical eye, those individuals seem *intent on creating* the confusion, friction, and malperformance that Drucker wrote about. Don't believe it? Just one piece of evidence: The comic feature *Dilbert* draws its enormous popularity from explicitly poking fun at such dysfunctional behavior. Creator Scott Adams credits his readers with providing many of the anecdotes—based on their own real-life work experiences—that inspire Dilbert's daily world.

While there is no shortage of top-notch business texts that address aspects of business success, there has not yet been a successful "unified theory" for organizational excellence. What is needed is an approach that identifies all of the relevant pieces and insights and then links them in a powerful, easy-to-remember, and easy-to-use framework of foundation principles.

Beat the Odds offers a nine-part framework that places just as much emphasis on little-discussed qualitative elements such as "purpose" and a get-it-done bias for action as it does on quantitative metrics. Blending clear descriptions of straightforward principles with real-life case studies and self-assessment tools that readers can begin to apply immediately, the book helps cut through the complexity that regularly distracts senior managers and derails improvement initiatives. *Beat the Odds* does not profile only those few companies that have lived 100-plus years, because that would mean studying only part of the equation. By including explorations of companies that have failed and others that have swung from periodic success to near failure, additional insights become available.

The book comprises four parts. Part I answers the question: "Why Nine Principles? (Aren't There Enough Business Books Already?)" It notes that quite a few of the companies highlighted in previous books on organizational performance have toppled off their pedestals. Similarly, some of those that have earned distinction as *Fortune* magazine's "Most Admired Companies" have fallen on hard times just a few years after being celebrated. Over a longer period, the Fortune 500 listing has seen some remarkable shifts as formerly great companies have fallen swiftly down the rankings and in some cases disappeared altogether. Part I explains why that can happen and lays the groundwork for each of the nine principles for sustainable organizational fitness and success.

The book's second part is its core—a detailed breakdown of each of the nine "Beat the Odds" principles. Each breakdown includes the following:

- A case illustration that introduces the principle and shows how attention to that principle will affect an organization's health and success
- A detailed description and explanation of the principle itself
- One or more well-known companies that exemplify effective commitment to that principle, and the resulting contribution to the organization's success
- One or more well-known companies that exhibit outrageous neglect of the principle, and the resulting damage to each organization

- An honor roll of companies that have been doing a commendable job of sticking to the principle, and dog house candidates that have done a remarkably poor job
- Key questions that the reader can use to begin assessing how well his or her organization adheres to the principle
- A "Yes, but ... " section giving some of the classic arguments with which resistant senior managers may push back, along with a recommended response

Part III walks the reader through real-life narratives that explore the totality of the nine principles as applied by three very different organizations. These lively "inside stories" illustrate how energized and aligned leadership teams in companies large and small, public and private, can harness the nine principles framework to secure their organizations' long-term success.

The last part of the book outlines Next Steps that will help generate the necessary insights and apply the nine principles to ensure success. In Appendix A, you will find detailed Assessment and Diagnostic Templates that are designed to assist you in pursuing Next Steps analysis and planning. These templates are based upon the key questions posed in Part II; used properly, they can provide deep insight into your organization's underlying challenges along with the factual basis for corrective action. The takeaway is this: Don't guess—assess! The next appendix, B, contains quotes from notable sources intended to inspire and entertain.

Part IV also illustrates other situations that relate to the nine success principles, and it asks the reader to analyze each situation. My goal is to make it easier for readers to identify where their organizations are versus where they should be—the all-important gap analysis. In addition, by highlighting the consequences of dysfunctional behavior, I hope to provide the motivation and the framework to help you commit to change on a personal basis, and as part of a more effective leadership team.

Each of us can be an agent of constructive change. In the long run, achieving positive change—in yourself, in your organization—can itself be one of your most rewarding and satisfying accomplishments. So if you find yourself in a "Dilbert-esque" situation, don't despair. Use the framework presented in this book to trigger vigorous dialogue and a rigorous assessment of your organization (or your part of it). That's the critical first step to building an effective corrective action plan that can impact the long-term health and success of your organization. It's also a necessary step to ensure that work is personally and professionally satisfying. Since our workdays occupy far more than half of our waking hours, work *deserves* to be satisfying. It should even be fun.

If you're not meeting these straightforward objectives in your working life, you owe it to yourself, your coworkers, and your company to pursue change in the organization. And if that option is not viable or not palatable? You've got one more choice: Find another situation where there is a better match.

2

WHY NINE PRINCIPLES? (AREN'T THERE ENOUGH BUSINESS BOOKS ALREADY?)

As I was heading into the final stretch of writing this book, I came across an article in my local newspaper headlined "Companies in 'Built to Last' Crumble Over Time" (see Figure 2.1). The article reviewed some of the "great" companies profiled in best sellers such as *Built to Last* and *In Search of Excellence* and looked at how they fared some years later. The story emphasized that quite a few of the previously identified "excellent" or "great" companies are no longer quite so great.[1] Is this further proof that the infamous "front-page jinx" really exists, or is there something more fundamental at work?

This book is designed to answer that question. I describe a fundamental framework that, if consistently addressed and applied as part of an organization's strategic guidance, will help to ensure long-term viability and success regardless of the economic, financial, regulatory, and technology factors that so forcefully buffet organizations today. The central theme in *Beat the Odds* is about building a resilient organization—one that can readily deal with and bounce back from the myriad surprises lurking in today's tangled and volatile business environment.

The ideas in this book are not the conclusions of academicians or uninvolved observers of business. The power and relevance of each of the nine principles have been demonstrated by a number of experienced business

Companies in 'Built to Last' crumble over time

Author says book was written to show principles of greatness.

By Peter Robison
Of Bloomberg News

Starbucks Corp. Chief Executive Officer Orin Smith says he was so taken with "Built to Last," a 1994 bestseller about 18 "visionary" companies, that he invited co-author Jim Collins to lecture top managers. Cypress Semiconductor Corp. CEO Thurman Rodgers calls it a "must-read."

Michael Holland, who manages $500 million at Holland & Co. in New York, hasn't read the book and says he doesn't want to.

"When you see stories about the world's smartest CEO or the world's greatest company, it usually is an indication that the stock's best days are behind it," Holland said.

Seven of the 18 companies featured in "Built to Last," including Boeing Co., Walt Disney Co. and Motorola Inc., have lagged the stock performance of rivals since the book was published on Oct. 26, 1994. Marriott Corp. split up, while Tokyo's Sony Corp. expects profit this year of less than half last year's 115 billion yen ($1.11 billion) as its stock trades at the April 1997 price.

As investment guides, management books often aren't built to last. "In Search of Excellence," a 1982 bestseller by Tom Peters and Robert Waterman, praised Atari Inc. two years before parent Warner Communications Inc. sold the computer-game maker, and hailed Levi Strauss & Co., a company that has had declining sales for the past seven years.

"Good to Great," Collins's latest bestseller, lauded supermarket owner Kroger Co. and drugmaker Abbott Laboratories.

Both stocks have tumbled more than 20 percent since the book's publication on Oct.

BOOKS PAGE D3

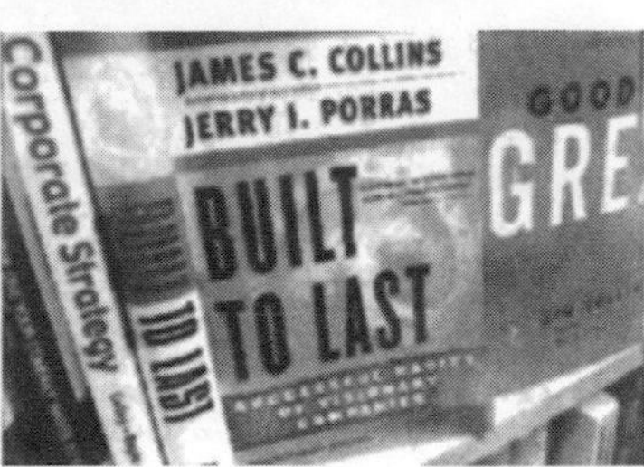

Daniel Acker Bloomberg News

'BUILT TO LAST,' a book by James Collins and Jerry Porras, sits on display at a Borders bookstore in New York.

Figure 2.1 Companies are not built to last. (Source: *Pittsburgh Post-Gazette*, April 8, 2004. Reprinted with permission.)

practitioners who have lived through the successes and failures of organizations, large and small, public and private, new and old.

The "Beat the Odds" concept first took shape during my personal experiences as a young officer of a well-known, struggling Fortune 500 American company: Bethlehem Steel. In its heyday, Bethlehem was viewed as one of corporate America's premier corporations—indeed one of the world's finest. Today, it symbolizes the formerly "great" organizations that fell to follower status and finally to "roadkill."

The basic "Beat the Odds" framework crystallized during those difficult years and was forged in the heat of an historic struggle for existence as the company approached but fell short of its ninety-ninth birthday. The concept evolved during my roles as a board or advisory board member of several private companies, and it was refined during interactions with hundreds of executives and companies when I was the chief procurement executive for the North American operations of Bayer, the long-lived European-headquartered conglomerate.

Gradually the framework began to fit the contours of a book, and eventually the completed framework and the manuscript were tested with an outstanding group of knowledgeable reviewers, including senior business executives, commercial bankers, senior management consultants, partners in major law firms, entrepreneurs, and organizational transformation experts. The framework was tested with input from executives of for-profit organizations with annual revenues ranging from $70 million to almost $10 billion. It was also used to guide the start-up phase of a now-successful software company. The diagnostic described later in the book has been applied with good results to companies as young as five years and as mature as 173 years.

As noted in Chapter 1, history shows that it is difficult for organizations to last more than 50 years. Statistically, beating those odds is very difficult. It requires close and constant attention to a set of critical, basic truths (or "principles" as referred to in this book), and vigilance in avoiding violation of those principles. A very good leader who follows most of the principles can perhaps achieve success for a period of time. But sustainable success will necessitate attention to all nine principles, no matter how good the individual leader might be.

INTRODUCING THE NINE PRINCIPLES

Many of the building blocks for success are present at the birth of any enterprise. Often these building blocks are implicit; sometimes they are explicit. But in almost all cases where the organization proves successful, the founder(s) have gone through a process that involved many of the principles for success.

Over time, as the organization matures and the founders leave, it is easy for the leadership to lose touch with the entity's origins. As the organization grows and new employees come on board, opportunities for misalignment abound. With growing size and complexity, the focus naturally shifts to *managing* complexity—and the inevitable result is that there is less focus on *leading* for the future.

It is fair to say that the framework of nine principles is fundamentally a leadership framework. In *Beat the Odds,* you will not find much discussion about policy manuals, procedure manuals, information technology, controls, or "attention to detail." Nor will you find checklists for such matters as capital structure objectives, logistics, procurement, and capital investment policies. Why not? Because these factors flow naturally from the nine success principles. And if you don't continually attend to the nine principles, the rest won't matter.

However, that isn't an invitation to cherry-pick the nine principles, starting with those that might be expected to meet the least resistance. There is far greater and longer-lasting company-building advantage in embracing the framework as a whole rather than, say, deciding to develop a clear world view (part of Principle 3), or just deciding to implement an appropriate metrics system (part of Principle 7). In other words, the whole (all nine principles taken together) is far greater than the sum of the parts. Just one piece of evidence: Some of the companies commended for their excellence in adhering to one principle still face major challenges in stepping up to other principles. Until they address *all* the fundamentals, their long-term success may still be in question.

A relevant analogy is to think of an organization as a living entity. The analogy is developed more fully in Chapter 12, but for now, just consider this idea: Each principle acts much like the basic mental or physical processes that inform and compose a living entity. Take one or more of these basic processes away and the living entity suffers. Optimize all of them and the entire being will thrive.

FRAMEWORK FOR THE NINE PRINCIPLES

Let's take a brief glance at the nine principles for sustainable organizational health and success. Table 2.1 outlines the framework and provides a short description for each of the nine principles. Figure 2.2 portrays graphically how the nine principles build upon each other.

How many senior executives know, quantitatively, how they and their organizations rate on each of these nine basic principles? Not many. Yes, it's important to embrace the framework intellectually, but its real value comes from understanding where you are and developing a corrective action plan to improve the organization's status with regard to each principle and with regard to the totality of the entire framework. As I describe in Part IV, that is best achieved by obtaining an assessment from four different perspectives:

- Top management
- Future leaders (the high-potential candidates expected to rise quickly in the organization)
- All other employees
- External constituents (suppliers, customers, bankers, and community leaders who know your organization well)

Table 2.1 Short Description of Each Foundation Principle

Principle	Short Description
1. Establish a Purpose	The fundamental reason-to-be underlying the organization's existence. The reason society would say the organization should continue to exist and prosper. Explains "what" you are seeking to accomplish, from the society/customer perspective.
2. Live and Defend Your Core Values	The moral and behavioral guideposts for the organization. Explains "how" you will conduct yourself and what you value.
3. Acquire a World View/Create the Future	Comprehensively and continuously monitor and assess developments that could affect your industry or activity (current reality and trends). Envision the future possibilities, and work toward making an attractive future happen.
4. Articulate an Inspiring Vision/Lead	Communicate—in a manner that employees understand and are excited about—"where" the organization is heading. Build excitement, alignment, and energy around the direction. Provide necessary information so that employees at all levels can contribute to Principle 5. Lead into the future.
5. Develop Strategies/Business Models/Competencies Consistent with the Foregoing, and Linked to Each Other	Following from the first four principles, develop strategies and business models to achieve the vision/future, and address changing customer priorities in a manner that is profitable for the organization. Provide the necessary competencies (in-house or in association with others) to support future activities.
6. Assure the Organization Is Aligned and Energized	Provide simple structures, processes, rewards/consequences, to align the entire organization with the behaviors and direction desired. Energize the organization as well, to build excitement and commitment.
7. Measure What You Want to Achieve (Steps 1–6), and Nothing Else	Focus everyone's attention on a few key leading indicators (areas that are predictive of future performance). Monitor a few key lagging indicators as well (areas that reflect what just happened) in a Balanced Scorecard.
8. Decide! Act! Get on with It!	Display and encourage an action-oriented culture. Make things happen, consistent with the foregoing.
9. When in Doubt, Use Common Sense	In the final analysis, when in doubt use common sense. Refer back to the purpose you adopted, the values you live by, and the vision you articulated.

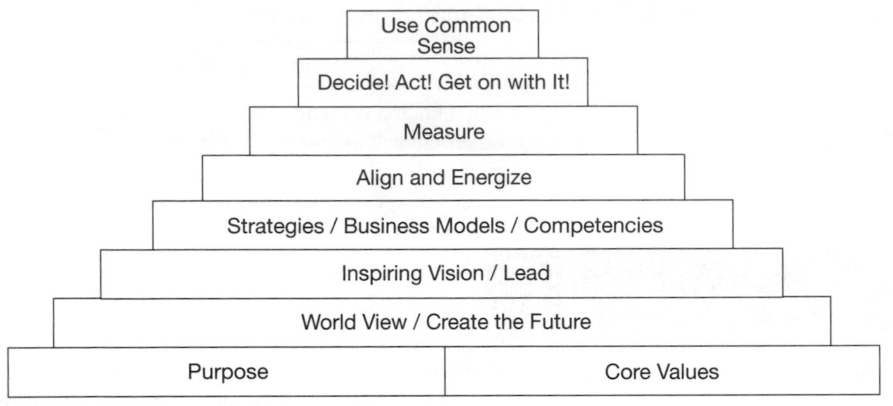

Figure 2.2 The building blocks of organizational success.

Obtaining an assessment from each of these perspectives, and then comparing those perspectives, can provide a wealth of insight and help create a roadmap for ensuring the future of your organization.

Let's turn now to Part II, where we'll explore each principle in depth.

Part II

THE BUILDING BLOCKS OF SUCCESS: NINE PRINCIPLES FOR ORGANIZATIONAL FITNESS AND SUCCESS

3

PRINCIPLE 1: ESTABLISH A PURPOSE

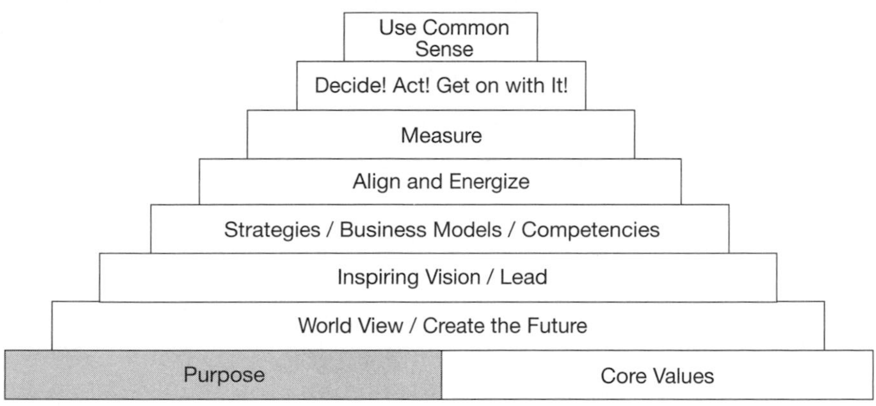

> "You are not here merely to make a living. You are here in order to enable the world to live more amply, with greater vision, with a finer spirit of hope and achievement. You are here to enrich the world, and you impoverish yourself if you forget the errand."
>
> —*Woodrow Wilson*

At most companies, the objective of "enriching the world" typically isn't found in the first paragraph of the chief executive's letter to shareholders. Yet some companies do embody that ideal while making a healthy profit and looking after their employees.

And then there are the companies that once lived up to that big objective but somehow let it slip away. A great case in point: Bethlehem Steel Corp., a manufacturing giant that once was an emblem of America's industrial might. Bethlehem Steel's rich history was characterized by such noble, early, and profitable "purposes" as the following:

- Helping to build America, by virtue of its heavy involvement in erecting many of the nation's first "skyline" skyscrapers and in building landmark structures such as the Golden Gate Bridge in San Francisco
- Helping to defend America during both world wars by providing armaments and battleships, including constructing more than 1,000 Liberty-class ships during World War II
- Helping to make America mobile by building equipment such as railroad cars and by providing materials for manufacturers of trucks, buses, and automobiles when America's transportation needs and infrastructure were booming

But in the last decades of the twentieth century, Bethlehem Steel ran into more and more challenges in its basic commodity business. Partly to raise cash and partly to "focus on its core," several generations of the company's leadership sold downstream operations. All of those operations were closer to end-use markets. Some of them had very attractive margins and growth prospects.

As the corporation neared its first century, and as its financial performance failed to improve, management continued its market retrenchment, cutting the field sales force, eliminating such "noncore" functions as competitive intelligence, and focusing heavily on head count efficiencies. After two decades of retrenchment, and with no distinctive financial performance relative to its competition, several senior Bethlehem managers were asked this question during a lunch break at an off-site meeting: "What is the *purpose* of our company?" The question was intended to determine what basic societal needs Bethlehem was addressing, such that the corporation deserved to survive and earn an acceptable profit. Although the managers gave compelling answers regarding Bethlehem's storied history, they were unable to suggest what the current or future purpose of the company was.

Not surprisingly, the lack of clear purpose contributed to problems at Bethlehem Steel. Employees were unsure of the future of the company and how they could contribute to its future success. Nontraditional competitors took advantage of the opportunities presented. The company's stock languished for many years, and the communities in which it did business no longer viewed Bethlehem as the driver of economic development that it once had been. Eventually, as a result of numerous fundamentals gone wrong, Bethlehem Steel filed for Chapter 11 bankruptcy protection, from which it did not emerge.

Sad though the story of Bethlehem Steel is, it provides a stark illustration of the need to have and to *hold onto* a fundamental purpose. Yes, of course, it is possible for an organization to have short-term "success" without having a defined "purpose." However, I'm not talking about success measured over a few quarters or even a few years. I'm talking about long-term, enduring success.

But what do I mean by "purpose"? Purpose is the *fundamental reason-to-be underlying the organization's existence.* It is perhaps best thought of as the organization's "North Star"—a perennial, perpetual guiding light. Increasing stockholder value is not synonymous with the purpose of the enterprise. Nor are boosting revenues or increasing profits, or any other traditional financial concepts and metrics. They are *objectives*—indispensable, of course, but they do not constitute a purpose.

Quite simply, a corporation's purpose can be viewed as the reason for society to conclude that the organization should continue to exist and prosper. Absent a clear answer to the question of which of society's needs it satisfies, the corporation's long-term success is in question. An organization's purpose is a keystone element—part of the critical foundation upon which ongoing success is built.

So is purpose just another name for social responsibility? It is not. Nor is it the same as a mission statement, which combines elements of other principles that we will address in other chapters. Corporate social responsibility (CSR) is indeed related to purpose, but it is not a substitute for having a fundamental purpose. CSR initiatives such as employment diversity, supplier diversity, environmental protection, safety, and corporate philanthropy are all important demonstrations of a company's value system, and often make good business sense as well, but they do not replace the critical need for an underlying purpose that benefits society either directly or indirectly.

Hewlett-Packard founder David Packard said it succinctly: "I think people assume, wrongly, that a company exists solely to make money. While this is an important result of a company's existence, we have to go deeper and find the real reasons for our being."[1] The enterprise's purpose provides guidance and inspiration to its employees. It also provides a framework for customers, suppliers, communities, and stockholders to understand and appreciate what the organization is seeking to achieve.

Purpose does not dictate specific areas of business activity, or even specific business strategies. It is not something to be accomplished by a certain date—to be checked off the "to do" list. And purpose must never change (nor should the organization's core values change, as I'll describe in the next chapter). Yet as the world changes around it, an organization may need to change its strategies, tactics, and practices in order to remain on a path true to achieving its purpose.

Organizations (for-profit *and* not-for-profit) that have a direct relationship with end users—the consumers of goods and services—may have an easier job constructing a purpose that links directly to generating some benefit to society. Then what do you do if your company is a *supplier* to the organizations that have those direct connections with end users? Does it make any sense to construct a purpose when you are one or more steps removed from those who may best perceive your purpose?

The short answer to that last question is "yes." Remember Bethlehem Steel's grand contributions to society. To be successful, your customers need to see you as part of how they satisfy *their* purpose.

Holding to a firm purpose is not without effort. It is all too easily subverted by short-term pressures and alternate management agendas. To catch a glimpse of how hard it can be to keep purpose held high, it's instructive to look at the case of The Walt Disney Co. For many decades Disney was clear about its purpose, namely, "To make people happy." Between 1984 and 1994, under the leadership of Michael Eisner and Frank Wells, Disney was reenergized and created enormous stockholder value by focusing on its purpose and its tremendous franchise, and executing well. That clear purpose and focus became somewhat diluted during the 1990s and early 2000s when Michael Eisner lost key members of his team to accidents (Frank Wells in a helicopter crash) and departures (Jeffrey Katzenberg). It was further aggravated as Eisner pursued the expensive acquisition of Capital Cities/ABC and as he presided over several corporate embarrassments, including the $140 million severance package for the 14-month tenure of Michael Ovitz. Some observers would say that Eisner's ego and micromanaging style further aggravated the loss of focus on Disney's purpose.

Eisner suffered an historic embarrassment in stockholder voting during the 2004 Disney annual meeting, and Disney itself was under attack by unwanted suitors. Let's be clear about one thing: Disney had other ills besides being distracted from its original purpose. For example, its board of directors was viewed for years as being composed of cronies of Mr. Eisner, suggesting that its corporate governance was weak. However, Disney's failure to maintain a clear, meaningful, and crisp focus on its original purpose—at the expense of executive egos and agendas—was a contributor to its performance difficulties. Not only was the all-too-famous Disney purpose lost in the shuffle, but in 2004, you could not even find Disney's purpose mentioned on the corporate Web site!

The Disney story is far from over. Disney's new CEO, Bob Iger, has embarked on a course of promptly addressing and correcting several of the fundamental miscues of the Eisner years. With regard to purpose, Iger hinted at the importance of reconnecting with Disney's roots when he commented that "animation is and will remain the heart and soul of Disney."[2] Shortly thereafter, Disney and Pixar Studios announced plans for Disney to acquire Pixar, making Pixar founder Steve Jobs the largest individual shareholder of Disney. Equally encouraging: Jobs, to his credit as a forthcoming Disney board member, uttered this statement about the Disney/Pixar deal: "Now everyone can focus on what is most important, creating innovative stories, characters, and films that delight millions of people around the world."[3] Between Iger and Jobs, Disney appears to have an excellent chance of returning to its core purpose, with all the attendant benefits.

WHO DOES "PURPOSE" WELL?

I've talked about companies that have not managed to hold onto purpose. There are so many more that don't have a clear purpose in the first place. But what about those that do? Following are a few of the corporations I would immediately put on an honor roll for their strong, clear purpose. Let's take a quick look at each of those honorees.

Merck. In a recent annual report, the pharmaceutical giant notes that the purpose of the company is " . . . to discover and develop the best of medicines and to bring those medicines to people everywhere."[4] Merck further supports its purpose in what it refers to as its five "values." Among them are two that clearly relate strongly to purpose and to Merck's understanding of purpose: (1) "Our business is preserving and improving human life. All of our actions must be measured by our success in achieving this goal." and (2) "We expect profits, but only from work that satisfies customer needs and benefits humanity."

Even though Merck is still struggling with court cases and reputation damage following multiple allegations that its Vioxx acute pain medication has caused deaths, the company remains true to the values that support its purpose. In September 2004, Merck voluntarily withdrew the drug and since then has been proactive in communicating about Vioxx to patients and doctors through publications such as the *New England Journal of Medicine* and via dedicated space on its corporate Web site, among other channels.

Procter & Gamble. Its purpose is combined with an expectation of the benefits of delivering on that purpose: "We will provide branded products and services of superior quality and value that improve the lives of the world's consumers. As a result, consumers will reward us with leadership sales, profit and value creation, allowing our people, our shareholders, and the communities in which we live and work to prosper."

Lowe's. This statement is found on the hardware chain's Web site: ". . . the company remains committed to offering quality home improvement products at the lowest prices, while delivering superior customer service." This simple declaration of purpose relates directly to what consumers in a developed, modern society are looking for.

Gerber. The baby food company makes these points on its Web site: "Gerber today is as dedicated to the well-being of babies all over the world, as it was when it began in 1928 . . . Gerber is committed to promoting good nutrition and healthy habits for children." Gerber's commitment to this purpose is supported by numerous corporate programs.

Medtronic. This medical products company, perhaps best known for its defibrillation products, personalizes its purpose in a unique manner. "Cofounder Earl Bakken presented the first Medtronic medallion to employees at Medtronic's 25th anniversary in 1974. Featuring the company's corporate symbol—a rising human figure—the medallion is personally presented to new employees by Earl or other senior executives at meetings held throughout the world." The corporate Web site goes on to note that the medallion ". . . symbolizes Medtronic's mission to contribute "toward full life" of patients.

The mission statement and the medallion unite Medtronic employees worldwide in a common goal—to "alleviate pain, restore health, and extend life in partnership with the medical community." In Medtronic's view, this shared mission has been fundamental to Medtronic's success and is the foundation for the company's future.[5]

Respironics. This leader in providing products and programs to manage sleep and respiratory disorders has a uniquely powerful approach to describing its purpose. It not only describes its core purpose in terms of value to the customer; it links that purpose to "core practices," many of which happen to coincide with key principles in the Beat the Odds framework (see Figure 3.1).[6]

CHECKLIST

As you consider whether or not your own organization has a strong and compelling purpose, ask yourself these questions:

- Do our organization's activities address one or more of society's fundamental needs?
- Does our organization have a clearly defined purpose, and is that purpose well understood by our employees and external constituents?
- Does our purpose provide guidance and inspiration to our employees?
- Does top management regularly speak about our purpose?
- Are we true to our purpose?

YES, BUT . . .

So you're skeptical that purpose makes a difference—or your boss is. You're certain that your chief operating officer or chief financial officer will greet your proposal to discuss purpose with a remark like this: "Yes, purpose is great, but right now we have to focus on turning this company around. We're bleeding to death!"

Here's how I'd respond to your COO or CFO. I'd say that in situations where the company is financially ailing, it's often best to first "stabilize" the situation through appropriate financial measures. As a veteran executive once

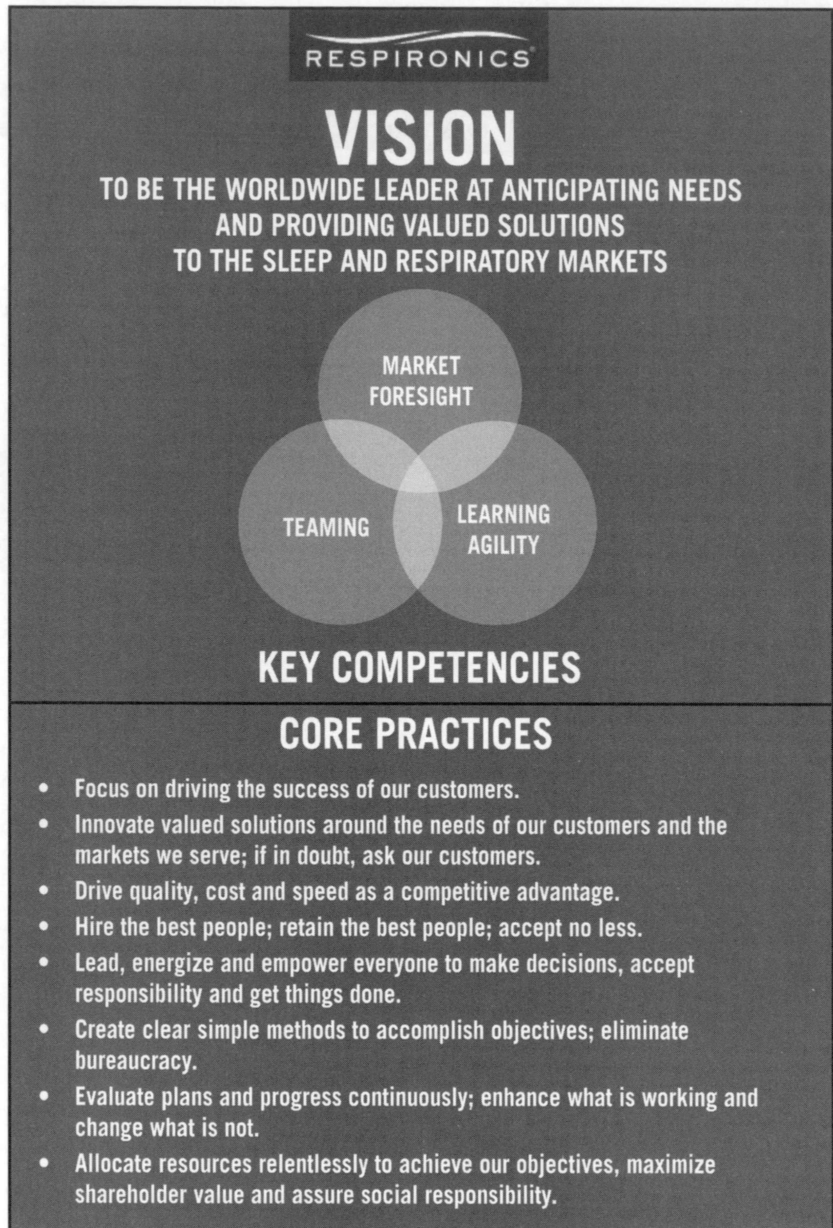

Figure 3.1 An example of purpose linked to other principles (© Copyright 2006 Respironics, Reprinted with Permission).

told me after his company had successfully weathered a near-death experience: "First you stabilize, then you improve, and finally you can focus on how to grow." And, growth requires, among other things, a fundamental purpose that relates to what society needs, a purpose that can drive an inspiring vision, stimulate an effective strategy, generate passion and commitment among employees, energize suppliers, and stir customers.

Can a company survive for a short while without a compelling purpose? Sure. But your COO will surely agree that the goal of every organization is not merely to survive: It is to thrive. And that calls for management to pay attention to all nine principles—starting with a true, fundamental reason-to-be.

4

PRINCIPLE 2: LIVE AND DEFEND YOUR CORE VALUES

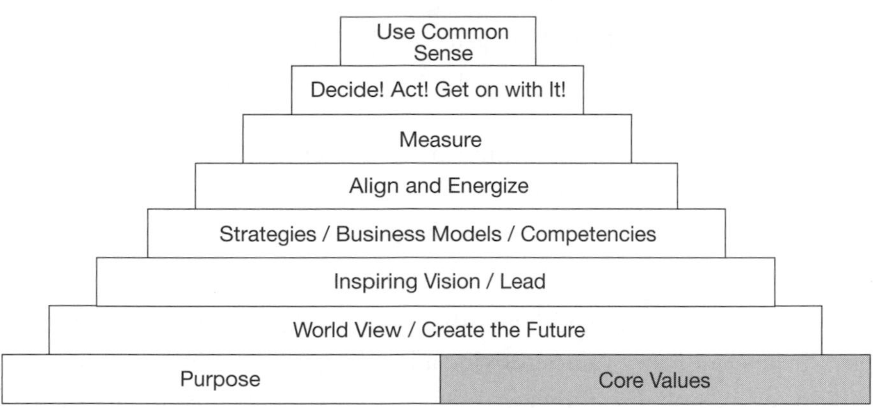

> "Treating people like numbers will prevent the company from meeting its numbers."
>
> —*Richard A. Moran, Fear No Yellow Stickies*

Follow me through this troubling scenario. A corporate officer loses responsibility for his company's business planning process after the reengineering team files its recommendations. Then, inexplicably, the executive is put in charge of employee benefits administration for all employees—this despite the fact that he is widely known for his lack of people skills, his shabby treatment of employees, and his view that employees are "costs" to be reduced. As if that were not bizarre enough, one of the company's stated "core values" is to treat employees with dignity and respect!

I'm sorry to say it's a true story.

Naturally, employees saw the new benefits chief's appointment as a demonstration that top management was not sincere regarding at least one of the stated core values. And not surprisingly, the move also raised questions about the top team's sincerity and commitment to the company's other stated values.

Core values matter. They are closely linked to a corporation's underlying purpose. History shows that long-lasting organizations are fierce defenders of their core values. They live those values all the time.

Most managers can readily reel off several typical core values. The best examples are these:

- Displaying honesty and integrity
- Showing respect toward and supporting development opportunities for employees
- Working with passion, commitment, and enthusiasm
- Showing continual improvement in everything we do
- Showing continual learning in every area and every activity
- Encouraging individual initiative and creativity

But listing core values and living them day-to-day are two very different things. Purpose and core values provide a bright guiding light for employees. Together they also offer a framework that helps external constituents such as customers, suppliers, government agencies, and stockholders to understand *what* the executive team seeks to accomplish (purpose), and *how* they and all other employees will conduct themselves (values). Core values must be authentic—they have to represent reality. The "walk" must match the "talk." Core values need to be easily expressed and genuinely believed and acted out in all respects. They are not negotiable and can never be compromised—not as a matter of policy, anyway. Any deviations from core value behavior must be quickly, decisively, and *publicly* dealt with.

Failure to live and defend your core values will undermine the foundations of your organization and contribute to its eventual decline. It's an issue of trust, a wispy attribute that is very hard to come by and very, very easy to destroy. These days, trust is evidenced not only at the point of sale. "A brand can be built up or torn down anywhere on that chain of touch points, from earliest impressions to after-sales service," observes Mercer Management Consulting in a recent issue of *Mercer Management Journal.* "Even old-line manufacturers are starting to recognize that there is a customer relationship continuum—the "before," "during," and "after" service components of their product sales."[1] The continuum reaches even further as online channels open up. Communications on a Web site that clash with messages conveyed elsewhere on the customer "touch-point chain" immediately detract from trust.

The purpose and the core values of an organization do not change once they are properly established. Strategies, tactics, and procedures can change—and as a rule they *should* evolve over time—but by definition, the purpose and core values offer their greatest value by remaining constant guideposts.

Those foundation elements were noticeably absent at Enron and equally ill-famed WorldCom in the early years of this century. I visited Enron's headquarters during 2000, a little more than 12 months before the energy conglomerate collapsed, and I had a firsthand opportunity to form an impression of the then-highflier. I was there because Enron's executives wanted to gauge the interest of Bethlehem Steel—my company at that time—in helping establish a market for steel product futures.

In hindsight, the meeting was an interesting foreshadowing of future events. It involved about a dozen Enron personnel, most of them relatively young and aggressive, trying to convince me, as Bethlehem Steel's sole representative, that the "Enron model" was a natural one for the steel marketplace. My goal was to discuss my team's view of the appropriate basis for proceeding, and to determine if there was commonality between our view and Enron's. The Enron team, on the other hand, was anxious to book one or more transactions as quickly as possible, and indicated that the strategy discussion could follow later. Their rush to book a deal, and the urgency with which they sought that first transaction with us, raised my antennae and gave me reason to wonder what was happening behind the scenes. Clearly a lot was happening. When Enron began to implode, it didn't surprise me at all.

Amid similarly sordid revelations from companies such as WorldCom and Adelphia, the Enron story gutted public confidence in corporate America. Media columnists and cartoonists had a field day. (See Figure 4.1.) And for every public outing of executives showing contempt for decent ethical standards, there were—and assuredly still are—plenty of examples of borderline

"It's an amazing coincidence, isn't it, that we all served on the same board of directors?"

Figure 4.1 © *The New Yorker* Collection 2000 James Stevenson from cartoonbank.com. All Rights Reserved. Reprinted with permission.

behavior in the boardroom that simply would not pass a Boy Scout test of what is right.

Not long ago, I was having a private conversation with a recently retired senior executive of a major U.S. utility company, and the subject of that company's internal culture and value system came up. Without hesitation, the executive outlined what he referred to as the two "hidden values" of his former company: There is no hard decision we can't walk away from, and there is no deadline we can't miss. In two short and chilling phrases, he had summed up what I'd already observed: an almost professional degree of procrastination that seemed to pervade that entire organization.

In the last 20 years, American business has seen Enron and other examples brought to light under the hot glare of media coverage and federal prosecution. Has the point about core values now sunk home with directors, executives, and senior managers, or will more outrageous examples emerge as soon as Sarbanes-Oxley is out of the headlines? Call me cynical, but I believe that a hint can be found in this short saying: "Where egos prevail, history repeats itself."

WHO DOES CORE VALUES WELL?

I'm glad to say you don't have to look far for great examples of long-lasting and genuine core values. The most stirring example I know of comes from the mid-1980s, when **Johnson & Johnson** won widespread acclaim for its handling of the Tylenol tampering cases and, in the process, preserved and even enhanced its reputation by putting its customers' welfare first. Two decades on, J&J's response is still the high-water mark for how corporate values can provide operational guidance. As every business school student learns, J&J's credo has been a guiding light since the early 1940s.[2]

Southwest Airlines is often lauded for considering its employees to be the company's premier asset, and for empowering its employees to have fun while doing the right thing. Other companies might say similar things, but Southwest has turned that simple idea into reality—and into a sharp competitive edge. For example, its ongoing efforts to eliminate bureaucracy, encourage its employees to act like owners, try new ideas, celebrate accomplishments, treat employees like the first priority, and treat customers like a close second priority have collectively resulted in customer service performance that still sets industry standards. That, in turn, continues to distinguish Southwest from other airlines in a very competitive environment.

You might be surprised to see **Tyco International** on the honor roll. Your memory is correct: Prior to 2002, the multi-industry conglomerate was indeed mentioned in the same breath as WorldCom and Enron—and for many of the same reasons. Who can forget the stories of former CEO Dennis Kozlowski's excesses at shareholders' expenses—the yacht, the art collection, even the

Roman-themed multimillion-dollar birthday party for his wife, much of it financed from the company's funds?

But Tyco has survived that shameful period and is recovering fast. Kozlowski will be behind bars for a long time. And new CEO Edward D. Breen acted promptly and decisively to replace virtually every senior corporate executive. He obtained agreement from the board of directors that they step aside to make room for a totally new and completely independent board. In his words and actions, Breen has consistently made it clear that the new Tyco adheres to the highest standards of ethics and business conduct. He quickly installed a senior vice president of corporate governance and established "whistle-blower" hot lines, framing his initiatives this way: "we set a different tone as to how the company is going to be run."[3]

The new governance chief reports directly to Tyco's board, as do two newly created positions: corporate ombudsman and the head of corporate audit. In addition, a guide to ethical conduct was developed and rolled out with a training program that included videotaped vignettes. And the executive compensation and incentive system was revamped to ensure that the right behaviors were encouraged and rewarded.[4]

Tyco's new leadership understood the need for strong, unequivocal core values. They acted decisively, not only averting catastrophe but laying the foundation for the prompt rebirth of the company. The stock price has recovered from the dark days of 2001, and revenues and operating margins have trended steadily upward and to the right.

CHECKLIST

As you consider whether or not your organization has strong core values, ask yourself these questions:

- Are our core values clearly defined and easy to remember?
- Are they regularly communicated and reinforced through daily actions?
- Are they authentic, and not just wishful thinking?
- Are deviations from the stated core values dealt with quickly, decisively, and publicly?
- Do we defend our core values passionately?
- Do our core values apply equally to all employees at all levels?

YES, BUT . . .

At worst, the concept of core values elicits snickers of contempt—although rarely publicly. More typically, it meets with indifference. Even when there is a willingness, there may not be a way. I've heard it put like this: "Yes, core values are a wonderful concept, but how do we design something catchy that is 'us'?"

Let me answer it as follows. Drafting a set of core values can start with top management, but it should not be finalized by top management in isolation. The authenticity of core values, and how those values are expressed, needs to be vetted by people from each level of your organization. Think of this as a focus group exercise. You have something you want to test, you have some willing "customers" (your employees), and you need a process that provides opportunity for open and candid debate, without risks to those who participate. Indeed, a formally facilitated focus group can be one avenue for drafting concrete core values.

Another approach is to utilize the diagnostic process described later in this book. One company that used the diagnostic gained insights into what its employees were concluding about its core values. It then used this reality as a basis for internal discussion and debate—and for crafting a more formal set of values.

5

PRINCIPLE 3: CREATE THE FUTURE

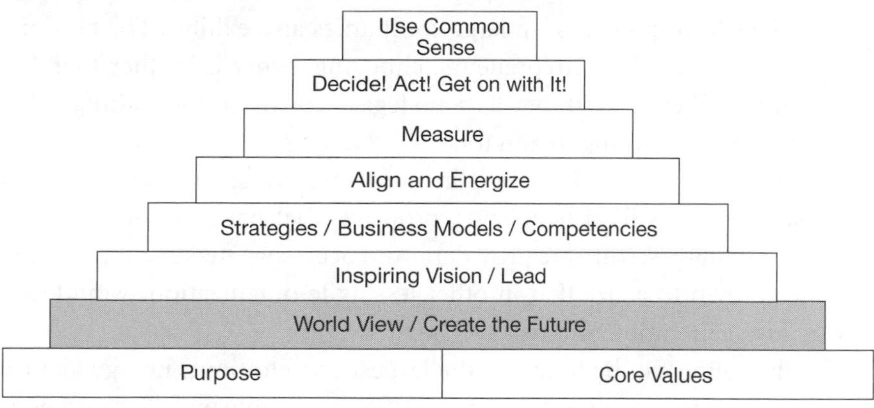

> "The future is not the result of choices among alternative paths offered in the present. It is a place that is created—created first in the mind and will; created next in the activity."
>
> —*John Schaar*

The Walt Disney Co. doesn't simply have engineers—it has *imagineers*. You've probably seen the handiwork of its Walt Disney Imagineering unit in the movie *Pirates of the Caribbean*; there's a good chance that you've enjoyed its creative output on a Disney cruise or at a Disney resort.

The Imagineering operation helps Disney to keep dreaming big—to take charge of its own destiny. The unit is responsible for the company's master planning, creative development, and research and development. Every company should have an Imagineering unit.

I know what you're thinking: Your organization has got it covered. But I'm referring to a function with a broader role than the conventional R&D department or even the business development group. I mean a group of individuals whose job it is to look around them and to look as far as they can over the horizon to imagine a future for their organizations—and then to help create it.

Call it "visioning" or "blue-skying" or "whiteboarding" if you like. I am referring to a discipline that transcends new product design and development and that is by no means limited to the corporate morphology made possible by the available merger opportunities. I think of it as "creating the future"—an externally focused principle that builds on the introspective focus on purpose and on core values.

It's the kind of discipline that entrepreneurs have in spades—and that the best so-called "intrapreneurs" in large companies also exhibit. The best practitioners in fact act like entrepreneurs, choosing "what if" rather than "yes, but" scenarios. They act as if they have no legacy constraints—nothing to hold them back, and everything to aim for.

Apple Computer has that discipline and then some—evidence the spectacular success of its iPod handhelds, products that have spawned an entire industry of imitators, software providers, and accessory makers. Yet Apple has long since grown to a size that in other less agile organizations would mean sclerotic idea generation and risk aversion.

The discipline can be found in the largest corporations. Energy giant BP has opted to define its own future by identifying its name with "beyond petroleum"—a position reinforced by its planned $8 billion investment over the next decade in alternative energy and expressed in the reworking of its sunburst logo to reflect environmental themes. And in 2005, General Electric launched "Ecomagination," a company-wide initiative pledging to cut the pollution its products create and doubling R&D spend on clean technologies. "Taking on big challenges" is one way that GE frames the initiative on its Ecomagination Web site.

GE is also applying similar thinking to China, which poses a fascinating double-edged sword for business executives. A large and fast-growing market, China has also proven quick to learn new technologies and become a new competitor. In the context of Principle 3, consider what GE chairman Jeff Immelt said in 2003: "Ten years out, 90 percent of our company's earnings will have no competition from China. Eighty percent of our businesses will be selling to China."[1] Immelt clearly has a world view of the opportunity and threat posed by China, but he also plans to create a future with respect to China that works well for GE.

While many eco-initiatives become easy targets for critics alleging clever public-relations stunts, there is no escaping the fact that companies such as Apple, GE, and BP have determinedly scoped out the changing world around them and set out to engage it—with strong roles for their own organizations. Management master Peter Drucker spoke out on the need for others to do what Apple and GE are doing: "It is absolutely necessary for every business to search for the idea that will make the future—and to start to work on its realization," he said. "By daring not to take the risk of making the new happen, management takes, by default, the greater risk of being surprised by what will happen."

Negative surprises are an unfortunate fact of life for companies whose constant primary focus is on reducing internal costs. That is not to diminish the importance of close attention to cost controls; it is simply to state that such inward emphasis is usually what your competitors are busy doing as well. It is far less likely to confer lasting competitive advantage than new-product or new-market strategies born out of deliberate scrutiny of external environments. Table 5.1 compares a recommended approach with that still taken by most companies.

In one example I know, a manufacturing company was suffering as the value it offered shifted to other organizations further downstream in the supply chain. At the same time, the company's management team, believing themselves hostage to labor unions, consistently agreed to excessive labor demands that the company could not afford in the long term. The company viewed both factors as beyond its capability to influence. The executive team could not see beyond existing customer segments—or around the labor issues.

In short, their captive mind-set (some might even label it a "victim" mentality) forced further attention onto cost cutting—an issue they felt they could control—and locked the company into a downward spiral. The company repeatedly missed opportunities to redefine and redirect itself.

The prerequisite to the principle of creating the future is what I call "acquiring a world view." It involves comprehensively and continuously monitoring and assessing the current reality and the developments that could

Table 5.1 Conventional Approach vs. Recommended

Components of Conventional Approach	Components of Recommended Approach
Periodic analysis of direct competitors.	Comprehensive and continual analysis of current and future competitors. Examination of nontraditional players who may be edging into one or more dimensions of the playing field.
Customer needs analysis (often focused on the physical product and its attributes).	Comprehensive, fundamental insight on how customer priorities are changing and how we need to innovate.
Extrapolating current trends to forecast the future.	Imagining the alternate futures (scenarios), and constructing plans to cause an attractive future to occur.
Mind-set: Certain factors are beyond our ability to control or influence. We are "captive" to certain events or factors.	Mind-set: It is possible, and it may be appropriate, to alter many factors in order to create the desired future.

affect your industry or activity, both near-term and longer-term. It also involves understanding how customer priorities are changing. It means much more than confronting current reality. It calls for understanding current realities and then appreciating and deeply understanding where those realities are likely to make an impact on your industry and your business, assuming no actions by your company.

The significance of that concept was underscored by A. G. Lafley, CEO of Procter & Gamble, in his bylined article in *Chief Executive* magazine. "So what are the unique responsibilities of CEOs who want to create . . . self-sustaining organizations? First, the CEO must create the conditions that are necessary for an organization to attack problems and seize opportunities. Most importantly, they have to get people comfortable with seeing things as they are . . . "[2]

"Acquiring a world view" can happen in many different and creative ways. In 1996, I took part in Carnegie Mellon University's Program for Executives (PFE). My 40 classmates for this intense four-week program came from all over the world and represented well-known global businesses. Three of them were from Samsung, which at the time was a large but relatively low-key South Korean firm that was not performing particularly well. In fact, a quick read of the 1997 annual report finds comments about "restructuring" and "finding a better balance . . ."

Hidden away in that report was a signal that something special was happening at Samsung. It came to light in a Q&A with the corporation's president and CEO, Jong-Yong Yun. The interviewer had asked about the CEO's management philosophy. His reply: "First, I believe that we at Samsung Electronics must elevate our ways of thinking, which means we have to be away from the fixed notions and formalism that have influenced us greatly until now."

This answer suggested an explicit attack on conventional thinking and captive mind-sets. But what I witnessed during PFE was even more revealing. Our daily schedule usually allowed one to two hours of informal time after classes and before dinner. Within a week, most attendees had fallen into a pattern of meeting in small groups in the early evening for impromptu discussions about the day's events or business in general, or to work out in the fitness center. I couldn't help noticing that the three Samsung managers always disappeared during that time.

Midway through the program, I had developed enough rapport with one of my Samsung classmates to ask him what was on my mind: "Where do you disappear each evening?" He responded with one of the few possibilities that I had not imagined. Each man retired to his room to write a report on the day's learnings (both classroom teachings and information picked up during the course of the day) and then sent his report back to Samsung headquarters in Seoul by fax (which, at the time, was the preferred electronic means of communicating). In Seoul, one person was receiving such reports from any Samsung employee who was on the road. His job was to read each report that same day and immediately disseminate the relevant information to anyone within Samsung who could benefit from the market intelligence therein.

I was impressed. Clearly Samsung had made a huge commitment to gathering business intelligence from all vantage points, with an equally strong discipline of extracting value from the data as rapidly as possible. Here was one indication that something special was under way at the company. Today, Samsung is indisputably one of the world's foremost consumer electronics brands.

With such a wealth of external data on hand, companies such as Samsung can far more easily envision the future state of their industries or activities, and launch to good effect the kinds of scenario planning exercises that lead to smart risk-managed initiatives. I applaud Samsung, BP, GE, Apple, and others like them for so resolutely working on creating their own futures. They have refused to become spectators in their own industries.

WHO'S GOOD AT CREATING THE FUTURE?

Samsung, BP, GE, and Apple are not alone in successfully acquiring a world view and creating the future. Here are a few others I'd put on the honor roll:

Amazon.com became the poster child of the "new economy"—the example of how to do e-business right. It also had plenty of doubters in its early days, particularly after the dot-com bubble burst. But CEO Jeff Bezos stayed the course with his original, create-the-future business strategy, and Amazon's current performance strongly suggests it has a winning view of the retail world. Amazon is, in fact, influencing the retail world's future. It is even making inroads into the grocery business.

In an innovative twist to the idea of identifying and examining nontraditional players that may be edging onto its playing field, Amazon has invited some competitors to sell their products right there on the Amazon site. Leveraging Amazon's efficient operation, this marketplace strategy expands Amazon's business model into one that becomes almost an open platform for retailers of any type. To say it another way: Amazon the online bookseller becomes Amazon the online mall. While Amazon still has other challenges to successfully address, it has demonstrated the importance and the value of focusing on Principle 3.[3]

Alcoa is a classic case of a formerly great company that by the mid-1980s had become a "wheezing industrial giant" according to *BusinessWeek*.[4] It was a company that could have gone into a long-term decline but did not. In fact, as other metals industries such as steel were entering a death spiral, Alcoa began a multifaceted effort that ultimately returned it to greatness. A large part of that effort involved an unconventional view of itself and the future it wanted to create. It was early to embrace the Internet. It was innovative in utilizing technology to enhance production and delivery times. It refused to live with the flood of Russian aluminum exports, acting as a catalyst of an international effort of aluminum producers and their governments to contain the glut. And, to top it off, it embarked on a series of acquisitions that today gives it nearly one-sixth of global aluminum production.

Cable TV companies such as **Comcast** created a new future for themselves with high-speed Internet access for consumers. As the Internet emerged, the local phone companies (the former "Bell" companies) were not very interested in pursuing digital technology as a way to meet consumers' demands for Internet access. For the most part, they were happy to offer a second phone line for the dial-up connection that most consumers initially used.

Comcast and others jumped right in with neatly packaged offers of digital broadband service, partly as a way to compete more effectively with *their* new competitors—satellite TV providers. Quite quickly, the cable companies established a huge beachhead in the consumer broadband market.

CHECKLIST

Here are the kinds of questions that you should ask yourself as you evaluate how well your organization is acquiring a world view and working to shape its own future:

- How externally focused are we? Are we really spending most of our attention on internal matters?
- Are we able to admit and confront the external reality of our business?
- Do we continuously monitor and assess economic, societal, geopolitical, and other external developments that could affect our industry or organization?
- Do we intimately understand how our customers are thinking, and how their priorities are changing?
- Do we invest time to envision the future state of our industry, and to change those things that make our industry difficult?
- Are we constantly on the lookout for nontraditional competitors who might surprise us?

YES, BUT . . .

It's human nature to push back against what we perceive to be impossible or nearly so. I've been guilty of it in my professional and personal life. The gut reaction of most managers to the question of envisioning their industry's future and then working to make it happen goes something like this: "But my industry is at the mercy of . . ." You can fill in the rest of the rebuttal.

That response belies a captive mind-set—the term that describes how people put constraints on their own thinking. The reasons for such a mind-set are many: preconceived notions based on incomplete information, assuming that historical patterns must continue, beliefs that the boss has a particular opinion, to name just a few. Management at Eastman Kodak certainly exhibited this attitude in the years prior to 2003, when they concluded that digital photography would only cannibalize their film business. The implicit assumption is that if you cannot change an external factor easily, or within some short period, it cannot be changed at all.

The first step in unlocking a captive mind-set is to identify its existence. That requires uncovering the assumption that drives it and testing the assumption against the hard facts—or against some fresh thinking.

Here's one quick example of how reevaluation of the status quo—coupled with patience, perseverance, and a creative, well-conceived plan of activities—got things moving again. Shortly after financier Wilbur Ross created International Steel Group from the defunct LTV Steel, he reached a mold-breaking agreement with the United Steelworkers of America. No one—other than perhaps Ross himself—imagined in his or her wildest dreams that such a breakthrough agreement could be reached in the contentious U.S. steel industry.

6

PRINCIPLE 4: ARTICULATE AN INSPIRING VISION—AND LEAD!

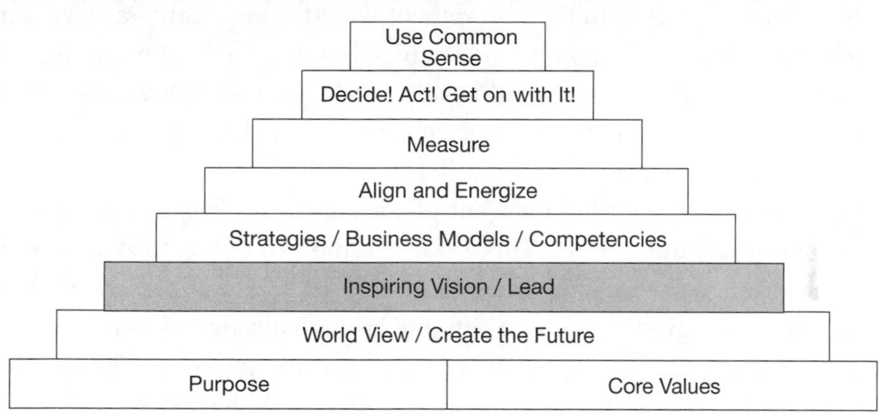

> "Leaders must challenge the process precisely because any system will unconsciously conspire to maintain the status quo and prevent change."
>
> —*Kouzes & Posner, The Leadership Challenge*

I don't know who said that "insanity is doing the same thing over and over and expecting different results," but I do know the quip gets grim smiles of recognition from every smart businessperson I've come across. Managers are just as guilty of such behavior as line workers—more so, in fact, since the consequences of their unthinking repetition are far greater. They're also guilty by omission—meaning that if they fail to lead and to inspire others to do things *differently*, nothing will ever change.

Which brings us to the fourth Beat the Odds principle: Once purpose and core values have been laid down, and after the ideas for creating the future have been set, it is critical to articulate an inspiring vision internally so that employees can understand and become excited about *where* the organization is heading. It is also important to communicate that vision externally—at the right time—to gain the confidence and support of external constituents as well. This is not just a job for the CEO and the top team. It is necessary for the vision to cascade down from leader to leader, right down to the line supervisors.

Conveying the company's future direction with vigor and passion is an area in which many companies fall down. I recall one company where executives, managers, and analysts would engage in "chart wars"—devoting considerable time to drafting, redrafting, and refining presentations, memoranda, and other *forms* of communication. Tellingly, however, if you asked employees to explain the *substance* of what the company was trying to achieve, what its vision was, what its strategy was, most would pause significantly and then—in a monotone that suggested lack of enthusiasm—deliver an incomplete recitation of some boilerplate language developed years previously by top management.

The message did not fail for want of time spent drafting the company's vision, objectives, and strategy. This was an example of failing to articulate an *inspiring* vision, one that employees could take to heart and mind, and that would excite and guide employee actions. Facing considerable internal and external challenges, the company was further constrained by employees who were neither as effective nor as energized as they could have been in helping to achieve management's vision.

But how to communicate vision? And whose job? Let me emphasize my earlier comment: It is the job of *all* leaders in the organization to evangelize about the vision. If it isn't built into their performance reviews, it should be. The methods can and should be many; it may be a regular CEO letter in the employee newsletter, or a motivating speech from the stage at the annual executive forum. It may well include communication through "management by walking around"—something that Randy Dearth, CEO of LANXESS Corp., is very good at and that employees appreciate, as you'll read in the case study on LANXESS later in this book. And it may involve formal but friendly special reports published on the Web site and in hard copy, to be disseminated to employees, clients, and suppliers alike.

The point is that there is no set formula for how to articulate the vision. It does not always have to be scheduled or scripted, and it does not have to be long. But it will happen best if it is conveyed through a variety of channels and media, and if it is expressed with some zest. Above all, it absolutely must be consistent and credible. In other words, the vision will not gain traction if a middle manager puts a very different spin on it than the CEO has done. And it simply won't take at all if managers' actions don't align with their words. The alignment refers to other core leadership traits beyond great communication. An executive can be as eloquent and persuasive as the day is long, but if he or she is not perceived to be a good leader in other ways, the impact of the message will be diluted.

From an employee perspective, understanding and being motivated by the vision is critical because it underpins efforts to act on other essential principles. First, it can build significant energy and help to align the workforce with the new direction. (See also Principle 6.) Second, it is crucial for employees to have the "big picture" information if they are to contribute effectively. (See also Principle 5.) Employees who don't "get" the vision also run the risk of focusing on the wrong activities and the wrong performance metrics (Principle 7).

The *Dilbert* comic strip sometimes aims its arrows at the way in which companies fail to convey their strategic vision. One of my favorite strips involves an exchange between Dilbert and his boss about strategy. The dialogue goes like this:

> ***Dilbert:*** *"How much budget do I have for my project?"*
>
> ***Boss:*** *"I can't tell you. If you knew what your budget was, you'd spend it all."*
>
> ***Dilbert:*** *"Can you at least tell me what our company strategy is?"*
>
> ***Boss:*** *"No, I don't want you to lose hope."*

So what constitutes an *inspiring* vision versus a regular vision? It immediately captures your heart as well as your mind. It engages you, grabs your attention. It's exciting and provocative. You want to sign up to be part of the effort. You're willing to make a substantial personal and professional commitment to the inspiring vision.

One of the most inspiring visions ever presented was President Kennedy's call for America to put a man on the moon by the end of the 1960s. It captured the hearts and minds of an entire nation. Early in the last century, Anglo–Irish explorer Sir Ernest Shackleton provided a classic example of outstanding leadership when he managed to keep his icebound crew alive and healthy during their 18-month ordeal in Antarctica. His success has been credited to outstanding leadership skills, including optimism, communication, courage, planning, discipline, and flexibility. Anyone who has read the account of the odds against Shackleton's expedition understands that he inspired his crew to do the impossible.

Obviously, a new corporate direction lacks the life-or-death urgency that helped Shackleton's messages get through. And clearly it lacks the drama and deep reservoirs of national pride that helped Kennedy inspire the Apollo landing. Pronouncements from corporate executives have another strike against them: Even the most passionate, energizing business leaders engender suspicion, mistrust, and sometimes outright disbelief if their words are known for not often matching their actions. Employees are rightly wary of management's latest announcements on the "strategy du jour."

That said, many companies *do* succeed in conveying clear visions. Which ones do you find to be inspiring? Which ones do you think most employees would find inspiring?

- "To experience the sheer joy that comes from the advancement, application, and innovation of technology that benefits the general public" [Sony]
- "Become #1 or #2 in every market we serve, and revolutionize this company to have the speed and agility of a small enterprise" [GE]
- "Be the Premier Steel Company" [Bethlehem Steel]
- "To build a motor car for the great multitude . . . It will be so low in price that no man making a good salary will be unable to own one . . . " [Ford]

Articulating an inspiring vision is one element of a broader subject: leadership practices. Leadership is not a subject for CEOs only. One of the greatest mistakes a company can make is to assume that only the CEO "leads." Even executive recruiters can fall into the trap of thinking about "leaders" as chief executives only. In a keynote presentation at a Chief Learning Officer (CLO) Symposium in 2004, Len Sherman, then head of the Learning practice at the global consulting firm Accenture, shared this anecdote with the audience:

> *A few months ago, an executive recruiter called to ask me if I had any ideas on who might be suited for a Fortune 500 CLO opening he was trying to fill. I asked him to tell me the job specs for the position, and he shared with me a number of characteristics primarily associated with the* ***technical*** *aspects of a senior education officer. The job spec included experience in individual and organization needs assessment, competency modeling, all aspects of training and development, performance technology, executive group facilitation, action learning, team and organization effectiveness, process engineering, consulting practices, and change management. In short, all the relevant professional learning skills.*
>
> *Now don't get me wrong. These are all necessary and important skills. But they are far from sufficient to succeed as a CLO of a large organization in today's challenging business environment. So I told my recruiter friend that I thought his client might be better served by a CLO who also . . . demonstrated [an] understanding of the key business drivers and profit levers of the corporation, a truly global mind-set, proven experience with delivering business results; an established track record in running a business entity; strong executive presence, communication skills, an ability to influence key stakeholders inside and outside the corporation and exceptionally strong leadership qualities.*
>
> *My executive recruiter friend replied that I must have misunderstood . . . he was looking for a C**L**O, not a C**E**O, who he thought would better fit the job characteristics I had just described. No, I replied. In my view, many of the attributes of both jobs are similar. Without strong management and leadership skills, neither a CLO nor a CEO is likely to succeed in their mission.*[1]

Let's be clear what is meant by leadership. There is a meaningful difference between management and leadership (see Table 6.1). Good managers successfully cope with complexity. But good leaders successfully guide and cope with change. Both skills are important to have in your organization. Not many individuals, however, possesses both sets of skills.

Table 6.1 Leadership versus Management: An Important Distinction

Leadership	Management
Create change	Control complexity
Set new direction	Develop plans
Create strategy	Allocate resources
Align people	Organize and staff
Promote positive outcomes	Prevent negative outcomes
Empower people and processes	Control people/processes

Source: Based on materials from John Kotter, Harvard University, and also Carol and Jack Weber, University of Virginia Darden School of Business.

Prior to 2001, Xerox Corp. certainly didn't demonstrate much in the way of real leadership. Its spectacular successes in commercializing photocopying technology and creating an entire industry in the mid- to late twentieth century were subsequently offset by a series of leadership blunders that saw several outstanding Xerox technology innovations commercialized by others. For example, several of the key features of today's personal computer originated in Xerox's Palo Alto Research Center but were not adopted by Xerox into its own product portfolio.

The story was similar at Kmart before its merger with Sears—and before the retailer entered Chapter 11 proceedings. Management failed to keep up with changes in the retailing business, and with the changing expectations of its customers. After the company emerged from bankruptcy in May of 2003, it still lacked a clearly articulated vision of what it would be and how it would distinguish itself from chief competitors such as Wal-Mart ("everyday low prices") and Target ("cheap chic"). Even the merger of Kmart and Sears, orchestrated by major Kmart stockholder Edward S. Lambert's ESL Investments, Inc., has not yet changed the picture. Without a clearly defined and articulated vision and strategy that is well led, the combined retailer's ultimate success as an operating retail business will remain problematic. That is an observation separate from the expectation that the merger—from a strictly financial and tax perspective—may serve as a useful platform for additional retail acquisitions.

Earlier, at Sunbeam, CEO Al Dunlap had attacked costs so savagely that he cut into company muscle—and damaged Sunbeam's ability to deliver on its

Table 6.2 Leadership's Five Essentials

1. Challenge the process
   a. Search for opportunities
   b. Experiment and take risks
2. Inspire a shared vision
   a. Envision the future
   b. Enlist others
3. Enable others to act
   a. Foster collaboration
   b. Strengthen others
4. Model the way
   a. Set the example
   b. Plan small wins
5. Encourage the heart
   a. Recognize contributions
   b. Celebrate accomplishments

Source: The Leadership Challenge, Kouzes & Posner.

promises to customers and Wall Street analysts. "Chainsaw Al," as he became known, repeatedly cut staff ranks and allegedly employed aggressive sales accounting tactics. At the same time, he failed miserably to excite Sunbeam's management ranks with any coherent vision of the company's future. These fundamental failures, combined with a personal leadership style that was characterized as "bullying," created a destructive environment at Sunbeam.[2]

Since leadership is fundamentally about creating change, let's take an executive tour through the subject of leadership and change. Many books have explored this subject. A classic is *The Leadership Challenge* by James M. Kouzes and Barry Z. Posner. The authors outline and elaborate on a five-stage process (five key practices) as shown in Table 6.2.

The purpose in "challenging the process" is to establish the belief that challenging the status quo is not only acceptable—it is desirable. The idea behind "inspiring a shared vision" is to develop excitement about where the organization is heading, and what management is trying to accomplish. "Enabling others to act" is about providing the support mechanisms that enable employees at all levels to succeed. The idea of "modeling the way" is to illustrate, through appropriate examples and small wins, the behaviors and results desired. And "encouraging the heart" refers to reinforcing the right behaviors and results and demonstrating positive consequences on a personal level.

Another classic leadership book is *Built to Last* by Jim Collins and Jerry I. Porras. Among other concepts, Collins and Porras introduce the idea of the BHAG (Big Hairy Audacious Goal), a common element among long-lasting, successful companies. A BHAG engages people. It is tangible, energizing, and highly focused. It takes little or no explanation. For his part, management guru C. K. Prahalad, coauthor of *Competing for the Future*, tells executives to think big. "Set ambitious goals and then figure out how to mobilize the resources to achieve them—rather than the other way around," he advises. "Most companies limit themselves because they focus primarily on what they believe they can afford."[3]

An essential element in building an organization of leaders is to provide feedback on leadership behavior and practices. The systematic practice of gathering feedback from direct reports, colleagues, and superiors—so-called 360-degree feedback—is invaluable for assessing the initial state of a leader's aptitude. Used periodically (annually or biannually), it can measure progress, or lack of progress, across key leadership practices and provide constructive input for improvements.

Equally important, a "360" can provide senior executives with a fact base upon which to make promotion and career planning decisions for aspiring professionals at all levels. Companies that are serious about building their leadership talent should build 360s into their annual performance review and succession planning processes. Simply stated: they must remove the hit-or-miss approach from their efforts to develop leadership talent. (See sidebar: "The 360 That Never Was.")

Successfully articulating a vision requires one additional insight: Not all people in the organization are equally receptive to change. Researchers and marketers break populations into six significant segments: (1) the innovators—that tiny percentage eager to be on the bleeding edge of change and new ideas, (2) the early adopters, (3) the early majority, (4) the late majority, (5) the laggards, and (6) the fraction who will never buy in.

When trying to initiate breakthrough change, many managers make the mistake of trying to convince those who simply won't be convinced. Their outreach would be far more productive if they started by identifying the innovators and early adopters in their organizations, and got them on board. Most of the rest tend to follow in due course.

THE 360 THAT NEVER WAS

Not long ago, a Fortune 500 CEO needed to replace his company's outgoing head of procurement. He proceeded to select a manager who talked a great story, in spite of past concerns about the manager's leadership skills. No professional assessment was conducted to confirm the manager's strengths or weaknesses. The CEO just "went with his feel" based on his personal rapport with the candidate.

One of the first acts by the new procurement chief was to meet with each of the new employees recruited on college campuses during the previous CPO's tenure. The message was simple, direct, and puzzling at first: You needed to spend at least four years in your entry-level buying job "to master the details" before you could be considered for a new assignment. Every one of the new hires immediately began to look outside the company for new jobs. Half did leave within 12 months, and word spread that the new CPO was working to reduce head count—cheaply—by encouraging employees to depart.

Trust in the new CPO was not enhanced by this approach to employees, and his effectiveness was further diminished by other actions that raised doubts about his understanding of procurement's role. Finally, in an effort to address the worsening results from the increasingly ineffective procurement organization, the CPO suggested that procurement be formally centralized. The CEO agreed, despite the fact that the company's organization structure favored strong business units. The result was a further disconnect between procurement and its internal clients, and a belief by the business unit heads that this CPO had a personal agenda that was inconsistent with their objectives.

In less than two years, a well-functioning procurement organization had been reduced to a tactical mess that was no longer contributing to the success of the company.

Message: Selecting the right leader cannot be done casually. It must be done with an understanding of the functional skills needed—and using hard facts to identify which candidates truly possess the critical leadership abilities.

(Adapted with permission from *Straight to the Bottom Line*™, J. Ross Publishing, 2005)

With a well-articulated, inspiring vision—plus the appropriate leadership practices at all levels of the organization—your employees will be *committed* to the chosen vision, rather than merely *complying* with requests and procedures. They will also have sufficient information and guidance on how they can contribute to the development of supporting strategies and tactics, business models, and competencies.

WHO LEADS WITH REAL VISION?

I have no hesitation in putting the following companies on the honor roll for their embrace of this principle.

Allied Signal/ Honeywell. Under Larry Bossidy, this company was a classic example of effective leadership. From his early commitment and personal leadership on Total Quality Management (TQM) and Six Sigma to his determination to instill a culture of action and execution, Bossidy exemplified some of the best characteristics of a leader.

I had the opportunity some years ago to see the videotape of Larry Bossidy's management meeting at Allied Signal relating to TQM. In that kick-off meeting, he very clearly discussed the need for TQM throughout Allied Signal, the training that would be made available to all members of management and ultimately all employees, and the leadership role he expected his managers to play. He wrapped up by very plainly stating that anyone who did not make a commitment to the program after the need was explained and the training was provided would not be part of the Allied Signal team. The presentation was highly effective, not because it was intimidating, but because the logic was inescapable.

Siemens. A different example of leadership was on display during the tenure of Heinrich von Pierer, CEO of electronics giant Siemens. In the mid-1990s, Siemens was exhibiting dismal bottom-line performance due to high costs, slow decision making (not atypical of some German companies), products designed *by* engineers rather than *for* customers, and other factors. Von Pierer recognized that generating breakout performance at Siemens would require, among other changes, adopting a more American-like business culture. Among his initiatives were the adoption of clear goals for management, introducing a strong link between pay and performance, placing importance on speed of decision making, making innovation a priority, and forcing product development efforts to deliver products pleasing to the customer. Von Pierer even adopted a few tricks from the Jack Welch playbook, including quarterly meetings in which business unit leaders met with him for an intense grilling.[4, 5, 6]

Continental Airlines. Continental is a testimonial to my belief that leadership can make a difference even in a "structurally defective industry" (to borrow the term used in the book *Confronting Reality* by Larry Bossidy and

Ram Charan).[7] CEO Gordon Bethune took Continental from the brink of disaster in the mid-1990s to the status of one of the few successful airlines, despite Continental's "hub-and-spoke" system design, which conventional wisdom said could not compete with the low-cost airlines.

CHECKLIST

How do you think your organization's executive team is doing in terms of articulating an inspiring vision and leading at all levels? Try answering these questions (and try them on your colleagues too):

- Do we regularly articulate an *inspiring* vision of our organization to our employees?
- How excited are our employees about where we are heading?
- Are our employees willing to make substantial personal and professional commitments to our vision, or do they simply seem to be complying?
- Does our organization understand the distinction between leadership and management?
- Do we have the right balance between leadership and management in our organization?
- Do we utilize BHAGs that engage and energize the organization?
- Do we select, develop, and promote those who are recognized as leaders by their peers, subordinates, and superiors?

YES, BUT . . .

Many organizations view selection of leaders as a risky undertaking. The thinking seems to be this: "Yes, leadership is important, but if we make a mistake selecting a particular leader, as a practical matter it is very difficult to correct that mistake promptly." Many more have only rudimentary leadership development programs—if they have such programs at all. And many leadership development programs often gloss over one of the most critical skills needed for successful leadership: how to make decisions.

True—it is not easy to offload poorly performing business leaders. But that problem can exist at any level, from the selection of a CEO down to the choice of a first-line supervisor. One answer: 360-degree feedback can help mitigate the risks of a mistake being made in the first place (refer again to the "The 360 That Never Was" sidebar).

But what if the mistake has been made previously? That depends on who you are. If you're the supervisor of the incorrect choice, then you must face up to the error. The sooner you do so, the easier it will be. In fact, delaying the action will only cause additional damage to the job's responsibilities, to yourself, and to the company. In other words, things will probably get worse with time. As Mike Krzyzewski, Duke University basketball coach, said in his book *Leading with the Heart:* "When a leader makes a mistake and doesn't admit it, he is seen as arrogant and untrustworthy. And 'untrustworthy' is the last thing a leader wants to be."[8]

The next step is to gather facts and observations. Arrange for a 360-degree survey for the purpose of *diagnosis.* A 360 can be done promptly, and the results known within a short period. If you prefer, you can conduct some informal "skip-level interviews" with people who report to the person in question, and with others who are his or her peers. Then approach the person with your facts and observations. You might be surprised to find he or she welcomes the opportunity to talk about a situation that the person may feel is not working out as intended.

Now let's say you're a subordinate of the substandard leader, and your boss's boss doesn't see the problem with the person you now report to. Sure, the situation is more difficult, but it's not impossible. How you approach it will depend on your company's internal workings, but the basic idea is the same: The person who made the selection needs the information and insight that you possess. Often the human resource department can be a good sounding board and ally. Sometimes it is possible to approach the decision maker directly, or through a mutual friend. As a last resort, write an anonymous letter. If you feel that is the appropriate avenue, you'll need to provide facts, not opinions, to have a credible communication.

7

PRINCIPLE 5: DEVELOP THE RIGHT STRATEGIES, BUSINESS MODELS, AND COMPETENCIES

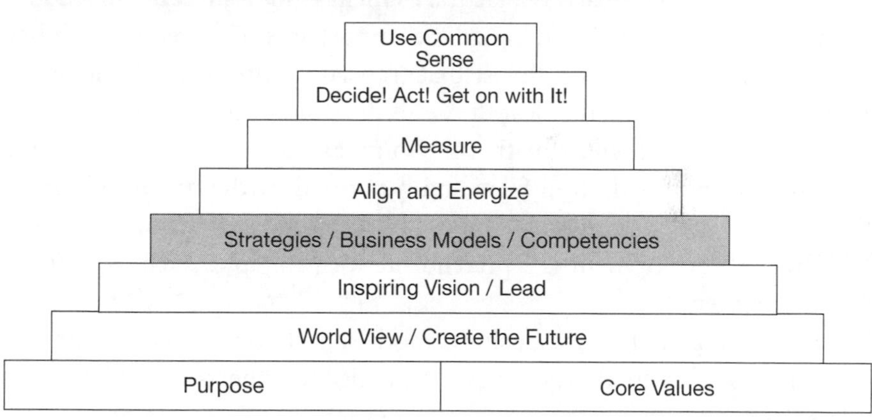

> "We must reverse a paradigm drummed into us from business school to the grave: 'What worked in the past will work in the future.'"
>
> —*Gary Hamel*

The experiences of the past often blind managers to the possibilities for the future. A case in point: a U.S.-based manufacturer that had to decide between investing heavily in product finishing operations at one of its older plants or starting from scratch with a new business model at a greenfield site. The new model would involve new technology, new infrastructure, new governmental incentives, new labor agreements, new transportation logistics, and so forth. If it opted for greenfield, the company would, over time, make further investments at that site while gradually "harvesting" the older plant.

Management played it safe—too safe. Unable to envision how they would manage the labor complexities of operating a "harvest" facility, they chose to reinvest in the older plant. In doing so, they sharply limited the potential returns available from the investment—and they stunted the company's strategic options. While the investment *did* lift product quality and the overall financial performance of the plant, it did nothing to alter the strategic terrain. Competitors moved aggressively into the older plant's market territory, utilizing greenfield investments and capturing a disproportionate share of the customer value opportunity.

Essentially, the manufacturer's management team confused operational initiatives with strategy. But who or what told them that strategy is synonymous with operational effectiveness or outsourcing or process efficiency or head count reduction or Six Sigma? Each is a tactical element—not a strategic direction.

In this chapter, I will emphasize the importance of developing and sustaining an effective strategic thrust that translates into business models and competencies. Revisiting the Beat the Odds pyramid of principles, you can see that strategy development is neither the foundation nor the pinnacle. It must be a *derived* activity—derived from and supported by the organization's core purpose, core values, world view, and well-articulated and inspiring vision. In turn, strategy development is a prerequisite for principles such as alignment and measurement.

I have grouped strategy, business models, and competencies within the same principle because they are inextricably tied together—and because great leaders approach them as a unit. (A good example is Randy Dearth, CEO of LANXESS Corp. You'll meet him in the case study on LANXESS later in this book.) Strategy is little more than hypothesis without the other elements; the business model and the competencies are the *organizational capabilities* needed to deliver on the strategy. Even if you have the right strategy and the right business model, it's still not enough because you must have the right people with the right skills in the right jobs at the right time to be able to deliver on the business model. (There is a related topic to the competencies discussion—energizing the workforce—in Chapter 8.)

Let's take a closer look at the popular misconception that cost reduction can be a corporate strategy. Over many years, Bethlehem Steel did a world-class job reducing costs and improving operational efficiencies, in an attempt to survive and eventually return to corporate health. But ultimately, the lack of an effective top-line growth strategy, in a company facing significant and increasing legacy obligations such as retiree pensions and health care, made the *business model math* inevitable: The company would fail. When it did fail, Bethlehem altered the business model math by declaring bankruptcy and shedding its massive pension and health care burden.

Yet for all of its current struggles, Ford Motor Company is getting the distinctions right. Chairman William Ford has made it clear that the automaker will focus on product innovation and top-line growth while it continues its battle to contain and reduce costs. Taking that approach is perhaps the only way to achieve reasonable business model math. Xerox Corporation faced the same type of challenge around 2000 and 2001, and CEO Anne Mulcahy wisely recommitted the company to investing in product R&D while bringing costs under control. Had she not done both, it is highly likely that Xerox would not be here today.

Let's walk through each component of this fifth principle and show how they fit together. It's useful to look first at the evolution of strategy development since the 1960s. Some notable milestones include the following:

- The concept of strategy as a tool to link the activities of a business and assess the organization's position relative to competitors (1960s). This often included a SWOT analysis (strengths, weaknesses, opportunities, and threats) to structure the assessment.
- The introduction, usually by management consultants, of 2 × 2 matrices to aid corporate planners in their development of plans for "market positioning" and "resource allocation" (1960s and 1970s).
- The emergence of "scenarios" as an integral part of the strategy planning process. The point of scenarios was to challenge conventional thinking about the future and to encourage the development of strategic decisions that would be sound for virtually all plausible futures. Scenario use in strategy planning reached its prominence in the early 1970s, particularly at Royal Dutch/Shell.[1]
- The Michael Porter "Five Forces" framework for assessing the competitive landscape (1980). Porter identified the threat of new

entrants, the bargaining power of suppliers, the bargaining power of customers, the threat of substitute products or services, and the in-industry competition as key determinants of an industry's competitive dynamics.

- A 1980s/1990s shift away from strong strategic planning groups to focus on reengineering and operational improvements.
- A 1990s/2000s evolving view that strategy is much more than assessing competition and developing plans for positioning and resource allocation. The emerging view is that strategy should focus on influencing the direction of your industry (creating the future). It should involve intimately understanding how customer priorities are evolving, and designing business models to address those changing priorities while ensuring good returns on investment. Furthermore, strategy should be directed toward identifying and assembling the competencies needed to achieve those future capabilities. In short, strategy is about organizational renewal and developing linkages to other organizations to supplement your internal competencies in order to achieve your organization's purpose and vision.

During much of this period, business schools gave their students the impression that strategy development was both the starting point and the pinnacle of the pyramid of activities to add value to shareholders. Regrettably, the concepts embodied in Principles 1 through 4 did not play a prominent role in the traditional business school curriculum. And yet, strategy development is fundamentally about creating the menu of "what to execute" in support of the direction and vision coming out of Principles 1 through 4. If strategy is not explicitly linked to the outcomes of Principles 1 through 4, that disconnect will inevitably cause problems.

Strategy also got raw treatment during the dot-com bubble. I remember a watercooler conversation in the late 1990s with a few of the 20-something employees at Bethlehem Steel. The young bloods were certain that a new paradigm would prevail—to them, the "old logic" was no longer relevant. Being well schooled and properly degreed from The Wharton School, I argued that in a sane world "value investing" fundamentals eventually would prevail.

Yet strategy clearly was not prominent at some of America's long-time industrial giants. Management at Goodyear failed to capitalize on Firestone's massive recall of tires during the period 2000 to 2003. The situation afforded a perfect opportunity to convert that event into sustainable market share gains for Goodyear's product lines. At the same time, Sunbeam, under "Chainsaw Al" Dunlap, did not have a viable business strategy. Instead, it had a slash-and-burn approach to reducing costs that was aimed, it seemed, to prepare the company for a quick sale. This shortsighted strategy—in combination with Dunlap's uniquely aggressive management style—contributed to its loss of ability to perform basic tasks such as billing its customers, sowed internal confusion and discontent, and ultimately led to an implosion of business performance and the ouster of Dunlap by his own, handpicked board.[2]

There's a happier story of strategy development—or rather, strategy adaption. In 2004, a new minority-owned company enthusiastically embarked on implementing its business strategy in the energy industry. Staffed with talented people, it began to arrange face-to-face meetings with its target customers (big utility companies) and with potential suppliers. Within 60 days of the initiative's start, a fundamental challenge revealed itself. The target customers all had the same concern: They were reluctant to help a minority business get started because—as regulated utilities—they had to explain every cost variance to their public utility commissions. As the gas buying departments knew, "helping" a minority firm to establish itself probably meant being a little flexible on pricing, and that pricing flexibility could mean headaches with the state utility commission. Nobody wanted to invite those headaches.

This reality caused an immediate rethink of the minority supplier's strategy, and the realization that what was needed was not a new strategy but *another dimension* to the strategy so that it involved initiatives and networking at three distinct levels: (1) the utility company's energy procurement department (operational level), where daily decisions are made, and the relationship must be based on demonstrated performance and personal trust; (2) at the executive level, where an executive sponsor would provide leadership, support, and guidance; and (3) at the public policy level (including the state utility commission and its staff), where support and understanding from the regulators can by itself remove the obstacle that the utility energy procurement department perceived it would have in doing business with the new firm. The rest of the company's story has yet to unfold, but the prompt strategy amendments opened up a much greater chance for success.

It is not the goal of this chapter to deliver a how-to on strategy. Suffice it to say that strategy development deserves serious time and attention whether it is accomplished by a formal, full-time strategy planning department or by periodic senior management meetings off-site. (Microsoft chairman Bill Gates takes a novel approach with his semiannual "think week." He holes up in a remote location for a concentrated week of reading white papers and contemplating the future. The sessions have been the catalyst for major revisions in Microsoft's strategy.)

Inextricably linked to the development of strategy is the design of the business model—that comprehensive system of assets, activities, and relationships that represents an organization's method of addressing customer priorities. It is the entire system of delivering utility to customers. It is "set" by the chosen technology, facility, and labor decisions, and it is "executed" through competencies. If strategy is the "what" to be executed, then the business model is the "how."

"How" a business does what it does must constantly evolve in order to satisfy the customer and the shareholder. If the "how" is static, the organization will eventually die. Business models have life cycles too; they eventually reach economic obsolescence. Value migrates to new models that are better able to satisfy customer priorities while delivering good returns to the owners. Two classic examples: FedEx designed its business model around overnight delivery, and Dell configured its entire supply chain to suit personalized orders by phone and by Internet.

But Kraft Foods didn't get it right. The company earns a spot in the doghouse for relying too heavily on brand extensions for strategic growth, and consequently failing to pay appropriate attention to creating new products. Kraft's lackluster performance contributed to its co-chief executive being ousted from her job in late 2003.

To say it another way: It is crucial to deeply understand what is really important to your target customers and to do it extremely well from two perspectives; first from the customer's perspective, and then from the stockholders' standpoint, by utilizing a business model that can profitably deliver what the customer wants. Successful organizations continually reexamine their business models to seek ways to renew competitive advantage. Pella, the longtime window and door manufacturer, is capturing new and profitable business with its custom design centers set up recently as "store within a store" kiosks inside Lowe's hardware centers.

So imagine that an organization has properly developed and followed the first four principles and also has developed strategies and business models that are consistent with the first four principles. Is success ensured? The answer to that question is heavily dependent on whether the right competencies, in sufficient quantity and deployed appropriately, are available to execute what has been designed.

A corporate competency is a set of skills that contribute to the organization's product or service offerings such that customers see real benefit. The most valuable competencies are difficult for competitors to imitate. For example, exceptional customer service—real empathetic problem solving as distinct from the perfunctory "have a nice day" responses—can engender strong customer loyalty, ensure repeat business, and even help recapture lost business.

Because strategies and business models are, by definition, forward-looking, a company's competencies must also support future directions. Thus, an important element of Principle 5 is to identify those competencies needed to support the chosen direction, to assess the gaps that may exist, and to develop plans specifically relating to building or acquiring the necessary competencies.

An important step in properly identifying and assessing competencies is to recognize that there are both strategic and tactical aspects to competencies. A common mistake is to think primarily about competencies in terms of the day-to-day tactical activities. Tactical competencies are clearly important, but they are often not the aspects that most fundamentally affect the development and execution of strategies and business models.

A useful exercise for any competency assessment is to develop a pyramid of the strategic and tactical components—from the most strategic at the top to the most tactical at the bottom. Figure 7.1 shows such a pyramid of one important corporate activity—the procurement function. The most strategic components are at the top of the pyramid, and the most tactical are at the bottom. The next step is to assess whether each component is presently available in sufficient quality and quantity, and whether it is deployed appropriately to execute the selected strategies and business model.

The classic horror story on this subject is the organization that assigns an entire pyramid of activity to one person or to one small team. Each day, that team will first ensure that the important, urgent tactical matters are taken care of. It is entirely natural that resources gravitate toward fulfilling tactical work first. If they do not, someone—perhaps a plant manager—will complain loudly that his or her immediate needs are not being met. The result is that at the end of the week, the tactical emergencies and priorities have been

Figure 7.1 Strategic and tactical components of modern procurement.

addressed. At the end of the month, the tactical items have been addressed. And, by the end of the year, the same has occurred. Very little time has been devoted to the strategic level, where great value lies.

At most large, complex corporations, it makes sense to organize a competency into separate but linked strategic and tactical teams. (See Figure 7.2 for an example based on the procurement of raw materials in the steel industry.) This structure has been used with great success at companies that recognize different objectives, different processes, different skill sets, even different career paths in each of the two major components of any function: strategic and tactical. Furthermore, each major component deserves to have dedicated resources managed in potentially different ways.

But is it crucial to have all of those competencies in-house? Leading organizations are increasingly recognizing that it makes economic sense to outsource many of the tactical work elements. Networking, alliances, and joint ventures are examples of mechanisms that can be used to leverage the strategic or tactical competencies of other organizations to accomplish your own vision (see Figure 7.3). One of the earliest examples of this concept in action

Figure 7.2 Organizing a competency into linked strategic and tactical teams.

was Chrysler Corp.'s "extended enterprise," which intimately involved key suppliers in product design, planning, and execution.

I would argue that for many executives, their foremost battle is against time. They simply have too little time to think through the big issues of strategy, and to think about how strategy informs the business model and is enabled by the organization's competencies. If that "think time" is not already a top priority, it must become one—and soon.

WHO DOES WELL AT DEVELOPING STRATEGY, BUSINESS MODELS, AND COMPETENCIES?

Although there is plenty to criticize when it comes to corporations' development of strategy, there is a growing list of companies for which strategy is clearly understood and business models are thought through and ably implemented. I'd put corporations such as General Electric and ITT (see the case study on ITT later in this book) on the list of exemplars. A few others who'd make the honor roll:

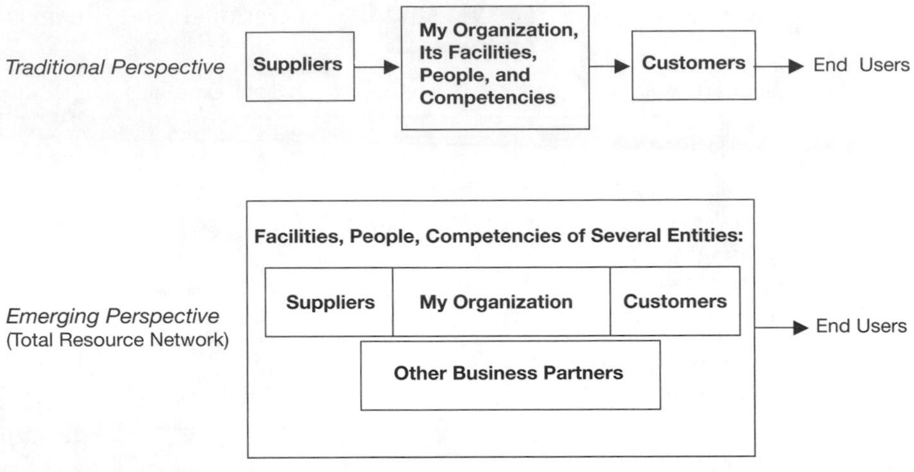

Figure 7.3 Expand the competencies available.

Amazon.com. Amazon.com earns a spot on the honor roll for its creative strategy and business model, its unrelenting dedication to that strategy and business model in spite of numerous naysayers' comments, and the creative extension of its original strategy to incorporate the products of other companies and also to leverage its Web technology to become a technology and logistics service provider.

Bright Horizons Family Solutions. This provider of on-site workplace child care and early-education services is a fascinating example of succeeding by going against the prevailing wisdom. In the mid- to late 1980s, its field was filled with companies that were running their franchises like commodity businesses; namely, keeping labor costs down, offering only the basics, and meeting minimal state licensing requirements.

Bright Horizons adopted an approach that was based on offering premium services. This approach, geared toward the corporate customer seeking a reputable and problem-free on-site operation, ultimately offered what the customer really wanted (high-quality services and high parent satisfaction), and offered Bright Horizons' stockholders a business model with acceptable returns. It's a classic story of designing and implementing a business model that responded to customers' needs while being good for the stockholders.[3]

Emerson Electric. This company is the quintessential example of robust strategy development. Emerson's process, well documented in MBA case studies, takes strategy development—and its operational and financial implications—to a new level of seriousness and discipline. The results—more than 40 consecutive years of earnings growth—speak for themselves.

IBM. IBM deserves mention on the honor roll for Principle 5 because of its successful transformation from a big-box hardware vendor to a company built on a services platform. That services platform is proving to be the engine of growth for IBM.

Xerox. Although Xerox may raise a few eyebrows for its inclusion as an honoree, it is absolutely true that prior to 2001, the company wouldn't have merited a second glance. Indeed, its lack of coherent strategy, combined with poor leadership, caused Xerox to almost implode. Today, under the leadership of CEO Anne Mulcahy, Xerox earns plaudits for its revitalized corporate strategy that "ditched the stagnant analog-copier market to embrace digital products and services,"[4] with particular emphasis on color products, the fastest-growing market segment.

CHECKLIST

As you consider whether or not your organization is doing an effective job of building strategies, business models, and competencies in order to ensure a sustainable future for the business, ask yourself these questions:

- Is our strategy process primarily focused on developing plans and allocating resources in relation to the activities of known competition, or do we spend significant time "creating the future," including understanding changing customer priorities and designing *new* business models?
- Is our strategy development process linked to our purpose, our core values, and our broad world view?
- Do we have a business model that can meet changing customer priorities in a profitable manner for our stockholders?
- Do we invest sufficient time and effort on innovation?
- Do we spend significant time and effort identifying and developing the necessary competencies to succeed?
- Does our organization believe, and demonstrate, that our people are key assets, or do we treat people as commodities and costs?

- Do we attempt to "own" all competencies in-house, or are we open to selectively utilizing the talents of our prospective business partners?

YES, BUT . . .

The counterargument against investing in particular competencies usually goes something like this: Sometimes it is necessary to cut employment costs, and in that environment everyone should share the pain equally.

You and I have heard those arguments before, usually from the bean counters. In effect, what they're saying is that they don't understand the link between competencies and strategy. Even if the CEO or the president "gets it"—thinks of strategy, business model, and competencies concurrently—it's a conceptual framework that must also be embraced by those holding the purse strings.

It comes down to the classic debate about effectiveness versus efficiency. If your organization is embarking on a round of internal cost reductions, should head count reductions apply to all areas equally? To offer some quantitative perspective to that debate, consider Figure 7.4, which is based on six years of data that I retained from my Bethlehem Steel days.

We found that for each additional full-time equivalent (FTE) resource that can be devoted to doing strategic procurement work, an additional $1 million of cost reductions can be generated one year later (the slope of the line is $1 million per FTE per year). Efforts to improve the "efficiency" of the overall procurement organization should be focused on reducing the resources devoted to transactional and tactical activities—that is, shifting the line as far to the left as technology and process permit.

However, applying head count targets to strategic procurement work would have had a very costly outcome. It would literally remove the capability to achieve cost reductions in the largest part of a company's cost structure—purchased goods and services.

Similar points can be made about the strategic and tactical competencies in other functions. One area that often gets short shrift in across-the-board cost cutting is innovation. Yet it is probably not an exaggeration to say that innovation must be part of a sustainable corporate strategy. It can come in many forms, the most fundamental being new product innovation and business process innovation.

Product innovations at Xerox Corporation's Palo Alto Research Center (PARC) during the 1980s and 1990s were among the most important and

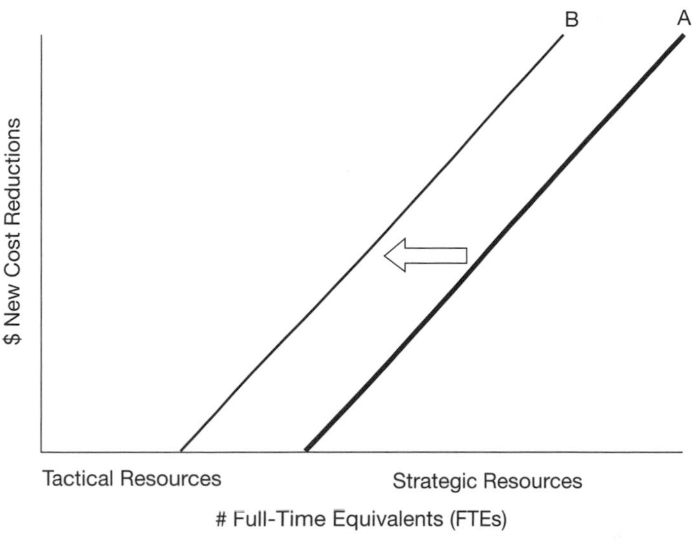

Figure 7.4 The efficiency–effectiveness debate: Some data.

valuable technology ideas of the last 25 years. However, as Xerox's pre-2001 experiences demonstrate, innovations by themselves do not create value for the innovator. Innovations must be incorporated into corporate strategy; and that, in turn, needs to be supported with a sound business model, and appropriate resources and competencies, to effectively launch the innovation and sustain it.

Product innovations, particularly those that might be viewed as having disruptive potential, don't always enjoy enthusiastic support from upper and middle management. As a result, to be successful with disruptive innovations, it is often necessary to establish a discrete business model, with dedicated resources—even geographically removed—from the incumbent organization.

Business process innovations can experience the same challenges. As a result, world-class companies often establish "program offices" under the CEO's umbrella. This program office jump-starts new business processes with dedicated resources, highly visible top management support, and experts in the business process who can help train and embed the new process in the incumbent organization. Such far-reaching business processes as strategic sourcing, Six Sigma, and lean manufacturing have benefited from such a program office catalyst.

8

PRINCIPLE 6: ALIGN AND ENERGIZE THE ORGANIZATION

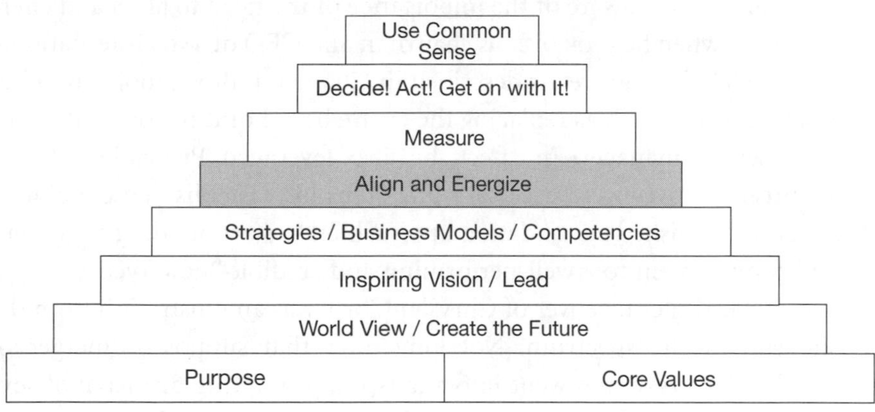

> "Nothing great was ever accomplished without enthusiasm."
>
> —*Ralph Waldo Emerson*

"So *what* if it's good for the company? If it makes me look bad, we won't support it here." That's an actual statement, and it's how one senior production manager of a U.S. manufacturer expressed his contempt for a new corporate-wide initiative to reduce costs.

Resistance to change is endemic in the business world, and it is indicative of several challenges: how to successfully initiate change, how to ensure all parts of an organization are aligned with corporate objectives, and how to ensure the organization is energized to do the right thing. In the situation just described, the company had not yet developed processes and incentives/consequences to ensure alignment of individuals with overreaching corporate initiatives and objectives. Furthermore, individual "blockers of progress," such as that production manager, were highly visible and continued to enjoy a career at the company. Their prominence and persistence had a severe adverse impact on the attitude and energy level of the many employees of the company who *were* receptive to change.

The sixth principle in the Beat the Odds framework means ensuring that the workforce is aligned with the corporate vision, wise to the strategy, clued in to the business model, and energized by them all. Principle 6 begins the transition to the execution and implementation phases derived from the first five principles.

Ed Breen was well aware of the importance of the need to align and energize employees when he took over as chairman and CEO of Tyco International after its steep fall from grace. As described in Chapter 4, Breen took a number of dramatic actions, such as replacing the entire board of directors and virtually every senior manager. In effect, he also leveraged Principle 2 (Core Values). Breen's moves were necessary first steps in reestablishing credibility, but they also established a foundation upon which to start building alignment with and commitment to a well-performing and credible "new Tyco."

The 1998 Daimler takeover of Chrysler Corp. was an illustration from the opposite end of the spectrum. Not long after that supposed "merger of equals," Chrysler's revenues went into a tailspin, prompting dismissal of several of Chrysler's American executives and the introduction of heavy-handed German oversight from Daimler headquarters. All of this created some skepticism about the original characterization of the transaction as a "merger of equals" and did not help the internal dynamics in the new company. It took the later introduction of an unusual German executive, Dieter Zetsche, to begin rebuilding employee trust and respect and to pave the way for a fundamental strengthening of DaimlerChrysler's American operations. Zetsche is a superb communicator.

To that point: An important first step, and one that is often overlooked, is to regularly communicate to the entire organization the results of Principles 1 to 5. Without this knowledge and understanding, members of the organization cannot possibly be as aligned and energized as they could be.

In addition, in order to achieve and maintain alignment, organizations first need to recognize that competencies matter. (That may sound naïve, but it bears repeating for the managers who persist in viewing their employees as costs.) Then they must have a thorough understanding of which competencies matter most for today's business needs—and for those of tomorrow and the day after. Leading companies think in terms of dynamic workforce *systems*—constantly shifting tapestries of talent that must be planned for, organized, and directed.

Next comes the need for focus on simple structures and processes, well-understood reward and recognition systems, simple and straightforward performance measurements (Principle 7), good leadership practices at all levels, and a bias for action—and results. While it is true that certain structures and systems help to "corral" the organization in the right general direction, only continual positive reinforcement will ensure a high degree of alignment. Equally important, there must be consequences for misalignment and shortfalls.

In tandem with efforts to align, organizations must provide "enablers" as well. These can be processes or leadership behaviors that literally encourage and enable members of the organization to become and stay aligned. Table 8.1 draws a distinction between certain conventional approaches to achieving alignment and the recommended approach.

To achieve true organizational health and success, you don't simply want people to be aligned. You want them to be energized. This is the fundamental difference between having *compliance* and having *commitment*. Truly successful organizations have tapped into the emotional energy—the hearts of their employees—with the result being high levels of personal commitment to, and passion about, the organization's goals.

The "symptoms" of an organization that is energized include the following:

- Good internal information sharing.
- Genuine teamwork across functions and across locations.
- People seek ways to help coworkers succeed.
- Regular recognition and celebration activities.
- A high degree of personal intensity and commitment to the organization's objectives.

Table 8.1 Fundamentally Different Approaches to Achieving Alignment

Conventional	Recommended
Tell each person what we want him or her to do (specific job duties).	Communicate the first five principles—where the organization is heading, why, and how (help people see total picture and rationale)—and show how their specific role supports the big picture.
Management focus (see Table 6.1).	Balance between leadership focus and management focus (Table 6.1).
Controls, procedures.	Well-understood objectives and performance measures; feedback on progress.
Across-the-board pay adjustments ("everybody shares equally").	Rewards for alignment and achieving results; consequences for misalignment and failing to achieve expectations.
"Just pay" viewed as the reward.	Higher level of rewards/satisfaction is also involved (contributing to organization's purpose and broad objectives).
Organization chart with hierarchical communications.	Multiple communication mechanisms.
Outcome: compliance.	Outcome: committed and energized personnel; results-oriented culture.

A prime litmus test for whether your organization is truly aligned and energized is the following: *Are employees (at all levels) willing to continually set aside personal agendas, egos, and personal preferences to do what is right for the organization's future?* You probably have an opinion about the answer, but can you be sure your view is correct? How can you develop a fact-based answer to this important question? (See Part IV of this book, along with the diagnostics templates in Appendix A, for some ideas on how to reduce the guesswork.)

Another litmus test is whether or not your organization exhibits signs of the Abilene Paradox. First described by Dr. Jerry Harvey, professor of management science at George Washington University, in a nutshell, it describes the situation "when groups take action that contradicts what the [individual] members of the group silently agree they want or need to do."[1]

Groups, or companies, that are "on the road to Abilene" can be identified by these characteristics: Individual members tend to agree, in private, about the underlying problem—and about appropriate measures to solve the problem.

However, once they are in a group setting, those same individual members tend to not communicate their perspectives, their observations, and their opinions. As a result, the group tends to acquiesce, by default, on a path that each individual member knows is incorrect, but no one is willing to raise their hand and say, "This is nuts!" If your organization has done a good job on the first five principles and has also truly aligned and energized the organization to do the right things, the Abilene Paradox should manifest itself rarely, if at all.

The Abilene Paradox surfaced at Xerox during 1999 to 2000, when the company's new CEO G. Richard Thoman—an outsider to the Xerox culture—sought to spur change at the then slow-moving corporation. Among his attempted changes was a restructuring of the sales force, an idea that was not new to Xerox but that had been avoided for years by the Xerox culture.[2] Thoman aggressively pushed that idea forward, but did so in a manner that arguably ignored the value of alignment and motivation. This was one of several attempted changes that contributed to his early departure. Successor CEO Anne Mulcahy said during a later interview: "We threw the whole sales force up in the air and didn't think about what that would cost us in terms of customer relationships, continuity and trust. *Everyone in the field knew it was stupid, but nobody said anything.*"[3]

WHO ALIGNS AND ENERGIZES THEIR EMPLOYEES EFFECTIVELY?

You can pretty much *read* strong alignment in the body language of employees who practice it—however unconsciously. They're clearly motivated; chances are they'll go out of their way to help each other and help to solve customers' problems. They're fundamentally happy. They're interested in what their company is doing and where it's going. Moreover, they can *tell* you in their own words, with some sparkle in their eyes—without reading off some boilerplate manifesto behind the desk or on the screen. You'll probably find that's the case at these companies:

The "fix" of **Continental Airlines** by CEO Gordon Bethune during the mid- to late 1990s is a classic example of aligning and energizing a workforce, from top to bottom. Over less than five years, Bethune was credited with a very effective overhaul of a severely sick corporate culture. The CEO utilized a combination of incentives, a significant personal investment in communication with employees and visits to employees at all locations, and a passion

The Org Chart Diversion

You may have experienced the following situation yourself. An organization is experiencing performance problems that just don't dissipate. The senior management team decides that the organization structure is at fault and that a "corporate reorganization" will give the necessary boost to performance. In come the consultants, and they happily redraw the complete organization chart. New divisions are created on paper, new management councils are designed, reporting relationships are changed, and new job descriptions are written. Much time and money are spent on "correcting" things. Management thinks it is about to fix its stubborn problem.

But performance does not measurably improve. In fact, in many cases such as this, performance worsens. Employees lose their focus, and also become disenchanted with senior management for not dealing with the root causes of the performance shortfalls.

Although a poor organization design can be an impediment to success, an organization design is rarely a driver of success. Furthermore, the temptation to apply the "org chart fix" to an enterprise ignores an important reality: The informal relationships and networks inside an organization are often more important than hierarchical org charts. And these informal ties are guided more by the organization's purpose, values, and vision than they are by somebody's recently published org chart.

Long story short: In such situations, it's crucial for management to make sure that the underlying problem is properly diagnosed before concluding that a new organization design might be helpful. The root problem could be associated with one or more of the principles between 1 (Purpose) and 8 (Decide! Act!). In the terminology of a later section of this book: "Don't Guess—Assess!"

about service levels and consistency in operations. He personally led regular reviews of how well Continental was doing relative to key objectives such as service performance and customer satisfaction, and instituted a system of feedback by employees on how well their supervisors communicated Continental's "Go Forward Plan." The result of all these coordinated activities was a motivated, happy, and fully aligned workforce that made the Continental of the past a distant memory.[4]

Starbucks Coffee, according to a feature article in *Fortune*,[5] ". . . is possibly the most dynamic new brand and retailer to be conceived over the past two decades." Starbucks' success, according to Chairman Howard Schultz, is heavily due to his early decision to give employees stock options. That, combined with better salaries and benefits than a franchise approach would allow, has helped to create a remarkable level of employee alignment and energy—some would say "zeal"—that is uncharacteristic of most "fast-food" businesses.

CHECKLIST

As you consider whether or not your organization is doing an effective job of aligning and energizing, ask yourself these questions:

- Do we regularly communicate our purpose, core values, inspiring vision, and strategy to our employees?
- Do we regularly communicate to our employees about the external realities of our business?
- Do we have simple structures and processes that support what we are trying to accomplish?
- Do we have well-understood reward and recognition systems?
- Are there truly consequences for poor performance?
- Are there consequences for behavior that is inconsistent with our core values? Are those consequences the same for senior managers and low-level employees?
- Are employees at all levels willing to set aside personal agendas, egos, and personal preferences to do what is right for the organization's future?
- If the organization heads down a path that individual members privately believe to be incorrect, is the work environment such that someone will be comfortable to stand up and say, "This is nuts!"?

YES, BUT . . .

I've heard the grumbling before: "Yes, alignment and energy are great theoretical concepts, but all I need as a manager are employees who can follow my directions."

That worked better when Andrew Carnegie was a steel baron, but it's a far less effective approach in a free labor market. Even if employees do not quickly vote with their feet, they can still act as a drag on operating efficiency if they do the bare minimum. At worst, disgruntled or merely dissatisfied employees can and regularly do alienate customers.

There is a huge opportunity for corporations to align and energize their workforces. According to a 2005 worldwide research study by human resources consultancy Towers Perrin, "just 14% of people are fully engaged on the job and willing to go the extra mile for their companies."[6] This indicates " . . . a vast reserve of untapped 'employee performance potential' that can drive better financial results—if companies can successfully tap into this reserve." If you have been following the logic of this book and this chapter, it should not surprise you to learn that the Towers Perrin's study also concluded that these same employees who are not engaged generally lack confidence in the ability of senior management to lead, inspire, act consistently with core values, and communicate key decisions.

The study also found a significant difference between the engagement levels of employees in for-profit organizations compared to not-for-profit. The not-for-profits enjoy greater commitment "because employees believe in their employer's mission."[7]

9

PRINCIPLE 7: MEASURE ONLY WHAT YOU WANT TO ACHIEVE

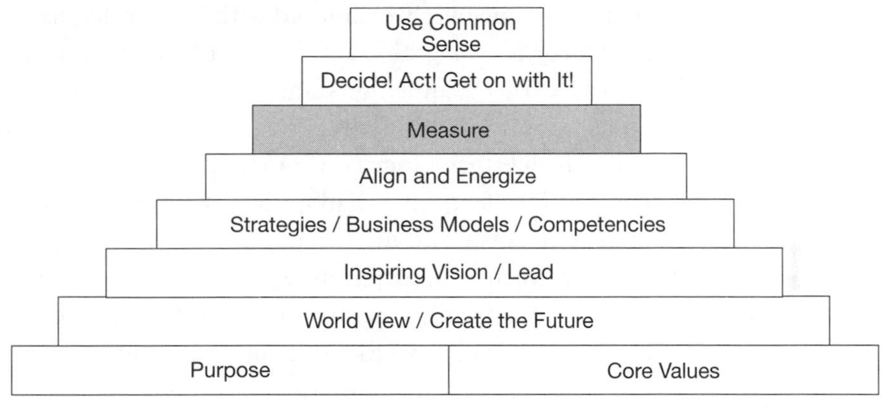

"You get what you measure."

—*Author unknown*

Early in its history, Southwest Airlines lived by a metric that made a big difference in its performance. The metric was its "20-minute turnaround" time, a commitment that it would turn around its planes at an airport gate in 20 minutes, cleaned, restocked, and ready to fly again. The metric proved to be a powerful internal operational discipline that resulted in cost savings, as well as a powerful marketing tool with customers.

By contrast, one U.S. manufacturer that will go unnamed began focusing on the wrong kind of measurement. The company had been going through a protracted period of downsizing. Over time, management seemed to adopt the view that head count reduction was synonymous with improved bottom-line performance. In fact, one of their most talked-about, measured, and reported "objectives" was head count. Indeed, the managers were so experienced in achieving head count objectives in successive waves of downsizings that they received benchmarking requests from major companies that were starting their first rounds of staff cuts.

Almost too late, the company began to notice examples where its *effectiveness* to accomplish important business functions had been eroded. It had become an example of "corporate anorexia." The objective and measurement of head count reduction (*efficiency*) had almost superseded the factors to which management should have given prominence in its performance measurement process (measures of *effectiveness*).

Communications equipment leader Cisco Systems got the wrong end of the measuring stick when it became overly enamored with its own acquisition prowess. A November 1999 *Fortune* magazine article about Cisco's acquisition system was headlined "Forty-Two Acquisitions and Counting."[1] Just a few years later, when Cisco fell afoul of the bursting of the high-tech bubble, its management team came to realize that a focus on "number of deals done" was shortsighted in the new world. In fact, Cisco had grown in an uncoordinated manner, resulting in enormous waste and inefficiency.

By late 2002, Cisco had formed a corporate-wide initiative, under the leadership of the senior manufacturing executive, to identify and eliminate waste. This effort, plus other core initiatives focusing on how to run a business well in good times and bad, reflected a maturation of Cisco's approach to measuring and guiding its business activities.[2]

The lesson here: Since you will only reliably get what you measure, you must measure what you want to achieve. The right performance measures drive appropriate focus, behavior, and results. Too many performance measures risk diluting focus, and thereby risk being counterproductive.

The Hackett Group points out that the use of key performance indicators is not a choice between focusing on effectiveness and focusing on efficiency. The strategic advisory firm's research shows that "world-class firms use efficiency as a means to free up funds to invest in high-impact people and technology—not as an end unto itself."[3] To say it another way, they use efficiency gains to fund adding additional resources to those activities (e.g., strategic themes), which can then drive fundamental business performance.

Performance metrics are either leading indicators or lagging indicators of performance. Examples of leading indicators include the following:

- Customer satisfaction
- Employee satisfaction and commitment
- Adherence to core values
- 360-degree feedback on leadership practices
- The number of supply chain alliances designed and implemented

Following are some conventional lagging indicators:

- Last quarter's net income
- Last year's return on assets
- Last year's cash flow
- The number of purchase orders processed per employee
- The average cost to process an invoice

Leading indicators give a clue to the likely future success of the organization. They indicate whether or not you are "building for the future," and can provide an early warning signal of future problems. For instance, persistent indications of customer dissatisfaction are an alarm bell about future order rates and revenues. Employee dissatisfaction can be a leading indicator of future key employee departures. Customer and employee indicators are among the strongest leading indicators of future performance. Lagging indicators are like looking in the rearview mirror. It's useful information about where you've been, but it's dangerous to steer by it. Financial performance, by its nature historical, is typically a lagging indicator.

Of course, metrics are nothing new. Stopwatch in hand, scientific management expert Frederick Winslow Taylor was gathering productivity data before the First World War. In recent decades, parts-per-million quality data helped drive the Total Quality movement in the 1980s just as net-promoter scores now help determine customer satisfaction at corporations such as General Electric. Supply chain metrics have gathered pace as supply chains have become the system to optimize; at the executive level, strategic measurement methods such as the Balanced Scorecard and newer financial metrics such as return on invested capital (ROIC) have become commonplace.

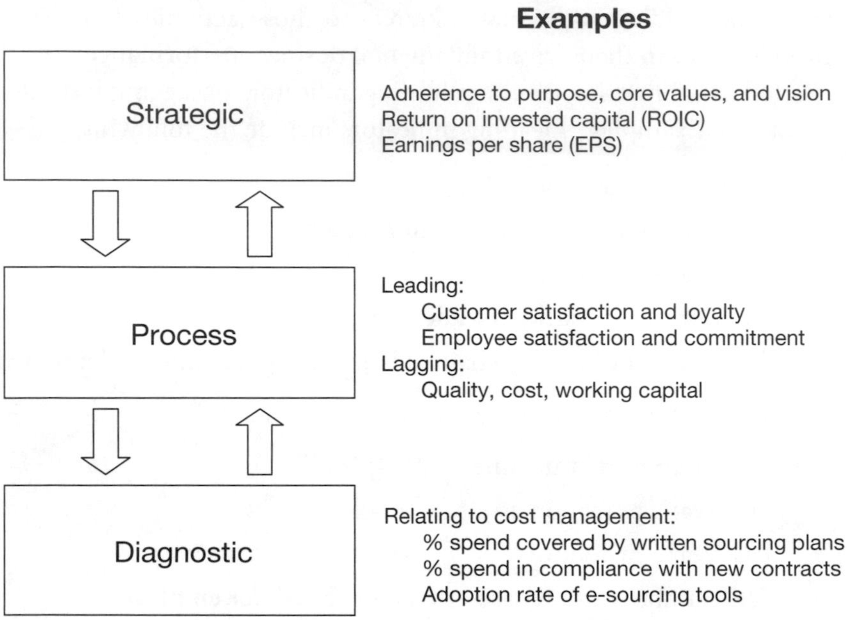

Examples

Strategic

Adherence to purpose, core values, and vision
Return on invested capital (ROIC)
Earnings per share (EPS)

Process

Leading:
Customer satisfaction and loyalty
Employee satisfaction and commitment
Lagging:
Quality, cost, working capital

Diagnostic

Relating to cost management:
% spend covered by written sourcing plans
% spend in compliance with new contracts
Adoption rate of e-sourcing tools

Figure 9.1 The hierarchy of metrics.

Technology systems are enabling far more data-driven decision making, certainly in terms of data gathering, data analysis, and data mining but also in the form of easily managed business-intelligence "dashboards" that give executives key metrics at a glance. Recent research by consultancy Accenture reveals that the use of data analytics for decision making has increased significantly since 2002. Organizations are now actively exploiting their enterprise IT systems to facilitate decision making. More than 30 percent of managers responding to Accenture's survey said they are using their enterprise systems for "significant decision support or analytical capability" compared to 19 percent four years ago. Importantly, the leading companies are taking care to measure only the performance factors that will truly distinguish them in their markets.[4]

So what's the best way to organize the internal discussion of goals and measurements so it facilitates the achievement of the right objectives and the right priorities—and does not inadvertently hurt your strategy and internal alignment? One useful framework is to recognize that there are three major categories of objectives. (Refer to Figure 9.1 to see how they cascade.)

At the top are the overarching "business-level," or strategic, objectives. These are the objectives that your corporation's senior executives and business unit leaders should be thinking about regularly. Prime among them are adherence to purpose and core values and vision; and two classic financial metrics: ROIC and earnings per share (EPS).

In the middle, supporting the strategic objectives, are "process-level" objectives. These provide indications of whether core business processes are performing well in support of near-term achievement of strategic objectives (typically measured with lagging indicators) and other indications of likely future performance (typically measured with leading indicators). Examples include leading indicators like customer satisfaction and employee satisfaction, and current levels of quality, cost, and working capital as lagging indicators.

If the metrics relating to processes indicate some unhealthiness, or a degree of suboptimization, then you should introduce the third level of metrics, sometimes referred to as "diagnostic" metrics. These enable management to identify and analyze underlying problems or root causes that are having an adverse effect on the process-level metrics (and that, in turn, impact the strategic objectives). Diagnostic metrics are also helpful during the early stages of innovation or process change, when you want to monitor adoption rates, and also measure how individual activities are changing as a result of the transformation you have initiated.

It is useful to measure both leading indicators and lagging indicators. But it is important to focus on just a few key objectives to which everyone can relate their activities. These measures should be highly visible and easily understood. They must be discussed regularly and monitored by all levels of the organization. One example of a measurement and management system that links it all together is value-based management (VBM).[5] Adopted by such leading organizations as Danaher and ITT, VBMs typically focus on generating value from the perspective of stockholders, customers, and employees. (See the ITT profile later in this book.)

VBM is expressed publicly as a "management system," and it becomes the tool that managers at all levels use day to day to gauge whether their units are on track against agreed-upon goals. It is also a tool for measuring the performance of the managers themselves. Here's how Danaher describes its system: "Success at Danaher doesn't happen by accident. We have a proven system for achieving it. We call it the Danaher Business System (DBS), and it drives every aspect of our culture and performance. We use DBS to guide what

The "Take This Job, Please" Index

On a humorous note, one of my former colleagues suggested a new index as a true leading indicator of employee alignment, commitment, and morale. It was to be based on the prevalence of office lottery pools. The suggested title was "Take This Job, Please"—a more refined form of the reaction to be expected from someone who had just won the big one.

The TTJP Index would be measured by the number of office lottery pools established when lottery prizes exceeded a predetermined level—$50 million, say. Two or more office workers pooling their purchase of lottery tickets would constitute one office pool. The metric is particularly interesting in a multifloor office building or a multibuilding office campus. If you noticed a growing number of lottery pools at your organization, what might that indicate?

After some watercooler debate, a refinement was suggested for the TTJP metric. Add this additional dimension: After the participants of a lottery pool are notified (by e-mail or phone) to contribute their share for the next round of the lottery, how much time elapses before the first person shows up with cash in fist? The metric and its analytical conclusions could be tabulated as follows:

First Person Arrives	Comment
(a) Next day:	Not to worry.
(b) Within one hour:	You have reason for concern.
(c) Within 10 minutes:	Your employees are desperate to get out.
(d) The participants prepay:	Don't you wish your employees were similarly energized and committed to your company?

we do, measure how well we execute, and create options for doing even better—including improving DBS itself."[6]

WHO MEASURES UP AT MEASURING WELL?

Metrics gauge the performance of every kind of organization, public or private, for-profit or nonprofit. To the extent that they are heeded, and to the extent that they are the metrics that matter, they also help to govern the corporate performance. So who deserves kudos for measuring well?

Alcoa has historically received high marks for its focus on appropriate measurements, and for its application of those measurements to fundamentally alter the company's culture. In the late 1980s, Alcoa began to introduce a discipline of measuring nonfinancial and financial metrics, combined with accountability for achieving objectives. That proved to be a powerful combination. In Alcoa's experience, a focus on improving safety proved to be a leading indicator of future productivity improvements and world-class operations. These, in turn, contributed to improved financial performance.

Similarly, **General Motors**, regularly in the financial doghouse during much of the 1980s and 1990s, began to show some signs of renewed vigor under the leadership of Richard Waggoner. Part of the Waggoner approach has been a focus on key measurements, to much more detailed levels than in the past. But it's not just the measurements themselves that add value. A critical step has been the utilization of monthly meetings of his 14-person management committee to actively discuss performance and to focus on process improvements and personnel (both of which were evidently understood to be leading indicators for future performance).[7] GM still faces plenty of significant challenges, including renewing top-line growth so that its business model math has hopes of working. Nevertheless, its attention to Principle 7 is an important element in its managing for the future.

Robroy Industries reached its 100th birthday in early 2005 and is being managed by the fourth generation of the founding family. In a bylined article, Robroy CEO Peter McIlroy offered these comments about the importance of measurement:

> *You can't know what you don't know. We have placed a premium on measurement and accountability. This is good business practice during the best of times and a life-saver during the worst. Over 100 years, we have made mistakes—some of them potentially catastrophic. However, in those instances, when our self-evaluations told us we had erred, we consciously worked to set aside egos and to promptly change our direction.*
>
> *For that reason, I urge all businesses to be metric-focused. If you cannot immediately—and I do mean immediately—summon statistical information specific to your top-line sales, the bottom line of your balance sheet and daily measurements of all vital production performance, you're at serious risk of going astray. Similarly, if your personnel have not been properly positioned with performance-based on-the-job objectives*

that can be accurately and fairly measured, you are at jeopardy of being lost without even knowing it.[8]

CHECKLIST

As you consider whether or not your organization is doing an effective job of measuring only what you want to achieve, ask yourself these questions:

- Do we rely on, and measure, only a few significant objectives?
- Do we measure mostly leading indicators, or are we looking mostly in the rearview mirror?
- Do we act on what we measure, or do we measure for measurement's sake?
- Are our measurements highly visible to all employees?
- Are our measurements easily understood by all employees?
- Are all of our employees linked to the same few performance measures?

YES, BUT . . .

"Yes, it sounds great to talk about measuring only a few important indicators, but my business is complex. I need to monitor lots of factors, both internal and external."

I've heard that response before. So have you, I'm sure. The desire of most leaders and managers to monitor many factors is not necessarily in conflict with the theme of this chapter. But the distinction is this: It is essential to measure a few key indicators that relate to corporate objectives. These key indicators need to be widely understood and highly visible, and embedded in the personal objectives of employees at all levels. They are the "super metrics," if you like. If you do this properly, these indicators will help drive appropriate focus and behavior throughout the organization and contribute to alignment.

So the monitoring of other factors by individual managers is fine, as long as it does not conflict with the organization's focus on the preselected "super metrics." To say it another way, each manager has full flexibility to acquire and evaluate all sorts of data for diagnostic purposes, but he or she must not let those metrics dilute the organization's focus on the few key objectives that have been determined to be strategically important. Monitoring of other factors serves the organization's overall purposes when it is used to gain insight and trigger relevant questions about what is happening internally and externally—and to get at the root cause of issues.

10

PRINCIPLE 8: DECIDE! ACT! GET ON WITH IT!

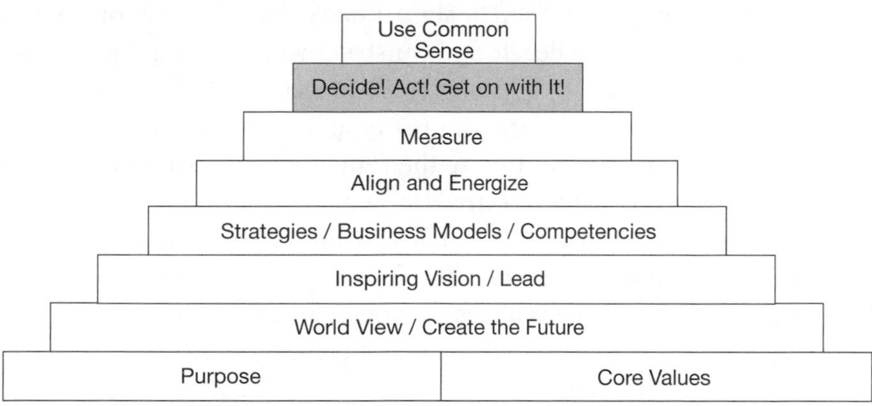

> "We trained hard . . . but it seemed that every time we were beginning to form up into teams, we would be reorganized. I was to learn later in life that we tend to meet any new situation by reorganizing; and a wonderful method it can be for creating the illusion of progress while producing confusion, inefficiency and demoralization."
>
> —*Petronius Arbiter*
> *Roman Navy, 210 B.C.*

If Petronius Arbiter were to join today's U.S. Marine Corps, he would not have that experience. The Corps holds firm to "the 70 percent solution." Its guiding principle: "If you have 70 percent of the information, have done 70 percent of the analysis, and feel 70 percent confident, then move. The logic is simple: A less-than-ideal action, swiftly executed, stands a chance of success, whereas no action stands no chance."[1]

Using today's terms, Petronius Arbiter might refer to his frustrating experiences as "busywork." And he'd probably be familiar with busywork's equally unhelpful cousin: "paralysis by analysis." For a good example of the latter, look no further than a certain midsized U.S. company that was characterized by a superficially "polite" corporate culture. In meetings, there was little debate and even less open dialogue. Disagreements, when they occurred, were private matters. Much time was spent lobbying behind the scenes for individual agendas. The staffs of certain executives spent incredible amounts of time preparing for "chart wars." In the unnaturally polite wars, one presenter would seek to take the initiative on a subject with subtly worded charts—in lieu of open discussion.

The senior management team finally acknowledged that the company had a cultural bias for avoiding debate and constructive conflict, and it took steps to alter its culture accordingly. As progress was made in this area, the executives found that the company was also better able to expand the list of possible actions to be considered, to make the right decisions from the expanded action list, and to execute the selected decisions.

Previously, the company seemed to be mired in inconclusive discussions—not to mention endless studies of data. Employees had characterized senior management as "slow as molasses" and believed they were afflicted with "analysis paralysis." To many, it seemed that meetings were held for the sake of holding meetings. (See Figure 10.1.)

Some years ago, Eastman Kodak suffered from an acute case of analysis paralysis. Its indecision regarding adoption and commercialization of digital photography proved to be a costly mistake. What is not well-known is that Kodak actually spearheaded digital photography with the first digital camera—as far back as the mid-1970s! But the company's chronically slow decision making, and its reluctance to adopt an innovative technology that some insiders viewed as having the potential to cannibalize its then-high-margin film business, caused it to be a second-rate player in the early stages of the fast-growing digital market.

The eighth principle of the Beat the Odds framework I call "Decide! Act! Get on with It!" There is simply no substitute for crisp, disciplined decision making followed by well-paced and effectively measured action. Once the first

"I'll begin by reading the minutes from our last meeting:
Higgins: 'If I don't get out of here my head will explode.'
Jennings: 'I feel like I'm trapped in a Kafka-like nightmare.'
Milbrooke: 'This is two hours of my life I'll never get back'..."

Figure 10.1 ©Mike Shapiro, 2006, All Rights Reserved. Reprinted with Permission.

seven principles have been effectively adopted and embedded, it becomes critical to the momentum of building a successful and resilient organization to display and encourage an action-oriented culture. It is necessary to "make things happen," and to do so in a manner that is consistent with the first seven principles. In other words, you must "deal with it" and move on.

But there are different levels of "dealing with it." An executive can excel at one type of execution and fail badly at another. Carly Fiorina, former head of Hewlett-Packard, was such an executive. During 2003, the business press generally was complimentary about HP's performance of Principle 8 under Fiorina's leadership. While there has been considerable debate about the wisdom of the Compaq acquisition strategy, what HP did do well was plan the project execution and the initial integration of the two large organizations. "With an elaborate playbook of action plans and time tables," noted the *Wall Street Journal*, "H-P Chief Executive Carly Fiorina has managed to succeed at the first chapter of the biggest high-tech merger ever: putting the pieces together."[2]

Unfortunately, project integration is one thing, but operational execution is another. As has come to light after the ouster of Fiorina, operational execution at HP left much to be desired. And, that is an important distinction to make regarding Principle 8. Success requires not only excellent planning and execution of projects of any nature and size but also excellent planning and execution of ongoing business activities. Perhaps that is why, as the *Wall Street Journal* subsequently reported, "Chiefs with the skills of a COO gain favor as celebrity CEOs fade."[3] And perhaps that is why HP is now headed by a consummate low-key operations man: Mark Hurd.

There is another vital facet to action: It is crucial to deal not only with the urgent matters but also the important ones. Too many executives focus on the firefights, and at the end of the week or the end of the month, the strategic issues have not been properly attended to. I once heard it said that too many corporate cultures lionize the "firefighters"—the executives who recognize and tamp down crises—but they fail to recognize the real heroes who prevent the crises from happening in the first place.

Simply doing more stuff faster is no substitute for doing the correct things. Actions must be completely consistent with the first seven principles, and thereby demonstrate and reinforce the appropriateness and importance of those principles. Done regularly and sincerely, action steps that are focused on the right things will build a virtually unstoppable momentum and help to establish an organizational culture—focused on action and results—that continually reinvigorates itself.

The important interaction of Principles 5 and 8 can be visualized in Figure 10.2. The combination of good strategy, well-executed, is the best of all worlds; it will generate good results fast. (The worst scenario is to have excellent execution of a bad strategy—you achieve bad results or even disaster, quickly.) Good strategy poorly executed often results in mediocrity. And, of course, poor strategy poorly executed will eventually yield the bad results that are to be expected.

A powerful, simple tool is available to help accomplish the intended actions; it is sometimes referred to as the "project workplan." While there are many variations on the workplan idea, the essentials are shown in Figure 10.3. The workplan identifies the action steps, the timeline, and the parties responsible or involved. It is a useful tool to organize your thought processes about a complex activity. It is a powerful tool for communicating, for coordinating, and for leading and managing activities toward timely results.

Figure 10.2 Interaction of Principles 5 and 8.

Project Name: Customer X Sales Plan
Team Leader: John Q. Smith

Project Objective/Deliverable: 12% higher sales in next calendar year with Customer X

Action	Who Leads	Jan	Feb	Mar	April	May	June
Kickoff Meeting (internal)							
Team Charter, Scope	JQS	■					
Finalize Project Timeline	JQS	■					
Data Gathering							
Issues	BM		■				
Opportunities	BM		■				
Value Proposition Development	FZ		■	■			
Account Resource Plan	FZ			■			
Plan Approach to Customer	EF			■			
Presentation to Customer	JQS				■		

Figure 10.3 Simple, powerful tool: The project workplan.

It is staggering how many intelligent leaders and managers do not use this simple and powerful tool as a regular part of their repertoire. (Why not? It's highly unlikely that the tools are unknown in this day and age. I believe I'm being more realistic than cynical when I say that some managers simply don't try to use the tools because they don't want to be held accountable. And in the absence of clearly defined roles and responsibilities, it is possible to escape

Week ending mm/dd/yy

Weekly STATUS Report
Project XYZ

Prepared by: Name, contact info

Current Status >

KEY PROJECT DELIVERABLES	**CURRENT WEEK PROGRESS**
Deliverable 1 Deliverable 2 Deliverable 3 Deliverable 4	☐ NO ☐ YES Add your comments here. Keep it brief.

EXPECTED RISKS / PROBLEMS	**ISSUES TO BE DECIDED**
☐ NO ☐ YES If YES, please provide details – Comment 1 – Comment 2	☐ NO ☐ YES If YES, please provide details – None

Figure 10.4 Companion tool: Weekly flash report.

accountability.) A companion report, the weekly status report, is essentially a flash reporting tool for communicating key points about the progress or lack thereof for a given project (see Figure 10.4) .

In addition to the project workplan tool, operational excellence in *everyday* activities is a basic need. Having streamlined, efficient, and *repeatable* processes can be a major contributor to enabling the right things to happen, avoiding the "killer re's" (rework, redesign, re-create, reengineer, reexamine, reinspect, remanufacture, reestimate, reapply, rebuild, and so on) and preventing unwelcome outcomes. These correct, repeatable processes can contribute to momentum building—and to effective execution of the prior seven principles.

WHO HAS A BIAS FOR ACTION?

An action orientation is something to applaud when the actions are backed with the right data, driven by the right plans, and flexible enough to roll with the punches when external factors change. Following are two corporations that I would certainly celebrate for their biases toward action.

Novartis AG. The Switzerland-based drug company exemplifies the "get it done" culture. Formed in 1996 from the combination of Ciba-Geigy and Sandoz, Novartis had an objective of becoming a maker of leading-edge cancer and cardiovascular drugs. Novartis CEO Dr. Dan Vasella realized that accomplishing that objective required top talent and a "make-it-happen" corporate culture. Unable to link up with a U.S. merger partner, and initially unsuccessful in attracting top scientists, Vasella took a straightforward, bold approach. He authorized his human resource people to offer competitive compensation packages, including stock options and performance-related bonuses, to top U.S. talent.[4]

At a later date, to further cement his commitment to research and to continue attracting top talent, Vasella made a decision to locate a major research facility in Cambridge, Massachusetts—not in Europe, as observers had expected. Since 1996, when he became CEO, Vasella has been credited with significantly enhancing Novartis's research capabilities and transforming a once-stodgy Swiss drug company into one of the world's premier pharmaceutical companies.

Kodak. Kodak also earns a place on the roster. I know that may surprise you, but I'm talking about the *new* Kodak. In the last few years, CEO Daniel Carp (a lifelong Kodak employee) and then-COO Antonio Perez (now CEO) made a clear and significant commitment to digital photography. By mid-2004, total corporate revenues were on an upswing, and Kodak was being viewed as a first-tier player in the digital market.[5] By early 2006, when Kodak reported its full-year 2005 results, a remarkable transition had occurred: Kodak generated more annual sales from digital imaging than from film-based photography. While by no means complete, this first stage of a strategic transition for Kodak was accomplished in record time, and "just in time" too, as the film market continued its dramatic shrinkage.[6]

CHECKLIST

As you consider whether or not your organization is doing an effective job of deciding and getting on with it, ask yourself these questions:

- Is our organization "action-oriented?"
- Do we focus on results rather than the procedures?
- Do we have clearly defined roles and responsibilities?

- Do our managers regularly utilize project plans to communicate, coordinate, and manage toward timely results?
- Do we have streamlined, efficient, and repeatable processes?
- Do we make it easy for innovative ideas to succeed?

YES, BUT . . .

"Yes, decision making is important, but the reality in our corporate culture is that we analyze everything to death. Decisions, if they are made, are often made too late."

I hear you. Analysis paralysis is common in many, many organizations. It may be recognized, talked about, and identified as a threat; yet it may still appear in pernicious pockets all over your organization. It often results from a culture that is unwilling to take risks, and therefore strives for complete and perfect knowledge—which, of course, is elusive.

So where does that attitude to risk come from, and how can it be managed? Risk can be favorably affected by doing a good job on Principles 1 to 7, and by communicating those principles to your employees and other constituents. Think of it this way: *In the absence* of the guidance that the first seven principles can provide, employees are much less likely to take action on their own. *With* the framework and guidance that the first seven principles offer, employees will be more likely to act because their actions will be supported and encouraged by the framework you have already provided.

There is another aspect of minimizing risk: providing risk management tools to your organization. The process of risk management involves risk identification, risk assessment (frequency and severity), the development of risk management options (retain, transfer, mitigate), and ongoing monitoring. In the absence of an understanding of the risks involved in a business activity, the natural human inclination is to do nothing. Providing a risk management framework and set of tools can help to provide a common basis for approaching risk analysis and a framework for considering how best to manage risk and move forward toward the right business outcome.

Organizational complexity is another pervasive impediment to action and decision making. Internal complexity can be a significant impediment to operational performance, to the development and speedy implementation of new ideas designed to create competitive advantage, and to a focus on external opportunities. But it's something we can change *if we choose to do so.*

I have found that internal complexity is often inversely related to the organization's performance in the first seven principles. In the case of one organization I've worked with, a root-cause analysis of its complexity amounted to a litany of weaknesses in those principles. When employees don't have the natural guidance that the first seven principles offer, things often go awry. This can prompt management to add "belt and suspenders" in the form of more layers of management, more complex organization structures, oversight committees, and so forth. As management does a better job on the first seven principles, there is a golden opportunity to simultaneously reduce complexity—with all that that means for the speed of decision making and resulting actions.

11

PRINCIPLE 9: WHEN IN DOUBT, APPLY COMMON SENSE

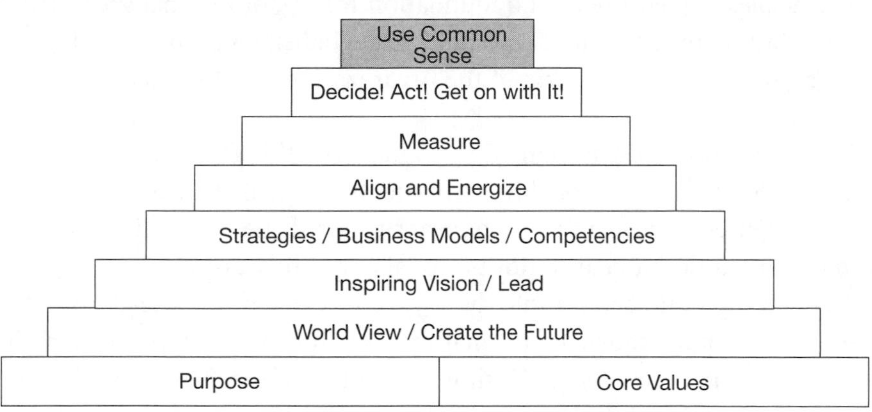

> "Never give in, never give in . . . except to convictions of humor and good sense."
>
> —*Winston Churchill*

You know it and I know it: Some executives do really dumb things. Worse, their colleagues and even their board members not only tolerate the daft decisions, but they permit the resulting actions. Unfortunately, there's no shortage of examples to choose from.

Case in point: American Airlines' attempt to implement plump executive pensions just when it was in dire financial straits and was seeking concessions from its unions.[1] Talk about self-serving! And talking of servings: How about the KFC ad campaign aimed at persuading people that fried chicken is a healthy food? In a complaint filed by the nonprofit Center for Science in the Public Interest (CSPI), the nutritional facts about fried chicken were detailed, in stark contrast to the impression left by the KFC ads.[2]

And then there is the complete absence of common sense demonstrated by the New York Stock Exchange when it granted outgoing executive Dick Grasso a retirement package valued in excess of $100 million. Arguably, Grasso himself lacked any semblance of good sense by accepting such a package in a society where there are fewer and fewer secrets and increased scrutiny is being applied to all public figures.

The ninth principle of the Beat the Odds framework I call "When in Doubt, Apply Common Sense." The first eight principles provide a framework and roadmap for organizational fitness and success. Understood and followed, these principles will ensure a solid foundation for organizational success and resilience. But there are plenty of questions and challenges even when all eight are woven tightly into the fabric of the organization. That's where common sense comes in.

So can common sense be taught? Is it a maturity thing? A judgment thing? Something your mother probably tried and tried again to teach you? Is it deeply enough embedded in your character to resist the temptations of ego-driven opportunities or chances for personal enrichment or reputation?

It's not my goal here to get into the psychology of common sense. But it is my intent to remind readers that it matters a great deal when doubts remain about issues or activities. Often it's simply a matter of carefully reviewing the other eight principles of the Beat the Odds framework and how they are being applied in your organization. It can be evidenced by taking the extra half-hour or half-day to revisit a decision—to avoid jumping to conclusions—or to go over the pros and cons with other managers.

For some specific issues or challenges, an additional common-sense structure or framework may be useful to further guide your thinking and actions. The design of this additional framework is based on the observation that managers and organizations often commit two errors: They fail to identify all principal alternative solutions before making a decision, and they fail to utilize a rigorous set of criteria to evaluate and select the best solution (that is, the best solution may seem "obvious").

In short, the common human error is to jump to the "obvious" option after failing to develop a full list of alternatives and to spend most of the time on the planning and execution of what may be the wrong path!

A. G. Lafley, Procter & Gamble's CEO, utilizes a simple yet elegant approach to decision making. Before making a decision or setting a new strategy, ". . . he always asks managers to give him two different approaches and present the pros and cons of each." Furthermore, " . . . at meetings Lafley says, 'Before you jump in and inject your own point of view, make sure you listen and truly understand the other's point of view.'"[3] Combine this "listen and learn" attitude with a culture that encourages debate, and you have a powerful combination.

But how to best identify those few approaches that deserve serious consideration? A rigorous, common sense discipline would be to:

1. Properly define and describe the core issue(s), often by asking fundamental questions (and, at the same time, avoid stating your own opinion, since that can skew others' thinking).
2. Exhaustively generate many ideas and potential solutions (without debating, at this brainstorming stage, the merits of any idea).
3. Determine the relevant and comprehensive criteria for evaluating the potential solutions.
4. Assess the potential solutions vis-à-vis the evaluation criteria.
5. Decide on the appropriate path, plan the implementation, and move forward (act).

Common sense? Absolutely. Practiced consistently by organizations and managers? Unfortunately, no. But this shortfall in common sense and mental discipline by the many is an opportunity for those few who *do* adopt it.

Longtime British prime minister Margaret Thatcher put it well when she said: "Do what is right, and in the long run history catches up to you." That's the benefit of the long view.

WHO USES COMMON SENSE BEST?

One of the best examples of common sense at work is **Johnson & Johnson's** much-celebrated response to the Tylenol tampering incidents during the 1980s. The conventional wisdom at that time might have been to try to downplay the incidents as something that was unlikely to be repeated and to try to avoid a costly product recall. But J&J went far further than that. Its managers absolutely did the right thing, not only for consumers but for shareholders as well.

Who else makes it onto the honor roll? Retailer **L.L.Bean** merits a place there for the courageous decision taken a few years ago by CEO Christopher McCormick—a decision that *reversed* one of his prior decisions. In late 2004, L.L.Bean had decided to build a call center near Waterville, Maine, a small community located about 60 miles from the company's Freeport, Maine, headquarters. A few months after construction began, T-Mobile USA announced plans to build its own center in the same area. In spite of having already sunk about $500,000 into the site, McCormick called a halt to construction, abandoned the site, and decided to open its center in Bangor, Maine—about 50 miles *further* away. His decision was based on a concern that the Waterville community could not adequately support the seasonal employment needs of L.L.Bean alongside the year-round employment needs of T-Mobile's planned center. Said one observer: "McCormick wasn't concerned about appearing wishy-washy. He simply wanted to make the best decision for the closely-held retailer."[4]

McCormick's willingness to change a prior decision is not typical. The natural inclination of most senior managers is to stick with the initial decision, for fear of inviting criticism of the initial decision, for fear of appearing indecisive, or born of a need to project a "confident, executive image." To reverse a prior decision takes a true leader—one whose personal interests are subordinate to doing the right thing for the organization's future.

US Airways gives us another example of common sense at work. Not long after American Airlines' executives were taking heat for their pay packages, US Airways' new CEO, W. Douglas Parker, rejected a $770,000 bonus that he earned in 2005. Noted one commentator: "Parker said that it would have been wrong to accept the payout before US Airways employees receive payments under a profit-sharing plan."[5]

CHECKLIST

Is yours a common-sense company? Ask yourself these key questions:

- When faced with a procedural, political, or moral dilemma, do leaders throughout our organization fall back on common sense to do what is right, or do other factors such as politics tend to sway decisions?

- Do leaders in our organization take care to properly define and describe the issues to be resolved?
- Do leaders in our organization take the time to identify all possible solutions to an issue before making a decision?
- Do leaders in our organization utilize a rigorous set of criteria to evaluate and select the best solution?
- What instances are there of our leaders exhibiting poor judgment, and how did it hurt the company?
- Were those instances rarities, or are there regular occasions when the good judgment of our company's leaders is called into question?

YES, BUT . . .

"Yes, it's great to say that common sense must prevail, but the world is increasingly complex. What might seem like common sense one day can appear foolish the next day."

For those who say that, I have a simple technique that may serve you well. It's called the "light of day" test. Would your decision or behavior, if widely and publicly known, be viewed positively or negatively? Would you want the story on the front page of the *Wall Street Journal*? In effect, would you and your reputation survive the information being exposed to the light of day?

If you doubt that this can be a powerful test, ask yourself how many of the corporate scandals of the past 20 years would have been averted if the individuals involved had considered their potential actions in the context of the "light of day."

12

IMPLICATIONS FOR THE ORGANIZATION AND FOR INDIVIDUALS

The organization's leadership and all of its employees should be involved in the design and application of the nine principles. However, their relative roles and involvement will differ.

RELATIVE ROLES

As shown in Figure 12.1, the organization and its senior leaders have a relatively large role in establishing and communicating the foundation principles. The role of teams and individuals picks up after the foundation principles have been laid down.

THE ORGANIZATION AS A LIVING ENTITY

An organization's capabilities and horizons are constrained if it is viewed solely as a moneymaking machine. In his book *The Living Company*, former Royal Dutch/Shell executive Arie de Geus notes that organizations can be thought of as machines or as living entities. Viewed as a living thing, an organization can have a quite different set of characteristics and capabilities—with

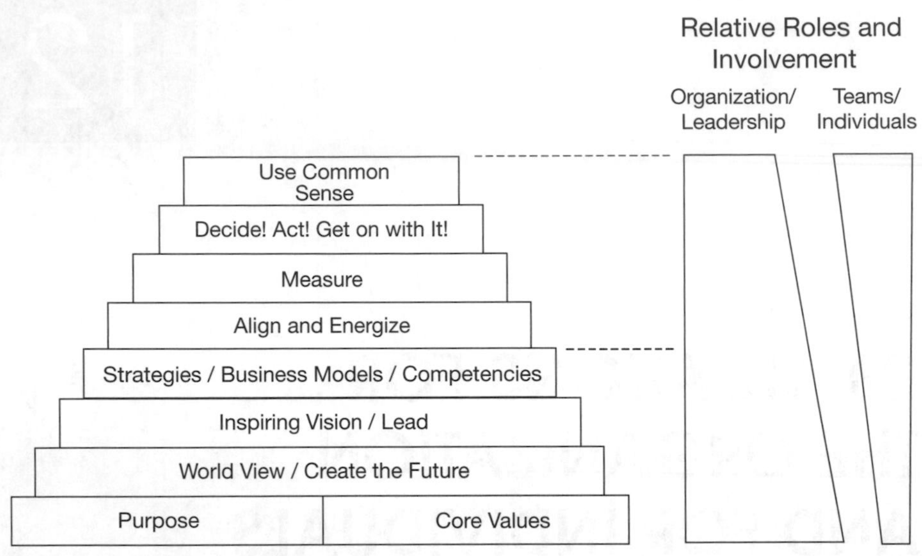

Figure 12.1 Relative roles differ.

significant implications for its ultimate success. It can be encouraged and expected to adapt, to learn, to manage and think, to develop an identity and character of its own, to become aware of its surrounding environment (and able to react to external changes is a timely manner), and to learn how to build constructive relationships with other organizations and entities.

As a living entity, the organization can also be expected to grow and develop until it eventually withers and dies. De Geus notes another "lifelike" characteristic of organizations: They are communities of human beings working together toward one or more purposes. As such, they can accomplish more together than they can separately.[1]

But, you might say, machines are eventually going to have similar characteristics and capabilities. After all, aren't scientists striving to create "artificial intelligence" (AI) that will enable machines to be more "lifelike"? Whether or not that AI goal ever reaches fruition, the point should be obvious: There is perceived value in having machines take on the characteristics and capabilities of living entities.

This "living entity" analogy can be taken a step further, by considering that each of the nine principles is analogous to one or more vital mental or physical processes. Taken as a whole, the nine principles can ensure the long-term health and resilience of an organization. But, just as with a living organism, the

Table 12.1 Organizations Have Characteristics of Living Entities

Characteristics of Living Organisms	Analogous Principle(s) of a Healthy Organization
Brain/intellect	Purpose, Strategies, Measure, Common Sense
Soul	Core Values
Eyes/ears/touch (senses)	Acquire a World View/Create the Future
Mouth	Articulate an Inspiring Vision/Lead
Heart	Purpose, Articulate an Inspiring Vision/Lead, Align and Energize
Internal organs that support the entire organism	Strategies/Business Model/Competencies; Align and Energize
Hands, legs, feet (motion)	Act! Decide! Get on with It!
Neurons, nerve paths	Articulate an Inspiring Vision/Lead (communicate); Measure (feedback)
Musculoskeletal system	Competencies
DNA	Purpose, Values

absence of even one vital mental or physical process (or in our parlance, "principle") can trigger a chain reaction that can prove damaging or even fatal.

Table 12.1 draws an analogy between the nine principles and some critical characteristics of living organisms. With the data in Table 12.1, it becomes clear why the absence of a single principle can have serious health consequences for an organization. It can cause immediate confusion, disarray, or difficulty and lead to much more serious outcomes if left uncorrected. But the table also indicates the benefits of practicing all of the principles in concert, all the time. A living organism is in good health when its organs, muscles, and respiratory, circulatory, and nervous systems are in peak condition. Similarly, an organization whose managers adhere to these nine principles will increase its odds of being in good health and enjoying lasting success.

Part III

PROFILES OF SUCCESS: THREE THAT ARE BEATING THE ODDS

Part III takes the reader through three case studies that amply illustrate the nine principles of the Beat the Odds framework.

The first exemplar is a well-known American manufacturer of premium musical instruments. Founded almost two centuries ago and led by six generations of the same family, the company now faces the very contemporary challenges of growth and pressure to consistently improve business performance while maintaining the reputation its products have earned over 173 years.

The second company is a large yet brand-new player in the global chemicals industry. A recent spin-off of an international giant, this chemicals company is skillfully blending proven strategic disciplines with a strong focus on execution to lay down a strong foundation for success.

The third subject, once famous as a serial acquirer in the conglomerate era, is a large NYSE-listed industrial manufacturer that is sharply focused on doing the right things right. Not satisfied with the company's exemplary performance, the top team continues to refine its "management system"—the tool kit that ensures minimal "leakage" between vision, strategy, and desired results.

13

SIX GENERATIONS AND STILL STRUMMING: MARTIN GUITAR

Not so many years ago, observant visitors to the C. F. Martin & Co. guitar factory might have noticed one or two workers peeking at their "little black books"—well-thumbed notebooks full of notations about specific work practices, tolerances, and quality standards. The visitors could have been excused for dismissing the notebooks as an anachronism—a throwback to an era that predated scientific management and a sharp contrast to the rapidly modernizing business practices typical of the last decades of the twentieth century.[1]

It would have been too hasty a judgment. The little black notebooks told two stories. First and foremost, they were eloquent testimony to a craftsman ethic that has always been absolutely central to the guitar company's being (Figure 13.1). Second, they represented job security—knowledge, much of it irreplaceable, that had been built up over decades and that was a bulwark long after Martin's labor strife had died down.

Today the black books are a rare sight, but many other elements of the craftsman era live on. Deliberately so: The 173-year-old family-run firm, now close to a $100 million annual revenue run rate, is steeped in a tradition of excellence. Its acoustic guitars, renowned for their quality of tone, are highly regarded by top musicians. Indeed, Martin has been the guitar of choice for the likes of Gene Autry and Johnny Cash. Today they are played by superstars such as Eric Clapton and John Mayer. Six generations of workers have taken

Figure 13.1 Visitors to Martin's facilities can take an hour-long guided tour of the factory, following a guitar's creation through 300 steps from rough lumber to finished product.

on the mantle of premium quality. The joke in the front offices is that sometimes Martin's employees have to be reminded that they can stop sanding—that their work is good enough for the next phase of production.

As rooted as it is in tradition, the Nazareth, Pennsylvania, firm is equally concerned about looking forward. Although change has not always come easily, it has come. Operating practices continue to shift, sometimes in startling ways: In one work cell at the main plant in Nazareth, a large industrial robot picks up lacquered guitar bodies and turns them carefully against large buffing wheels. Today the company's management processes are increasingly collaborative and less hierarchical. There is greater emphasis on sharing knowledge rather than hoarding it in the little black books. And there is growing use of best practices everywhere from manufacturing to planning and market forecasting.

The outcome is very positive. C. F. Martin is positioned well in its market; it has, over the last two decades, come to embody many of the elements of the Beat the Odds framework. The company is now more robust, healthier, better prepared, and more alert to market needs and market forces than at any time in its 173 years.

THE EFFECTS OF DANCEHALL DISCO

It was not always thus. In fact, in the early 1980s, C. F. Martin came close to shutting up shop. Then almost 150 years old, the company had already beaten the odds. (See earlier stats in Chapter 1.) But its prospects looked bleak. The symptoms were plain to see, and they were not at all pretty: Production of guitars had fallen drastically, from a 1971 high of 22,000 units annually to just over 3,000 by the early 1980s. Labor unions, hardened in many a battle over the fate of Eastern Pennsylvania's cement mills, helped precipitate a bitter nine-month strike. Pay cuts were the order of the day. The company had three times more debt than equity, and the company's principal lender insisted on a loan work-out. "We were hand to mouth with the bank," recalls chairman and CEO Christian ("Chris") Martin IV, then just leaving college.

The causes were many. Certainly the external market had withered: Acoustic instruments had been eclipsed by the rise of electronic music starting in the 1960s—from dancehall disco to keyboard and synthesizer sets in hotel bars. But many of C. F. Martin's woes were of its own making. Decision-making processes were fuzzy; many crucial decisions turned into struggles that were characterized more by personality than by procedure. And Frank Herbert Martin, the head of the firm and Chris Martin's father, had embarked on a bid to create a music conglomerate, purchasing, among other businesses, a banjo company and a drum maker. The financial consequences of the acquisition spree lingered long after the loan had been worked out and the last non-core business unit had been spun off.

THE BIRTH OF A BUSINESS

This was not what Christian Frederick Martin—Chris Martin's great-great-great-grandfather—would have wished for. Yet the company's German founder was himself no stranger to strife. Like other cabinet makers that made instruments in early nineteenth-century Germany, he had run afoul of the protectionist Violin Makers Guild. Concluding that the guild system would limit his opportunities, C. F. Martin Sr. emigrated to the United States in 1833, setting up shop on New York's Lower West Side before moving six years later to the small town of Nazareth in rural Pennsylvania.

Business grew in fits and starts; barter was typical in the retail trade. With the death of the founder in 1873, his son C. F. Martin Jr. assumed firm command, building an extension to the factory some years later. The hand-built guitars' designs changed over time. In the 1850s, Martin introduced the guitar top X-bracing system used in all steel-string Martins today, a construction method that is largely responsible for the marque's tonal qualities. By 1859, a proper factory was built to cope with demand. During the 1890s, the company, led by the founder's grandson Frank Henry Martin, was especially successful in selling mandolins, then popular in banjo and mandolin orchestras. It was Frank Henry Martin who, in the preface to the 1904 catalog, codified the ethos of quality: "How to build a guitar to give this tone is not a secret. It takes care and patience. Care in selecting the material, laying out the proportions . . . Patience in giving the necessary time to finish every part."

By 1928, annual guitar production stood at more than 5,200 units, over four times the output of 1920. However, the Great Depression nixed further expansion plans; guitar sales were virtually halved, and the company cut wages and instituted a three-day week. Energy went into product development, leading to a larger model known as the "Dreadnought," whose fortunes were soon to soar with the rise of country, bluegrass, and folk music—particularly in the years after World War II. With the end of that war, C. F. Martin III took over. Postwar prosperity helped propel demand, so much so that by the early 1960s, the company was back-ordered by as much as three years.

With few exceptions, the guitar maker had, for more than 130 years, held firmly to one of the core Beat the Odds framework elements. Under C. F. Martin III's helmsmanship, the company was crystal-clear about its purpose as a maker of top-quality acoustic guitars.

However, things began to change during the 1970s. While C. F. Martin remained chairman, his son Frank Herbert Martin became president. The new leader oversaw the launch of the company's custom guitar unit, where Martin players could help design the personalized instruments they wanted. However, the company clarity of purpose was compromised as the president launched his acquisition run. Conglomerates were a popular business design at that time, and the president saw benefits in expanding into banjo production, drum sets, strings, and more. The loss of focus did not serve the core operations well, and debt escalated. "The only good acquisition was the strings business," Chris Martin says. (Today strings are one of the company's most profitable product lines.)

The acquisition initiatives were not the only worry, however. F. H. Martin's management style was mercurial and hierarchical—much more Theory X than collaborative, and more so than was typical of the times. His approach did not engender cooperative problem solving and did not encourage development of, or support for, disciplined management controls. Although the management team was unable to change the situation, the board was eager to do so. The solution came when, as a stipulation of the loan work-out, the bank insisted that Frank Martin retire early. His father, C. F. Martin III—then well into his eighties—came back from retirement.

BACK FROM THE BRINK

Young Chris Martin never intended to join the family business. Although he had boxed guitar strings as a small boy and worked in the offices and factory as a teen, and although the business had clearly been part of his life from very early on, he had not envisioned it as the path for his career.

His grandfather changed Chris's mind. Chris Martin joined the company full-time not long after graduation from Boston University in 1978, working in many departments and learning how the business functioned from the bottom up. After his grandfather's death in 1986, C. F. Martin IV was appointed chairman and CEO. His was a monumental task. The death of C. F. Martin III triggered a valuation of the company, and the calculations were ominous. The projection indicated that if everything worked out right—*everything*—the company would lose less money than in the previous year. The strong recommendation from external advisors: sell—and soon.

The prospect was unthinkable to the new CEO. His instinct was that he could not betray his family legacy. His immediate strategic decision was music to the ears of the workforce: "We're just going to make guitars," he told them.

But this is not the story of a heroic leader. It is the story of how a successful family-run firm evolved into a well-integrated, professionally managed, specialty manufacturer of premium products. When he took over in 1986, Chris Martin already knew that success could not be defined as his father had defined it.

As a new young manager, Chris had allies among many of the longtime managers. But he turned to outside advisers as well: industrial engineers and management consultants who helped him standardize many of the manufacturing work processes, improve the production workflow, institute a formal one-year strategic plan, and prepare the organization for the Theory Y collaborative approaches then starting to make some headway in U.S. business.

Figure 13.2 Chairman and CEO Chris Martin IV is the sixth-generation Martin to head the 173-year-old company.

However, many of the old management practices persisted. "We didn't have a team—we had a bunch of rugged individuals," says the CEO. "In meetings we had a great tendency to talk over each other."

Chris Martin (Figure 13.2) worked hard to broaden the product range—the little portable Backpacker model appeared in 1991—and to expand the "limited edition" to include signature models of major artists such as Eric Clapton. He authorized steady updates to the manufacturing operations—polishing, cutting, assembly forms and fixtures, and much more—consistent with the challenges of modernizing production of three-dimensional wood products and with meeting the required product quality levels. Inspired by an

OUTWARD BOUND HELPS GUITAR MAKER REBOUND

Enthusiasm for off-site leadership programs usually extends only as far as the first bowl of nacho dip. Few managers really find themselves getting excited about trust falls and rope-bridge exercises.

Which makes the managers and coworkers at C. F. Martin & Co. a little different. Each year, a group of Martin employees spends five days on an Outward Bound course—one of the most recent being in a city environment. The purpose, as with most such courses, is to open up new lines of communication, to foster team building, and, of course, to have fun. At the guitar maker, the programs effectively serve as new-manager orientation sessions.

The program got its start in the early 1990s as an outgrowth of chairman Chris Martin's move to promote more open styles of management and communication. Martin had been on a course some years earlier. "It really turned around my head," he says. He had his top management team attend in 1992. Since then, he has participated in most of the company's Outward Bound trips and has recently asked president Keith Lombardi to lead the group of managers and coworkers who go on the company's next expedition.

early Outward Bound experience (see sidebar), he pushed further and faster with collaborative work practices. "It's about time we ask the people who do the work what they think" is how he phrases it.

Chris Martin wouldn't have put it this way, but by this time, several elements of the Beat the Odds framework were falling into place. It was apparent that the company was refining core values such as employee involvement and was working hard to craft a cohesive and inspiring vision of what C. F. Martin & Co. could become. Every quarter, the CEO would share operating details with each employee. And a profit-sharing plan was introduced, giving the workforce a much clearer stake in the company's future.

Fortune smiled in the late 1980s: The backlash against electronic music was well under way, and there came a resurgence in the popularity of singer-songwriters, most of whom used acoustic guitars (Figure 13.3). "We were ready when the phones started ringing again," says Chris Martin. The Backpacker travel guitar proved very successful—and it ventured to the North and South Poles and around the world on the space shuttle. The signature series was a hit, backed now by a formal marketing program called "artist development." Prominent musicians such as Tom Petty, Willie Nelson, Joan Baez, Sting, and David Crosby lent their names to guitars, actively participating in product

Figure 13.3 Willie Nelson is one of many famous owners of Martin guitars. Joined here by Dick Boak, Martin's director of artist relations, Nelson is debuting the N-20WN Limited Edition Signature Model.

design. At one trade show, the 00042-EC Eric Clapton model sold out within hours, "if not minutes," says guitar marketing director Dennis Tenges.

By the late 1990s, it was evident that a new spirit was coming back. C. F. Martin was overcoming much of the worker–management animosity of earlier days. Sales were strong; production was steady. In 1999 the Nazareth factory almost doubled in size, and the company shipped its 700,000th guitar. Examined through the lens of the Beat the Odds framework, C. F. Martin was starting to score well in terms of alignment and energy. Leadership was much more effective all around, with strong and open communication. And common sense was increasingly on display.

BOOSTING LEADERSHIP BENCH STRENGTH

Reviewing the company's future early in 2000, Chris Martin knew that his titles of chairman, CEO, and president were one title too many. Yes, he had grown C. F. Martin to become a successful $40-million-a-year organization, but like many a gifted entrepreneur, he would be challenged to manage a complex, sophisticated company several times that size. He had to decide if he could run the business day to day while continuing to articulate the future of the family firm in which he held 60 percent of the equity. After much soul-searching and help from an executive coach, he decided to share the challenge.

The search began for a president and COO. Martin insisted on recruiting an experienced leader who would act collaboratively over the long term, and with whom there could be constructive give-and-take within a healthy partnership. Sitting down to lunch one day with Keith Lombardi, he knew he'd found his new COO. Lombardi, a University of Chicago MBA with a sterling operations background in the health care sector, asked a lot of questions and acted like a team member from the start. He was a rare find: Not only had he heard of the private Pennsylvania instrument maker, but he knew all about it. As a youth, he'd been on several factory tours because his father was a self-confessed Martin guitar fanatic.

Although Martin had made sure that Lombardi interviewed with the managers who would report to him, there was no guarantee, after the new president had been hired in November 2002, that he would have their trust. Experienced managers all, they had long been used to direct access to and decision making by the CEO. A few had expected to be sitting in Lombardi's chair themselves. The new boss would have to earn their trust. At the same time, he had to move quickly to tune up many of the business processes that had not been tested against best practices or progress-checked with meaningful metrics.

ACCELERATING THE IMPROVEMENTS

For all its successes, Martin still had plenty of improvements to make at the turn of the twenty-first century. Gauged simply in terms of hours per guitar, efficiency was low and had been trending down by at least 5 percent a year since 1997, due in part to increasing product complexity. At the same time, materials management was not integrated across the supply chain; purchasing was often handled by manufacturing, sometimes to the point of order placement. Inventory management needed an upgrade, particularly in the distribution channel. And the new Mexican production facility—a maquiladora (also called maquila) for building Martin's lower-priced models—needed attention.

Lombardi and Martin had a list of work processes in need of tightening. The priorities were to focus on the basics—get rid of surplus inventory, straighten out reporting lines, ensure that every necessary function was identified and capably led. By the second half of 2004, the focus had switched to brand management and customer support, addressing the tricky issue of dealers who'd had considerable control over deal terms and who were prone to undercutting the brand by, for instance, discounting older inventory. Lombardi puts it this way: "We had this unbelievably great brand and product being sold through way too many dealers—and many of them were treating it as a pure volume game, just buying from us and adding a small markup." The remedies were to limit supplies of product and to start trimming the U.S. dealer network—it's already down from 699 at the end of 2004 to 565 at the start of 2006, and will fall further.

In 2005, the emphasis switched to balance sheet issues. Although the company was well able to self-finance out of cash flow, it was still necessary to improve inventory turns and to accelerate the transition of lower-end product from Nazareth to the new maquiladora plant in Mexico, in part to free up capacity at the main plant. And labor utilization deserved scrutiny—particularly the levels of indirect activity such as rework.

As president and COO, Lombardi bears the bulk of the day-to-day operational burdens, and he and Chris Martin lead the strategic decision making. For the most part, they're completely in sync, but one of their ongoing debates concerns strategic planning. Lombardi believes in formal three-year planning cycles. Martin thinks such plans become theoretical after a year. But what's healthiest is that the leaders are having that debate in the first place and are turning their strategies into plans that cascade down through the organization—and that are all tied to common objectives.

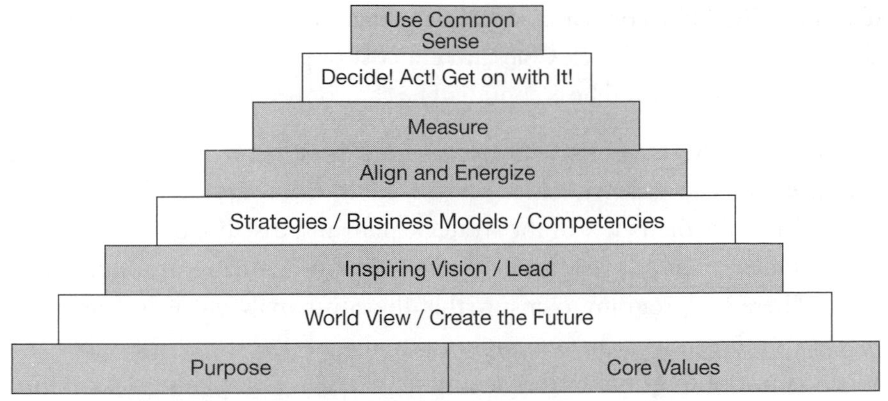

Figure 13.4 Areas of significant strength at Martin Guitar.

The company's senior managers are moving into alignment with the new disciplined direction set by the CEO and president. "People started to believe when they began to see results," says Lombardi. It is now clear that many elements of the Beat the Odds framework are firmly in place (see Figure 13.4 shaded areas).

Asked to gauge Martin's performance using the Beat the Odds queries, the leadership team expresses confidence that the company has a crystalline purpose and a robust set of core values, and that its teams are aligned with and energized by its purpose and values. Their responses also signal that the company can get better at improving its strategy process, its measurements, and its aptitude for action. And there is recognition that its monitoring of activities in the outside world has room for improvement.

Progress to Date

On many counts C. F. Martin is well placed to weather storms ahead. Here are six areas in which big improvements have been made to date.

Financial Measures. Revenue growth is settling down into a stable stream: 8 percent year on year compared to the 10 percent-plus surge seen in 2004 to 2005. Worldwide market share is robust; C. F. Martin has more than 40 percent of the premium sector of the acoustic guitar market—steel-string models costing $2,500 and up—and it ranks in the top 24 musical instrument and sound suppliers worldwide, according to *Music Trades* magazine. Product pricing is stronger and more disciplined today, and there is a clearer understanding of sector contributions. For example, guitar strings are very lucrative. On the cost side, supply chain chief Nick Colesanti cut cost of goods sold by more than 10 percent over last year, and he is confident he can continue that rate of reduction.

Workforce Management. Employees are now part of the communications stream. Each quarter, Chris Martin, Keith Lombardi, and other executives deliver a detailed view of the strategic plan and disclose operating results. Workers' ideas regularly lead to upgrades in manufacturing processes in particular. There is a program to ensure that the company's Mexican workers feel involved by hosting exchange trips for many of them. At the same time, Martin is promoting more cross-training. And it is sharpening up on hiring interviews, no longer viewing the 90-day probation period as a time for remediation. One outcome: Martin is now considered a "cool" place to work by younger recruits.

Leadership Development. C. F. Martin now clearly recognizes the need for strong leadership development efforts and succession planning at several management levels. Human resources vice president Debbie Karlowitch has led an effort to identify and nurture "high-potential" managers. She is pleased with the company's leadership training partnership with the local community college. And she is exploring the involvement of the Center for Creative Leadership in order to develop specific leadership development programs.

Operations Management. C. F. Martin has made big strides with planning and forecasting, starting with a more rigorous approach to strategic planning. A three-year planning cycle has largely replaced a year-by-year focus. "It doesn't matter what year you're in," notes Lombardi. "Think of it as a 36-month rolling process so that in Month 8, say, you know what is going to affect things in Month 14."

The management team is also well along with a formal sales and operations planning process that is enabling the company to do a much better job with capacity planning, forecast accuracy, margin mix, hiring plans, and more. The smoother planning process has improved the quality of hires. The company is also moving away from relatively informal agreements with suppliers to structured 24-month scheduling with consequent requests for improved pricing terms. Supply chain director Colesanti is debuting radio-frequency identification (RFID) scanners to track materials and work-in-progress in real time, tying the data feeds into the company's enterprise resource planning

(ERP) systems. A perpetual inventory system is in the works. And international manufacturing director Bill Hall is streamlining how production of some guitar models is transferred to the Mexico facility. On the demand side, the company is improving channel management, setting more stringent terms with dealers, tightening up on accounts receivable, and clarifying what demand looks like with structured feedback from user groups and at trade shows.

Organization Structure. Operations have been segmented by function as well as by product: strings separate from guitar making, marketing distinct from sales. And the new plant in Mexico is the site for product families that sell at lower price points—making cost containment crucial—or whose production requires fewer steps, omitting capital-intensive operations such as lacquering, for instance.

Corporate Culture. At C. F. Martin, there is now more readiness to measure and to accept being measured. And there is less and less tolerance for poor performance.

NEXT ON THE AGENDA

C. F. Martin has plenty on its plate, including making further improvements in planning and forecasting. On the demand side, the team is working on improving sales and marketing leverage with dealers, fine-tuning the product mix, securing and enhancing the brand, and getting better payment terms. A new print advertising campaign in music magazines is setting the right tone, using a simple picture of a Martin guitar in a homey setting accompanied by a few lines from a well-known song by a famous Martin user. But there is more to do to extend demand. Although very popular in Japan, Martin guitars are not marketed aggressively elsewhere.

Internally, Lombardi and HR chief Karlowitch plan to extend cross-training among employees, to expand leadership development efforts, and to kickstart formal succession planning programs. That issue still hides many unanswered questions. Chris Martin has repeatedly stated that he plans to retire by 2014, when he turns 59, although most expect him to scale back his involvement gradually and nobody will be surprised if he remains an active participant for years after that.

Increasingly, the company faces the question of how to manage workforce growth, with all that is implied for the company's culture and collective knowledge base by mixing the necessary new hires with the existing employees. The management team also has to narrow the gap between a guitar's total production cycle time of several weeks (or months, in the case of some high-end models) and a total "touch time," when work is actively being done on the guitar, measured in days. And they must continually revisit the "stop sanding" argument—walking an ever-finer line between aggressively improving manufacturing efficiencies and maintaining the product's "craftsman" appeal. "As good as today's guitar is, tomorrow's has to be better," declares Martin.

What the Beat the Odds framework shows is that overall, the guitar maker is in a very strong position, with some work to do to improve its use of metrics and to sharpen its decision-making skills. Those are two of the areas where there is a wider gap between the responses of senior managers and the high-potential up-and-comers.

TO BE CONTINUED

The Martin story continues to unfold in fascinating ways. In marked contrast to the dark days of the early 1980s, banks now hammer on Martin's door seeking business—not loan repayments. Demand is steady, market share is solid, and cash flow and profitability are strong. A diverse, experienced, and disciplined management team is at the helm—and looking far forward. As mentioned, new young recruits view C. F. Martin as a cool place to work. And Chris Martin is setting sights on annual revenues of $150 million.

Although much has changed, especially in the last 20 years, a lot more has to change. Product development will change as scarce woods become scarcer. The corporate culture will shift as new recruits join the company's long-timers. Leadership development and succession planning must grow in sophistication as revenues grow—and as Chris Martin nears retirement.

But one of the most interesting aspects is that there will be no change to the fundamentals, such as the company's purpose and its core values. Weighing the company's resilience through the Beat the Odds framework, both the top management team and the up-and-coming leaders give good scores to the characteristics that matter most. The company's keen self-awareness is perhaps the best armor of all.

For all of its ups and downs, C. F. Martin & Co. has already demonstrated that it has the bones to beat the odds. It may not yet have the patina of a 14-generation family firm such as cymbal-maker Zildjian or the sheer size of family-run conglomerates such as Anheuser-Busch or Levi Strauss. But now, after six generations, it has the crispness of purpose, values, leadership, operationalized strategies, structures, and momentum to help it succeed for another 173 years.

14

STARTING OFF ON THE RIGHT FOOT: LANXESS CORPORATION

For the people who live near America's great river ways, the busy flow of barge traffic is routine—a cause for occasional curiosity, perhaps, about a cargo or its destination. For Tom O'Neill, it's anything but humdrum. The barges mean money in motion—specifically working capital in play. That's why he's been giving some of those barges and their cargoes so much scrutiny lately.[1]

O'Neill is the chief procurement officer for LANXESS Corporation, the U.S. arm of the LANXESS Group. Like other senior managers at the company, O'Neill has been acutely aware of the need to maximize the use of working capital. So when he found out that LANXESS took title to a key raw material it was buying to feed one of its U.S. manufacturing plants when the product was loaded onto the barges, and that this product was on the water for several days, he requested contract changes of the suppliers.

Long story short: Today LANXESS does not take title until the material is offloaded at its facility, allowing the company to conserve a welcome slice of working capital. This raw-material title transfer change is just one of several similar initiatives from O'Neill's procurement department—collaborative moves that speak to a new sense of empowerment and energy across the chemicals company.

Similarly, the procurement operation has helped LANXESS Corporation's Law & Intellectual Property department to set terms for and then outsource some of its services. O'Neill's group has also worked closely with Finance to expand use of the Procurement Card—effectively a credit card for corporate purchasing—to save significantly in payables-processing costs such as approving and cutting checks. "We have more people coming to us than ever before," says O'Neill.

His collaborative experiences are echoed by other top managers at LANXESS Corporation. But then, the company's new ethos of cross-functional teamwork shouldn't be surprising because LANXESS itself is a brand-new company, born from the spin-off of a collection of mature, chemicals-related businesses.

THE MAKING OF A BRAND-NEW BUSINESS

LANXESS Corporation exemplifies the type of open and self-aware organization that is embracing many of the elements of the Beat the Odds framework. In doing so, it is positioning itself for long-term success in the highly competitive global chemicals market.

The senior management team at LANXESS and the company's up-and-coming leaders have already participated in the Beat the Odds diagnostics. Later in this profile, we'll take a closer look at how they responded. But let's first take a step back to look at where the company has come from—and how far it has come already.

The 20-second overview: The LANXESS Group was carved out of the Bayer Group in July of 2004 (Figure 14.1). The previous November, the management board of the 140-year-old German conglomerate had voted to exit the low-margin chemicals business and define a new strategic core in life sciences and material sciences. Bayer Chemicals had been one of the industry's leading players; ditto for some of Bayer's plastics and rubber businesses in their sectors. But none of these businesses meshed with the company's view of its future. Products were heavily commoditized; two-thirds of the businesses were running at a loss, and margins were low in the others.

The news of the move hit employees like a hammer blow. Many had worked for those businesses for decades. "I had people in my office crying that this was their job, their life," recalls LANXESS Corporation President and CEO Randy Dearth, then head of Bayer Chemicals in the United States. He didn't

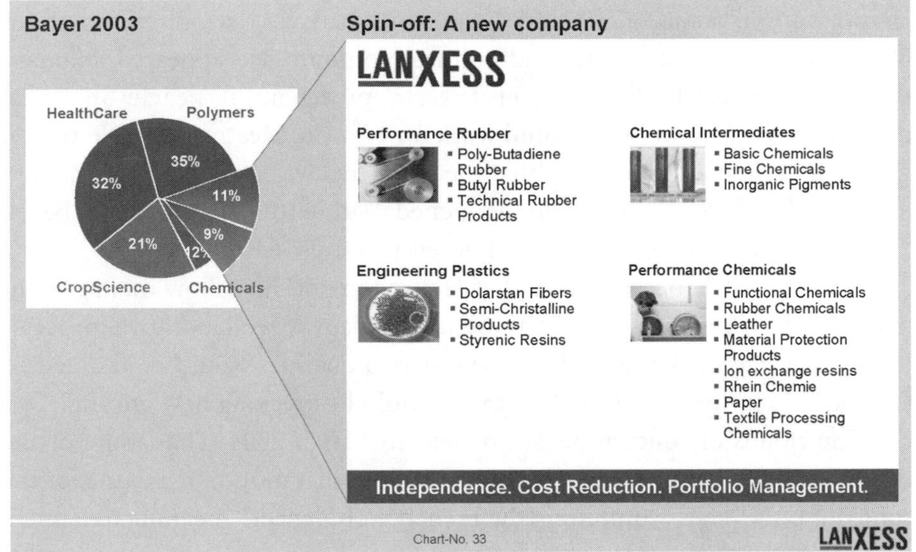

Figure 14.1 LANXESS is a new company—built on polymers and chemicals (Source: LANXESS Corp.).

have a lot of detailed answers; at that point he couldn't have. Consolation would be a while in coming.

February 2004 was as gray and chilly in North America as it was in Leverkusen, near Cologne, the main offices of Bayer Chemicals. The weather reflected the mood. That month, Bayer organized and assigned employees to the as-yet-unnamed business that was targeted for spin-off. However, "NewCo," as it was labeled, was still too nebulous a concept for many of its "new" employees; anxiety was sometimes joined by anger when word spread that a loss-making first year was almost preordained, since two-thirds of the business units being inherited from Bayer were unprofitable. The feeling that they'd be joining part of a "collection of underperforming businesses" (as one LANXESS manager puts it) wasn't the nicest feeling in the world. The term "stepchild" crept into hallway conversations.

FAST DECISION MAKING

But most employees weren't to know what kinds of conversations were being held in Leverkusen. Bayer had selected a young, assertive, independent-minded Bayer executive—Dr. Axel C. Heitmann—to run NewCo, and

Heitmann and some of his new lieutenants had very strong views about NewCo's direction, structure, and cultural contours. He appeared adamant that neither Bayer's traditional asset-driven approach nor its heavily analytical decision-making techniques would work for NewCo. Meeting with Heitmann for the first time, Dearth recalls that the new CEO was making decisions very quickly—far faster than it had happened within the much-larger Bayer. "*Everything* was fast," he says. In fact, it felt positively entrepreneurial.

It immediately became clear that Heitmann and his fellow management board members wanted NewCo to be agile, adaptive, collaborative, process-driven, and highly disciplined. Those last two qualities would be familiar to any Bayer long-timer. But the first three would be breaking new ground.

The clouds of concern began to clear in March 2004. The labors of the marketing team became evident with the rollout that month of a name for the spin-off: LANXESS—combining the French verb "lancer," meaning to launch, with the word "success." The carve-out teams had been active for months, preparing everything from the customer contracts to signage and stationery and to dedicated IT systems. As employees—now *LANXESS* employees—began to receive their specially prepared "welcome" folders containing their new employment information, and as executives including Heitmann began to visit plants and offices, the worried frowns began to dissipate. You could almost hear the collective sigh of relief.

On July 1, 2004, the work of the carve-out teams was just about complete: LANXESS began to operate as a separate legal entity in the United States. The Web site started up. Inauguration parties got going. A new 20,000-employee organization was "born." Six months later, LANXESS AG would be listed on the Frankfurt Stock Exchange.

LANXESS began with more than 50 companies at 50 sites in 18 countries (Figure 14.2); annual revenues in fiscal 2005—the calendar year—came to more than \$8.5 billion, with net losses but with EBITDA (earnings before interest, tax, depreciation, and amortization) margins of about 8.1 percent. The company comprised four business segments: performance chemicals such as additives for plastics; chemical intermediates, which include agrochemical intermediates and inorganic pigments; engineering plastics; and performance rubber, such as polybutadiene rubber for vehicle tires.

With about a third of LANXESS's global revenue coming from the U.S. businesses, it was not difficult to decide to locate the support organization—LANXESS Corp.—in the States. Bayer Chemicals had been located in the

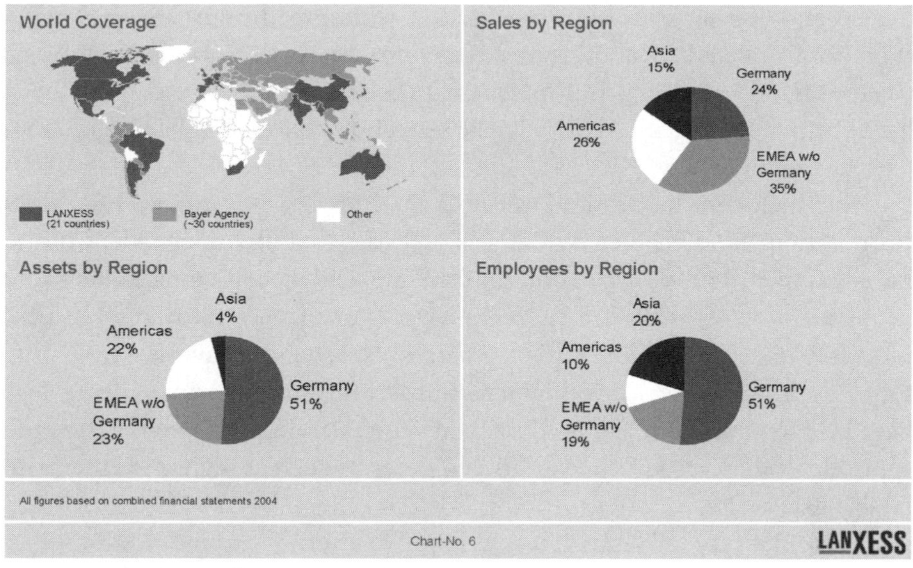

Figure 14.2 Global presence (Source: LANXESS Corp.).

Pittsburgh, Pennsylvania, area; Findlay, a community just outside the city, had a modern four-story office block available, and that became LANXESS Corporation's new headquarters. Like Heitmann, Randy Dearth saw real cultural value in having all the functional service units and most of the business units in one building. There were clear benefits for communication, collaboration, and faster decision making. LANXESS's new headquarters in Findlay supports 16 business units across the United States and more than 4,000 customers.

GETTING DOWN TO BUSINESS

The champagne glasses had barely been put away as LANXESS got down to business. The first order of business was a hard line on costs. CEO Heitmann had set expectations for Bayer, for the new investors, and for LANXESS employees that EBITDA margins had to approach 10 percent in the short term. That put a premium on cash management and overall cost control. And it has led to two aggressive rounds of restructuring. The first round has already cut capacity within existing product lines, with some plant shutdowns and job losses. The second round has involved selling off complete product lines—the paper chemicals business, for instance, and the fibers business.

Execution against those decisions won widespread praise. Several managers said privately that decisions could not be made so swiftly at Bayer Chemicals, and planning and marshaling the resources for execution would have taken even longer. LANXESS managers and employees alike find the new pace invigorating.

The high-communication, act-now culture is pervasive at LANXESS Corporation—and enabled by the new premises that are independent of the Bayer campus. Randy Dearth and his team are acutely conscious of their role in managing costs—as Tom O'Neill's barge story indicates. Many business processes that are not core to U.S. operations—such as payroll—were outsourced early on; others are under constant scrutiny by department heads who have far more freedom and accountability to make decisions than before the spin-off. And there are far fewer "nice to haves"—such as high-end enterprise IT software tools.

There is a very deliberate push to improve internal communications, too. Dearth himself is a natural communicator—an "open-door" manager who invites chance meetings with employees as much as he hands out praise and thanks—and who expects the same traits of his lieutenants. Formal communication is encoded in the company's *Xpress* internal magazine and in the four times yearly "town hall" meetings that Dearth holds with all U.S. employees. "He's always concerned about what employees think," says internal communications manager Angela Wheland. Dearth is in sync with Heitmann, who visits plants regularly to listen to employees and to be very candid in his assessments of the business. "Heitmann is not afraid to tell the ugly," says Dearth.

There are clear parallels between the Beat the Odds framework and many aspects of Dearth's and Heitmann's actions and behaviors. They are clearly focused on good execution underpinned by the appropriate business models and competencies and by strong purpose. It's worthwhile looking more closely at how they have defined value before studying their Beat the Odds diagnostic.

REDEFINING VALUE

LANXESS's management board has been crystal-clear and very consistent in its messaging about what constitutes value. At a global senior managers' retreat in Austria in 2005, it was expressed in a manifesto, agreed to by all present, that they should (1) always seek solutions, (2) take ownership of problems and actions, (3) keep things simple, and (4) think new and act fast.

Those behaviors were very much on display a few weeks earlier. When Hurricane Rita pounded the Gulf Coast, it damaged the LANXESS manufacturing facility in Orange, Texas, and left many employees homeless. With an initial focus on providing humanitarian assistance to fellow staff, employees in the Findlay office effectively self-organized a crisis center that involved several HQ departments and the LANXESS Leadership team in Orange. In Finance, staff drew out a sizable amount of cash, purchased food and emergency supplies, and literally drove down from Pittsburgh to the Gulf to deliver everything. And Legal helped to set up The LANXESS Foundation—again, in a matter of hours—to provide ongoing assistance to employees affected by Rita. To ensure that the company's operations would not be compromised, buyers worked round the clock to arrange the purchase and delivery of urgently needed supplies and services—they even managed to locate a replacement flare stack and get it delivered within 48 hours.

LANXESS has mapped out a value framework that comprises four key principles.

Clear Structures. Heitmann understands well the importance of clear structures—both for the businesses and the services. The LANXESS goal was for all shared services to be centralized and shared—and they are. There are also simple business reporting structures: Each global business-unit leader reports to one of the three management board members in Leverkusen. The focus is on clarity in structures and processes: easily understood metrics for performance, for resource allocation, and for portfolio management.

Defined Responsibilities. The emphasis here is on complete ownership. The leader of each business unit is completely and directly responsible for the unit's performance wherever its plants and offices are located. There are no geographic matrices to blame; regional entities don't have a separate set of objectives that may conflict with global business objectives. And the service units are now free to collaborate across departmental boundaries to better serve the needs of the business units. "We gain acceptance by doing something useful for someone," says Procurement's Tom O'Neill.

Strong Incentives. LANXESS has structured its rewards simply. For the managers, four-fifths of their bonus target is based on the company's financial performance globally, with the remainder driven by the performance of their unit or their department. There are similar compensation structures for the rest of the employees. But incentives are not limited to compensation. Randy Dearth has set a powerful precedent because he is quick to praise and to thank employees for their work—and not just at formatted times such as the "town hall" meetings. When he learned about the expansion of the Procurement Card program, he bought lunch for the employees who were driving the program.

There are other soft incentives in the form of active talent development. At least twice a year at LANXESS Corporation, Dearth and his senior managers meet with employees who are considered to be the company's up-and-coming leaders. The company has also initiated a mentoring program and offers numerous management and leadership courses to employees at all levels of the organization.

Focused Metrics. LANXESS also prizes consistent and easily understood performance metrics because they lead to transparency and they support unambiguous goals. For example, procurement chief O'Neill worked with his global counterparts to craft a simple guideline for regular measurement of cost savings achieved by Procurement, across the full range of purchased products and services and regardless of contract type.

INSIGHTS FROM THE BEAT THE ODDS FRAMEWORK

During 2005, just one year after LANXESS's birth, LANXESS managers and up-and-coming leaders took the Beat the Odds poll. Their overall rating is not surprising: in general, LANXESS performs well against the Beat the Odds principles (Figure 14.3). One of the most interesting findings is that there is good alignment between the responses from senior managers and those from the future leaders—something that CEO Dearth takes as a good sign.

The up-and-comers clearly believe that Dearth and his management team think of their people as assets. They are closely in sync with their bosses in terms of inspiring vision, core values, and common sense. They are confident that their senior managers can execute well ("Get on with It!").

PROGRESS TO DATE

So far, so good. LANXESS AG is growing, paying down its debt, and controlling costs. For 2005 sales revenues were up nearly 6 percent over the previous year. EBITDA margins were up to 8.1 percent against 6.6 percent in 2004—

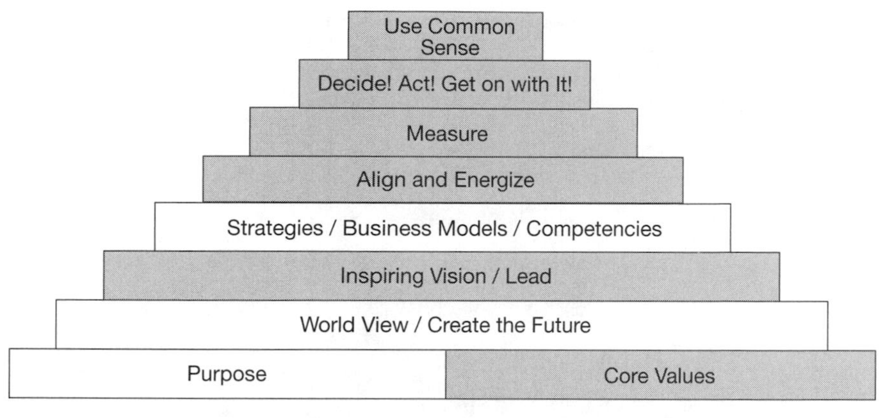

Figure 14.3 Areas of significant strength at LANXESS Corp.

right on target. And the stock price rose by nearly 70 percent in 2005. EBITDA margins improved further during 2006, to 9.7 percent in the third quarter.

The LANXESS team is demonstrating first-rate financial management, holding firm to the "price before volume" strategy to successfully pass along increases in the costs of raw materials, and its working capital discipline is helping pay down debt quickly. The belt-tightening continues: In a first phase of restructuring, the portfolio of products has been adjusted by shuttering two unprofitable fine-chemicals facilities and cutting back capacity in styrenic resins.

A second, more aggressive phase has seen the shutdown of a handful of smaller production sites with unfavorable cost structures on both sides of the Atlantic. (See Figure 14.4.) At the same time, the company has sold off entire operations that it considers noncore: its Dorlastan fibers business, its paper business unit, and iSL-Chemie, a subsidiary of Rhein Chemie that manufactures color pastes and specialty coatings for plastics. "I'm convinced that restructuring, in principle, should never end," CEO Heitmann told *Chemical Week* magazine.

Meanwhile, the company is readying for the growth phases that it expects will follow restructuring. There are significant investments in sectors with strong growth potential, such as butyl rubber. A host of product innovations are in the pipeline. (These include an invisible coating that can be applied to large secure areas; disturbances, such as footprints, quickly show up when the

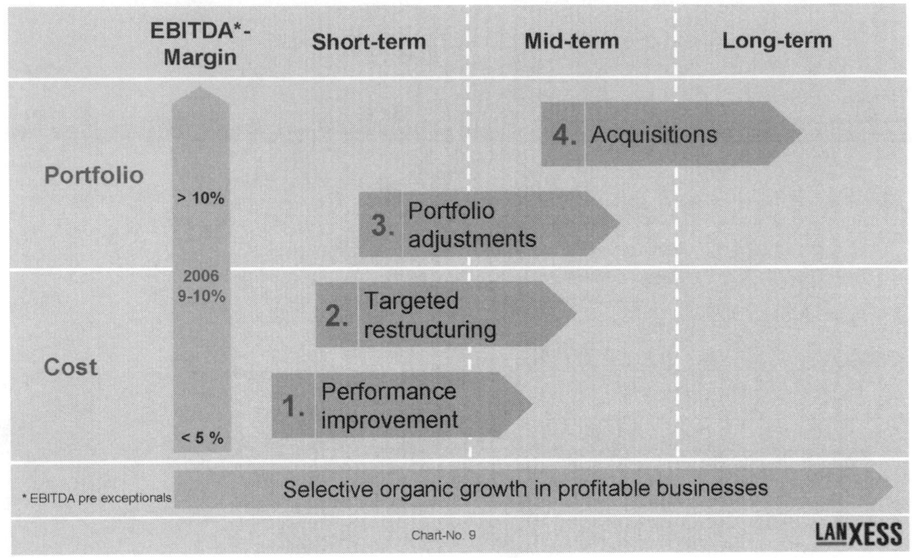

Figure 14.4 "Step-by-step approach" to creating value (Source: LANXESS Corp.).

coating is exposed to a particular light frequency.) True to the first syllable in its name, LANXESS has launched its fine chemicals unit as a standalone business unit named Saltigo. And the company is positioning to exploit opportunities in China, dismantling its entire hydrazine hydrate plant in Baytown, Texas, and moving it to China.

LOOKING AHEAD

LANXESS is a youngster—a feisty, focused one, but a youngster nonetheless. The company's story has only just begun. "I'm very pleased to say we are doing well. We are already making significant progress, but LANXESS still has a long way to go," CEO Heitmann told the *Pittsburgh Post-Gazette* during a 2005 visit to the LANXESS Corporation offices.

There is no shortage of challenges, both external and internal. The chemicals business is acutely competitive, and will remain so unless there is significant shakeout or consolidation in the industry. Towering longtime rivals such as BASF will not easily give ground. The expansion of India's and China's economies hints at competition from new potential global players—a concern for which LANXESS may need to be better prepared, according to the results of the Beat the Odds diagnostic survey.

On the cost side, margins are elusive: Feedstock costs—particularly petroleum-based raw materials—put procurement departments in a headlock. And there is the worry over what happens to demand if the global economy softens. Although the U.S. economy remains robust into 2006, there are plenty of warnings about an approaching slowdown.

Strategically, LANXESS's management team must soon move toward its midterm goal of growing the company by making selective acquisitions. It has to find more ways to participate more quickly in China's remarkable market growth. And it must keep looking at how to lessen the volatility of some key sectors, such as engineering plastics.

While the company has much to celebrate, everyone seems to understand that there is more work to be done and the future holds new challenges. "The restructuring story is not news anymore," says one manager. And a review of the company's responses to the Beat the Odds diagnostic shows that there's still progress to be made in terms of expressed clarity of purpose, core values, and a focus on the future—particularly when it comes to presenting a "future vision" of the company to customers, prospects, investors, and future employees. But that's not surprising in a one-year-old company.

That said, LANXESS has so much on its side. There is strong financial momentum as its debt overhang recedes, as capacity is matched to demand, as operational cash flow improves, and as the "price before volume" strategy bears out. For the first nine months of 2005, for example, the company was able to raise prices by an average of 9 percent while reducing volume by 3 percent. EBITDA is moving toward its double-digit goal.

But it's the cultural characteristics that will serve LANXESS best. Many organizations answer economic challenges with the conventional sequence of cost-cutting, restructuring, and a return to acquisitions—as if that is all that matters. But LANXESS clearly demonstrates that successful change calls for something more profound. It calls for principles of good conduct, of sound values, of strong purpose, all working wholeheartedly and in concert to support the right responses to change.

The new hallmarks are evident in the answers that managers and future leaders gave on the Beat the Odds survey. It is clear that there is a new openness at work at LANXESS. Managers and workers alike demonstrate a determined sense of ownership, and there is a willingness to take appropriate risks. Those attributes aren't found on the balance sheet. But they are really the most valuable assets of all.

THE NEW GYM: AN EXERCISE IN ENTERPRISE

There is an exercise center at LANXESS Corporation's headquarters offices. The gym is managed by a third-party provider for the exclusive use by the 400 or so employees there. It was built at management's request when the building was being fitted out for the new occupant.

That fact is completely unremarkable in North America today. But for the company's 2,000-plus employees across the United States, it was big news indeed. It proved to be a very powerful emblem of change—a sign of independence, a signal that things would not be done as they had always been done before. Recalling the uncertainty and concern that were endemic after Bayer announced it was selling the chemicals and polymers businesses, one manager notes: "People were very excited about the gym."

On that basis alone, the investment in the fitness center has been amply repaid already. But just in case someone starts questioning the facility's ongoing value, President and CEO Randy Dearth has an answer ready that has nothing to do with keeping employees healthy. "It's a great way to meet other people," he says. For a company that already collaborates across functions more effectively than many, that is good news. It's fair to say that LANXESS's exercise center is aligning and energizing—in more ways than one.

15

RETOOLING THE MANAGEMENT TOOL KIT: ITT CORPORATION

If *Fortune* magazine one day sets up an award for corporate self-critiquing, ITT Corporation will without question be a front-runner for the top prize. "We all know that one of the biggest risks to continued success is complacency," wrote chief executive Steve Loranger in a recent issue of ITT's employee magazine. Since joining the multi-industry company as CEO in June of 2004 and becoming chairman later that year, Loranger has propelled an already successful and self-aware organization to new levels of alertness.[1]

He is not about to ease up. Opening the company's 2006 leadership forum, Loranger posed these and other questions to the 500 or so senior managers: "What's going to happen to this company when very competent Asian competitors start entering our markets—as they've already done to several of the ITT units here in the room? . . . What's going to happen if we don't have a best-in-the-world cost standard for all of our products? . . . How long are our customers going to pay more for our products than they have to?"

Loranger tempered his strong call to action with abundant recognition of ITT's many wins. He praised individual managers by name and celebrated a range of their accomplishments. But he left his team in no doubt that if they—and he—did not deal quickly and conclusively with the issues he was raising, ITT would be "left behind."

THE PURPOSE OF PURPOSE

Try to launch a conversation about an organization's purpose with most chief executives and chances are you won't get far. Try it with Steve Loranger and the conversation gets interesting. In fact, he has already expounded on the idea to his managers at the 2005 leadership forum. The ITT chief is the first to admit that he does not yet have a tailor-made answer. But he can quickly parse the discussion into distinctions between familiar financial goals and what he terms "content-based purpose." He is also careful not to equate social responsibility outreach or ITT's laudable tsunami-relief efforts with the idea of purpose.

So is it somehow about being "the water company"—the provider of sustenance to humankind? Does it even have to be so lofty? Loranger is drawn to the notion of a transcendent purpose for a for-profit corporation such as ITT, but he is not about to try to craft a purpose for the sake of doing so. To him, an organization's declared purpose has to have practical payoffs for the company's stakeholders—without necessarily being translated into balance sheet numbers.

The CEO hints at some ways in which purpose might be made tangible: as a way of attracting the right kind of talent, or of creating a strong sense of worth at work. "It's when you go home at night energized, refreshed, because you were working on the right things," he has told ITT's managers.

Loranger may not yet have the definition of purpose ready to write into the company's management system, but he recognizes its importance and is certainly getting a lot closer.

At first glance, Loranger's concerns seem overstated. ITT is near the top of its game: The global engineering and manufacturing company produced 2005 revenues of $7.4 billion—a 17 percent lift over the previous year—with a 20 percent gain in adjusted operating income. Including first-half 2006 results, the company has now turned out four years of consecutive quarterly revenue growth, and it continues to spin off cash. "A lot of our success is generated because our businesses are very close to our customers," notes Scott Crum, the corporation's senior vice president of human resources.

ITT is the world's premier supplier of pumps, systems, and services to move, control, and treat water and other fluids; it prides itself on playing key roles in all parts of the water cycle, from extraction and supply of clean water to treatment and recycling of waste water, and doing so worldwide. It is also a major supplier

A PURPOSEFUL RESPONSE TO THE ASIAN TSUNAMI

Within hours of the first report that the 2004 Indian Ocean tsunami had contaminated water supplies, CEO Steve Loranger was getting e-mails back from ITT managers worldwide confirming what the company could do to help.

Inside a few days, a senior-level task force came together to help on a vast scale. And over the weeks to come, ITT—the world's largest fluid technology company—made a huge difference to the lives of countless people suffering in the aftermath of one of the most devastating natural disasters in memory. "Within three weeks, we were producing clean water for half a million people," says Scott Crum, ITT's human resources chief.

Partnering with Sri Lanka's Industrial Services Bureau and with USAID, the ITT team moved quickly to get water-purifying equipment into that country. Logistical and bureaucratic hurdles were abundant. But the team successfully installed clean-water equipment in nearly 60 sites along the southern and eastern coastlines of Sri Lanka.

ITT's spontaneous, immediate, and wholehearted response reflects many of the tenets of its own management systems and some of the strongest elements of the Beat the Odds framework. Identifying an issue much more momentous than earning profits, the company demonstrated a clear sense of purpose. It illustrated adroit, determined leadership. And it excelled in terms of getting a crucial job done well. Tsunami relief patrons George Herbert Bush and Bill Clinton expressed it this way in a letter of thanks to the company: "ITT reflects America at its best, reinforcing our nation's fundamental values of community, compassion, and responsibility."

of sophisticated military defense systems, and provides advanced technical and operational services to a broad range of government agencies.

The company's successes have not gone unnoticed. ITT recently topped the *Forbes* list of Best Managed Companies in America for five-year annualized total shareholder returns in the conglomerates category, beating out contenders such as Fortune Brands, 3M, United Technologies, and GE. And gauging the company against the Beat the Odds framework, ITT not only yields high absolute scores on many of the key questions, but it demonstrates a remarkable degree of alignment in perspectives between the executive team and the company's up-and-coming leaders—a very good signal indeed.

But Loranger and his top team are well aware that success is a fragile thing. They worry (that's the word that many of them use) that ITT is not yet premier—that although it may have surpassed United Technologies and GE in

Forbes' listing, it does not yet have the good bones that those blue-chip multi-industry majors do. They are concerned that they cannot break out beyond organic growth. They want to avoid the limitations of the defense sector's profits picture. And even though ITT's stock has done well, they are anxious to win the enduring trust of the investment community.

Before exploring how the ITT leadership is responding, it is instructive to walk quickly through the company's history as a multi-industry player.

A LEGACY OF MANAGEMENT DISCIPLINE

ITT is remembered as one of the most muscular corporations of the conglomerate age—a sprawling organization run under a holding company headed by legendary leveraged buyout master Harold Geneen. During the 1960s, ITT included everything from car rental giant Avis to the Sheraton hotel chain to the Hartford insurance company. By the late 1970s, as profits sagged, Rand Araskog became CEO, and he saw it as his task to deconstruct and rationalize the conglomerate. By 1989, many elements had been sold: The company's telecommunications products business—one of its earliest operations—went to Alcatel, and its long-distance phone service unit was eventually acquired by what would later become WorldCom.

The watershed came in 1995 when the company split into three public companies. ITT Hartford became The Hartford Group. What was then ITT Corp. merged with Starwood, the hospitality chain. And the manufacturing business—until July 2006 known as ITT Industries—stood alone, with annual revenues of about $3 billion and a high debt-to-capital ratio.

ITT Industries' first CEO, Travis Engen, led the company from the time of the split until 2000. Engen had already begun to embed accountability and tight measurement systems in the company, encouraging "value-based" management disciplines to ensure that all decisions, acquisitions, product developments, and process improvements would be based on hard data that showed exactly how those moves would create economic value. The chief executive who succeeded Engen, Lou Giuliano, pushed management operating disciplines even further and faster. In his first report to shareholders in 2000, Giuliano emphasized the value of continually improving business processes as well as products— "an important part of the management approach," he said. That year, ITT launched its value-based Six Sigma (VBSS) initiative designed to implement more efficient and production operations company-wide.

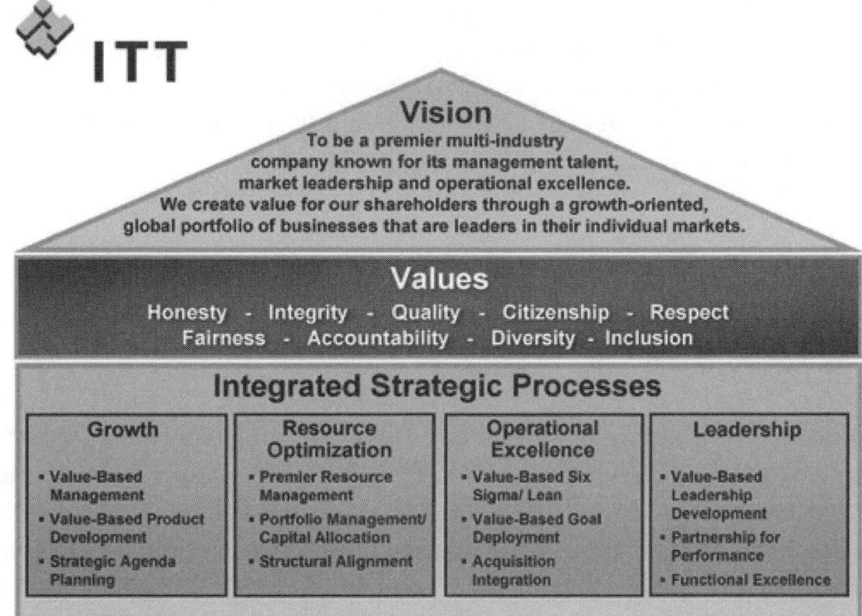

Figure 15.1 The IMS keeps ITT on track.

Giuliano sharpened the focus on business systems from then on. The cover of the 2001 annual report featured a photo of one of the company's VBSS "black belts." Inside, the chairman and CEO told shareholders: "An important part of our strength as a multi-industry company is our commitment to a consistent way of doing business. During the year, we formalized the elements that make up our management system. We didn't change the way we do things. We simply documented the tools and disciplines that define the ITT Industries approach."

The consistent fundamentals he was talking about referred to a shared approach to financial management, leadership development, and operational improvement. "Employees now have a blueprint that will help them develop the skills they need to succeed anywhere in our company, and investors can now see the system—the engine—that is driving ITT Industries' overall success," he said. Under Giuliano, the ITT management system (IMS) became a compass for managers throughout the company. (See Figure 15.1.)

When Steve Loranger joined from Textron halfway through 2004, he saw results that could be chalked up to the growing influence of the IMS. "You've tripled the value of this company in the last 10 years!" he told managers at the

2005 leadership forum. Loranger took to the IMS like a duck takes to water. He understood and was completely in tune with the vision; he "got" and agreed entirely with the values. The integrated strategic processes made sense to him, too. And he saw IMS as a robust and essential tool kit to keep the company on track.

A LOOK INSIDE ITT

ITT Corporation (the new name as of July 1, 2006) is headquartered in White Plains, New York, and comprises three major operating segments, or "management companies," as ITT calls them: Defense Electronics & Services, Fluid Technology, and Motion & Flow Control (for financial reporting, the company still reports in four segments). Each management company comprises units referred to as "value centers"—all of them run as independent profit-and-loss centers and many of them wearing brands that are household names in their markets. All together, ITT employs a little over 40,000 in 57 countries.

Since becoming an independent entity in 1995, the company has bolstered the management centers with a series of acquisitions (Goulds Pumps and Kaman Sciences, among others) and with selected divestitures. For example, in September 1998, ITT sold its automotive Electrical Systems business to France's Valeo SA for $1.7 billion and its Brake and Chassis business to Continental AG in Germany for $1.9 billion. (Together, the two businesses accounted for approximately $4 billion in annual sales.)

Defense Electronics & Services—currently the largest of ITT's business sectors—builds products such as digital combat radios, night-vision goggles, sophisticated satellite imaging systems, jamming devices that guard military planes against radar-guided weapons, and air traffic control systems. (See Figure 15.2.) In 2005, ITT won a sole-source contract for night-vision goggles worth a potential $560 million, along with a five-year contract to operate and maintain communications and information systems for the U.S. Army in southwest Asia and Africa. About 44 percent of the business segment's sales come from contracts for technical and support services that the company provides for the military and other government agencies.

The **Fluid Technology** segment contains ITT's pump businesses, including brands such as Flygt, Goulds, Bell & Gossett, A-C Pump, Lowara, and Vogel, making ITT the world's largest pump producer and a leading provider of water treatment equipment. The company sees sizable opportunities

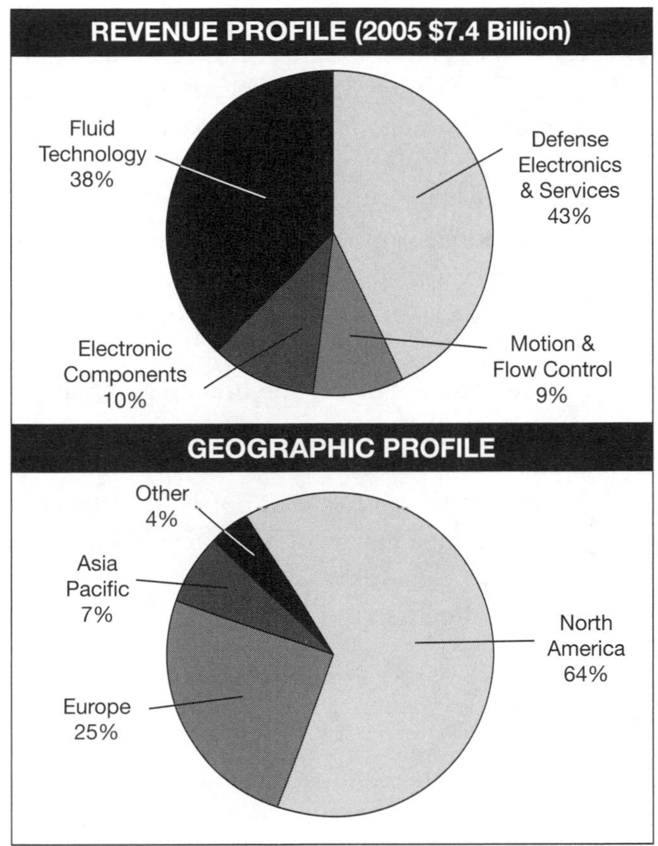

Figure 15.2 Breaking down ITT's revenue.

throughout the water cycle in 137 nations in which it does business, driven by the fact that water scarcity will remain a challenge for mankind for the foreseeable future.

The **Motion & Flow Control** companies make products for the marine and leisure markets, such as specialty shock absorbers, friction materials, aerospace controls, and electronic components. Koni shock absorbers are among its best-known brands. Motion & Flow Control has recently absorbed the connector business of what was previously the Electronic Components management center. Marketing under the Cannon brand, that group included connectors, switches, and cabling.

Collectively, ITT's products and services go to market under the ITT brand. In the last two years, the corporate brand has been the subject of some attention; in many of its markets the name of the value center—Jabsco or Flygt or Koni—was far better known than ITT. So senior vice president and corporate relations director Thomas Martin spearheaded an initiative to elevate the corporate brand, resulting in the creation of a distinct visual brand identity—it's an abstract of yellow engineered blocks—along with a corporate tagline, "Engineered for life," that carries a dual meaning: durability of ITT's products as well as a corporate commitment to advancing human progress. "People want to feel that they work for one unified company," explains Martin. "Whether they sell Flygt, Koni, Goulds Pumps, or one of our other brands, they work for ITT."

Martin hosted a breakout session on the branding initiative at the most recent leadership forum, and the session turned out to be one of the highest rated at the forum. That fact speaks volumes: first of all, that ITT has systems detailed enough to measure the performance of its leadership forums, and second, for what it says about the impact of a unifying brand on hiring, training, leadership development, global expansion activity, and capturing internal leverage and synergy opportunities.

THE PUSH TO "PREMIER"

The drumbeat at ITT's corporate headquarters is about the "path to premier." It may not be voiced that way every day or in every meeting, but there is no doubt that it's what drives the executive team forward. The term "premier" has very specific connotations for ITT's top team: it means ITT is considered an equal in a group of top-performing multi-industry companies such as United Technologies, Illinois Tool Works, General Electric, and Danaher. It means ITT's long-term revenue growth, cost structure, market potential, earnings record, cash flow, credit ratings, and standing on Wall Street are all up there with those of the UTCs and Danahers. "This is a club we would like to be in. We're not premier, but I think we're on the threshold of being premier," Loranger told managers at the 2005 leadership forum.

The new corporate branding is just one visible step on the path to premier. What is less obvious are the long strides toward functional excellence in every value center, leadership at every level, and accountability throughout. The message is "premier"; the method is constant reinvention.

Reinvention was on display recently as ITT acted to simplify its organization structure, bringing together businesses and brands that share a customer focus and can benefit from sharing people, products, and technologies. One impressive result was streamlining the organization from the previous four management companies to three, and 26 value centers to just 15. Each value center now averages about $500 million in annual revenues; each now can exploit broader economies of scale to help break into China's markets and to consolidate procurement, among other benefits. The shift is reflected in the naming of the value centers—oriented by market, such as Friction Materials, instead of product brand name.

By streamlining the value center structure, ITT could more clearly examine its business portfolio. In doing so, the management team was able to apply its value-based management strategic planning tool—one of the IMS keystone processes—to pinpoint seven market segments that will generate the most value: water, wastewater, advanced water treatment, defense electronics, space and intelligence systems, advanced engineering and services, and leisure marine.

The IMS itself has come in for a tune-up in order to make it less like a to-do list and more like a tool kit. Previously, it included a section titled "Improvement Priorities," but that implied that the IMS had an in-built expiry date. The Vision has not changed, but the Values section now has two new areas—diversity and inclusion—to demonstrate the company's wish to expand its talent pool with people from all geographies, cultures, and backgrounds.

In turn, the IMS has helped the management team to lay out the improvement priorities for 2006. Among them were the following:

- To drive growth by increasing sales in Asia and by enhancing the company's global water leadership position
- To accelerate global sourcing and lean production
- To deploy and execute value-based leadership development (VBLD) at the value centers

AN EMPHASIS ON GREAT LEADERSHIP

That last point merits broader explanation. Leadership themes take up half of Loranger's time by his own admission—and even more, according to some of his lieutenants. Indeed, excellence in leadership is one of the three fundamentals referred to years before: "Lou Giuliano realized we didn't have the bench strength we needed," explains HR chief Scott Crum.

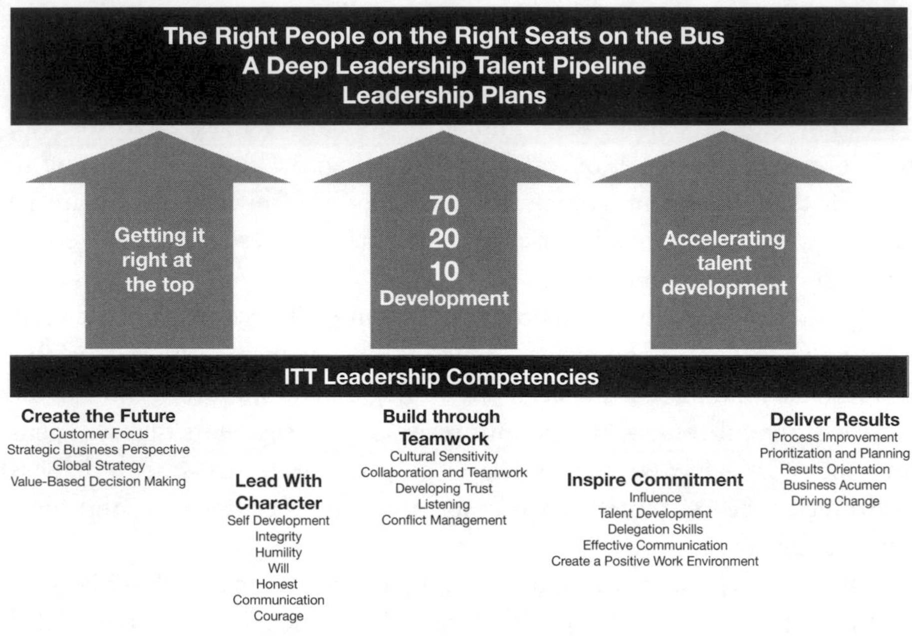

Figure 15.3 The leadership development model.

Several new positions have been added in the last two years. There is now a senior vice president of global workforce strategy, tasked with charting and improving ITT's diversity and inclusion efforts. A former segment leader, Brenda Reichelderfer, has become senior vice president and chief technology officer. And John Williamson joined recently from Danaher to fill the new role of vice president of operational excellence.

From here on, ITT will look to "grow its own," aiming to fill more than three-quarters of its available senior management positions from the inside, according to Crum. A key objective is to ensure that every leader is intimately familiar with and an assertive user of the IMS. A foundation element of the IMS is VBLD—now being pushed deeper into the organization in successive waves. (See Figure 15.3.) For those positions that will be filled from the outside, hiring is already becoming a lot tougher, and the recruiting cycle longer. In some cases, well-credentialed external candidates have been rejected because they lack a highly desirable trait: humility. Explains Loranger: "You want to make sure people are putting the company ahead of themselves."

The performance bar for ITT's managers is getting higher too. The company has recently instituted formal "fit checks" for all executives, gauging them against the five VBLD leadership competencies. The checks, held with Loranger, occur twice a year and are not negotiable.

The management teams meet formally and often. Aside from the usual executive council meetings—Loranger and his most senior team—there are three major gatherings a year, such as the leadership forums, drawing together as many as 500 of the company's managers. Launched in 2002 and orchestrated by communications chief Martin, the events are eagerly anticipated for their fusion of formal information sharing, networking, and employee recognition, with a meaningful and high-caliber award program.

Meanwhile, ITT is forging ahead with another of its fundamentals: operational excellence. The company sees ample opportunities to improve its cost structure and is targeting $200 million of incremental cost reductions between 2007 and 2008. Six Sigma and lean production practices are central to those efforts—to operational excellence in general. At the same time, the company is mounting a major push to source much more from low-cost regions. Of the company's annual $2 billion in purchased materials and parts, "we're getting less than 10 percent from low-cost regions," says Chief Financial Officer George Minnich. By 2009, the goal is 25 percent. The stretch goal—as much as 35 percent—is what ITT's benchmarks have determined is the standard for other premier-league companies.

This is where Williamson's operational excellence group comes in. Set up with a firm cross-functional and cross-company mandate, his team is charged with chasing cost out of procurement, finding commonalities in buying patterns among value centers, and encouraging joint bids and selected engineering changes where the sourcing benefits merit them and where they don't hurt competitive differentiation.

The operational excellence team also oversees the company's Six Sigma and lean initiatives. Addressing one lean "boot camp" recently, Williamson urged the lean team leaders: "My challenge to you is to make this worth it—you and everyone on your team. First of all, admit you have a lot to learn. Challenge others to admit they have a lot to learn. Collect your lessons learned. Then have a plan to apply your lessons learned. If you and your people are not feeling uncomfortable about the pace and extent of change, you're probably not pushing hard enough."

Excellence in operations pervades staff departments too—functions such as finance and HR. Minnich's team is moving to expand its capabilities in planning and analysis. "We were doing a lot of reporting but not a lot of analysis," he says. Two potential benefits: He expects to be able to assess best practices in closing the books—particularly benchmarking the premier competition—and to analyze whether it makes sense to begin buying back stock with some of the cash that ITT has generated.

Similarly, Crum's HR teams are setting up centers of excellence in areas such as talent development, compensation and benefits, and human resource operations. And Martin's communications group is actively soliciting and weighing the feedback from the company's executive gatherings.

THE IMPORTANCE OF THE "FLIGHT MANUAL"

As a pilot himself, Loranger is familiar with an aviator's flight manual, and he uses that metaphor to convey the importance of the IMS—particularly the value-based management systems. With operational excellence and leadership development as ITT's first two fundamentals, the third is financial management, which breaks down to an emphasis on three crucial metrics: operating margins, cash flow, and return on invested capital. Boosting operating margins calls for increasing the size of the revenue opportunities, he says. Stronger cash flow comes from working faster. And better ROIC stems from working more efficiently. "It's easy to move any one of these metrics, but it's kind of hard to move all three of them in the right sequence and in the direction you want. That's why we're going to follow a balanced strategic plan," he explained to managers at the 2005 leadership forum.

Value-based management is what guides that strategic plan. And value-based goal deployment (VBGD) is the IMS discipline that ensures that the plan is broken out into pragmatic steps—and followed. "It's a very efficient way to make sure the organizations under you are doing the things you need them to be doing," says the CEO. Nick Hill, president of ITT's Motion & Flow Control segment, shows how operating charts break the VBGD systems into specific targets, with names and dates attached to them. "It's a hard-wired matrix of the actions we need to take," he says. (Tongue-in-cheek, Hill also describes the processes as "spinach.")

Loranger sets the pace. Interviewed recently in *Leaders* magazine, he said: "I'm a stickler for accountability . . . if we decide we want to get something

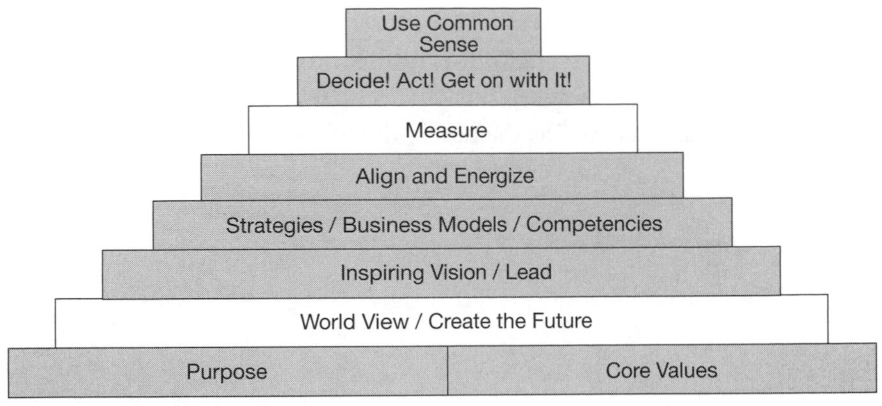

Figure 15.4 Areas of significant strength at ITT.

done, I insist on getting it written down and linked to metrics. I don't want ideas explained through anecdotes, but rather through action plans, with regular review processes built into those plans. All my plans are written down, and I expect everyone else to write down theirs too."

OUTSIDERS' EYES ON ITT

ITT is justifiably proud of its "Best Managed" citation in *Forbes* magazine—and of its "Most Admired" 2006 ranking in *Fortune* in the Industrial & Farm Equipment category, beating out formidable contenders such as Eaton, Parker Hannafin, and Dover. And the company's yardsticks stack up well against the "Beat the Odds" framework. Participation in the survey questionnaire was exceptionally strong—several hundred ITT managers responded, making for very robust calibration. Not only were the absolute scores high compared to the baseline, but there was strong alignment between the responses of the top executive team and the leadership at large. The readings on "purpose" and "core values" were impressive indeed. (See Figure 15.4.) But what is even more encouraging is Loranger's reaction to an overview of the Beat the Odds results. He homed in at once on the few areas needing improvement—for example, alertness to new, nontraditional competitors and the response gap on questions such as how quickly and decisively deviations from core values are dealt with. Not only that, but Loranger declared his intent to address those areas—a signal of his adherence to ITT's value-based management systems, and his dedication to dealing with any self-critiquing insights.

ITT would still prefer stronger and more consistent approval from Wall Street. The cadre of analysts who follow multi-industry companies think well of ITT and grade it appropriately, but the company's leaders would like to be held in the same high esteem as the blue chips such as GE and UTC.

A HINT OF ITT'S NEXT DECADE

ITT has an arm's-length list of specific initiatives to get busy with—from driving lean processes, to helping with the competitive hunt for talent, to accelerating its growth in the Asia Pacific region, which still accounts for only a few percentage points of the company's revenues. Senior managers are self-critical of the company's market research competencies and aware of the need to identify cross-company engineering commonalities that can be refined and supported in a corporate research and development center. And Loranger concedes that for all its forward vision, ITT could do a better job of scenario planning.

There is also a desire to enhance capabilities around ITT's acquisition prowess. "We need to build a stronger core competency in acquiring businesses," says CFO Minnich. His comment is especially relevant to the Fluid Technology group, where there is plenty of room to grow by acquisition but where the bulk of the targets are smaller companies. Some are concerned about ITT's ability to maintain momentum given the significant changes it is going through. "Change is good, but too much change is bad. Can we continue to perform at these levels? Do we have the strategy and the leadership team to do that? Can we grow up and still be the company we are today?" asks Scott Crum.

Valid though they may be, these concerns are the expressions of a passionately self-critical culture. The fact is, ITT is in many ironclad markets and in favor with many good customers. The company has demonstrated solid financials. It has a clear code of conduct and strong ethical stance endorsed personally by the CEO. It sets goals aggressively. It is clear about its strategic objectives, its vision, and its values. It has made overall talent development a priority—leadership development in particular. The company measures results, holds leaders accountable, and acts quickly on the results of those metrics. If all that isn't enough to put ITT on the path to premier, it is hard to know what would.

Operations excellence chief John Williamson ponders what the company's legacy will be, looking back from year 2036. "Did we create the mechanisms, did we have the right talent to drive tangible results over the next five years?" he asks. "The needle is moving in the right direction."

At ITT, with its continual state of self-examination, that is bordering on satisfaction.

Part IV

NEXT STEPS

16

THE PATH TO ENSURING LONG-TERM HEALTH

Once the nine-principles framework is understood, the challenge becomes to apply it creatively and diligently in your own organization. That requires the following:

- The ability to see yourself accurately ("what is")
- The ability to see the difference between what is and what should be ("gap analysis")
- The ability and willingness to make the necessary commitment to change

This chapter assists with the first two of these points by describing how to gain insights about where you *really* are today compared with where you should be, and by explaining how to use those insights to build an effective plan. In the next chapter we provide numerous illustrations and case study exercises relating to the nine principles of success. The exercises will give you additional experience in gap analysis. In addition, by highlighting the consequences of dysfunctional behavior on the organization's health and lifeline, Chapter 17 can provide the motivation and the framework to make the personal commitment to change.

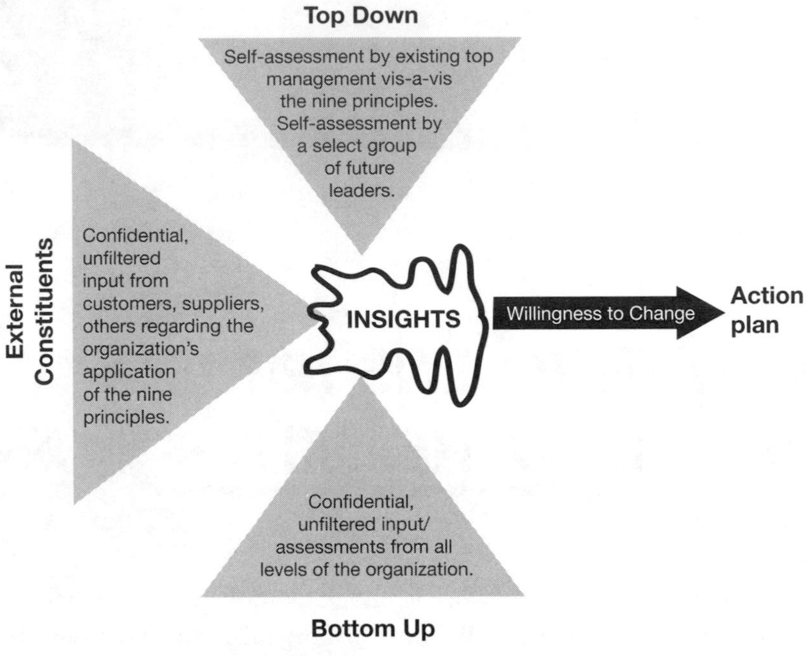

Figure 16.1 The four perspectives in developing an action plan.

THE PATH FORWARD

To properly develop an action plan, it is important to gather information from four perspectives (see Figure 16.1):

- **Top down (senior executives).** It is crucial to obtain confidential input and assessments from members of the top management team. Don't assume that a group discussion among the senior executives will suffice to bring out their perspectives. What you want is candid input on the diagnostic's dimensions, without concern for being politically correct or wondering what the career impact might be.
- **Top down (future leaders).** In this phase, you obtain confidential input and assessments from those you consider to be the future leaders of your organization. The same comments apply here as for senior executives.

- **Bottom up (other employees).** This phase involves collecting confidential, unfiltered input from all levels and all areas of the organization. You don't have to survey everyone. But you should select a sample of meaningful size and variety from employees at many levels and in many roles across the organization.
- **External constituents.** Here you get confidential, unscreened input from customers, suppliers, bankers, and others outside the organization who know you well. Suppliers in particular can be a valuable source of information about your organization, and about how they can contribute to your organization's future success as part of your team.

Before we go much further, let's deal with one misconception about gathering employee feedback. A common belief is that face-to-face "exit interviews" with departing employees can provide a wealth of honest feedback about the state of the organization. Don't believe it for a minute. I have personally witnessed colleagues adopting the attitude of "I don't want to burn any bridges." As a result, their exit interviews were relatively short events, often built around a single, safe message: "I couldn't turn down this new career opportunity." In fact, some of them could have been a valuable source of insight, but they were concerned that being candid would be counterproductive to keeping their options open.

Employees who have departed can provide valuable input if they have an opportunity for *anonymous* feedback. One way to do that is to include them in an anonymous diagnostic survey.

As mentioned earlier in the book, the nine-principles framework is not a menu to be cherry-picked. There is far greater and longer-lasting company-building advantage in embracing the framework as a whole rather than, for example, deciding to focus on one particular principle for improvement. Why? The whole—all nine principles taken together—is far greater than the sum of the parts. And until all fundamentals are addressed effectively in your organization, long-term success—even survival—may be in question.

Appendix A contains several assessment surveys, based on the core questions for each principle discussed earlier. These surveys can assist you in preparing for and conducting your own assessment and diagnosis across all nine principles, and for each of the major constituencies (Figure 16.2). The bottom line here is very simple: Don't guess! Assess!

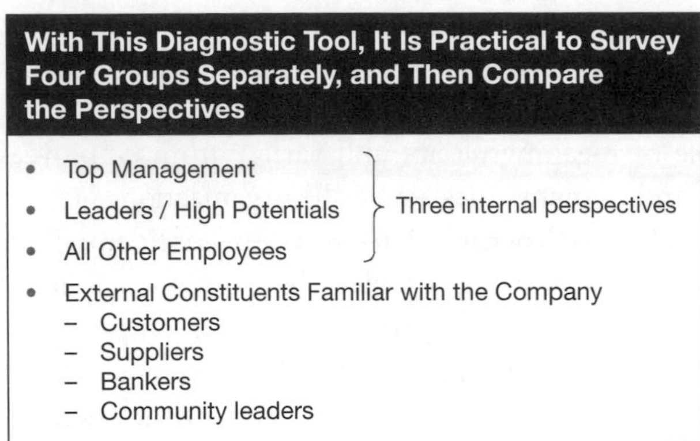

Figure 16.2.

You will find separate assessment surveys for each of the internal audiences (Senior Execs, Future Leaders, Rest of Employees). The questions for each survey are worded somewhat differently to reflect the differing perspectives of each audience. For the external audiences (Suppliers and Customers), the surveys focus on the same nine principles but are considerably shorter and are geared to elicit their outside perspectives.

The best starting point is to conduct an assessment of the senior executive and future leader groups and then to compare the results (see sidebar). What you are looking for are themes and viewpoints shared by both groups as well as marked differences in perspectives.

A word of caution: If you believe that the most important perspectives in your organization are those of the management team, then you'll probably plan to stop right there. Don't do that. Go the next step. Add the perspective from "all other employees." It will test the assumption that most of your workforce understands the foundations you've established for your business and is aligned with the perspectives and directions set by management. You need to know whether or not that is true, rather than assuming it is so.

Of course, in this survey-fatigued world, it is rarely popular to add another survey to the working day. So my advice is to carefully plan when and how you introduce this diagnostic to your organization. You want people to take it seriously and respond in earnest to the questions posed; importantly, you also want them to view it as a healthy indication of management's interest in the organization's future. For greatest impact, the CEO or the entire senior team should sponsor the survey and promise follow-through with the

ADDITIONAL ADVICE FOR CONDUCTING YOUR OWN ASSESSMENT

The sample assessments in Appendix A represent core questions that can be the basis for an assessment and diagnosis. It is often appropriate to expand the list of topics surveyed for each principle, based on the unique issues within your organization. When I assist companies with their organizational assessments, I often use an expanded diagnostic that contains about 25 percent more survey points than the sample core assessments in the appendix. I also give them averaged data to show them how their survey results compare to the survey database.

Once any new diagnostic questions are identified and worded according to good survey structure (not a topic covered in this book), they can be easily incorporated along with the core diagnostic questions into an online survey that you manage. Online research services such as Zoomerang, SurveyMonkey, and others offer survey tools that are easy for the surveying manager to use and simple for the survey participant as well. Very importantly, as independent third-party services, they provide confidentiality regarding the survey participant's responses.

Once the surveys are ready to go, all you need to do is provide e-mail addresses for your intended recipients. The survey software takes care of distributing the appropriate survey and then capturing the recipients' electronic responses. Some of the survey tools also offer a "reminder" feature that can be sent to your survey population a week or two weeks after the initial e-mail, reminding them to complete the survey if they have not already done so.

With most of these online survey tools, you can watch the results build as participants complete their surveys—which can be an exciting if unnerving process. Most of these tools have fairly easy reporting and graphical depictions of the results, making preliminary analysis easy. For more detailed comparisons—for example, testing whether the responses from one group are different (in a statistically significant sense) from the responses of another group—you may need to download the raw data from your survey software into an Excel spreadsheet, which allows you to conduct T-tests and other statistical analyses. One note of caution: A few of the core questions are "reverse questions"—statements in the negative. These should be removed from any averages so they do not distort the results.

As mentioned earlier in this section, it is worthwhile to survey several internal groups separately, and maybe to poll external constituents as well. It is especially instructive to highlight areas of agreement and areas of statistically significant differences in perspectives. It is also enlightening to study each survey group's responses from the perspective of which questions indicate the greatest organizational strengths and which reveal the greatest opportunities for improvement.

Once the baseline assessment has run its course and generated insights and a plan, follow-through becomes key. Make this a responsibility of the senior team, and plan to report progress to the organization and, as appropriate, to your external constituents as well. Finally, you should periodically reassess to confirm progress and adjust direction. Given what is at stake, a fresh survey every 12 to 15 months is not too frequent.

results. As a final step, you can add the external perspectives to the picture you are developing. Often, outsiders who know you well can see the forest more clearly than those standing among the trees.

Still not convinced? Consider the example of Home Depot, which was prominently featured as the positive cover story in the March 6, 2006, issue of *BusinessWeek*. The article argued "that the command and control discipline [CEO] Nardelli has imposed is getting financial results."[1] Just a few weeks later, the magazine's Letters to the Editor section introduced numerous customer letters about the original article with this comment: " . . . a deluge of letters, online posts, and message board responses—nearly 300 in all—indicates that the overhaul has come at a cost . . . Only two correspondents praised America's largest home supply store."[2]

To that negative customer feedback I can add anecdotes from the supplier side. In two completely separate meetings *unrelated to Home Depot* during the early part of 2006 (one of the meetings occurred before the *BusinessWeek* article appeared), one prospective supplier and one incumbent supplier volunteered their negative impressions of the "new" Home Depot. To say they were passionate about their feelings is to put it mildly.

So how do you develop useful insights about the gaps and the opportunities for change? What's needed are candid comparisons not only between the different internal and external perspectives but between those viewpoints and what you would like to see. Also needed: open, constructive, ongoing debate about the learnings from these separate assessments. If needed, you can use an internal or external facilitator to ease the process and make it as productive, painless, and nonpolitical as possible. (One company I know decided to use "breakout sessions" at one of its management meetings as a way to delve deeply into the underlying reasons for low scores on one Beat the Odds principle.)

The insights gained, *when combined with a willingness to change*, provide the impetus to develop a meaningful action plan for change. The key word here is "willingness." If you're one of those leaders who takes advantage of every opportunity to learn and to improve performance, what is described above will be adequate motivation: You now have the insights and tools to make a real difference. You're off and running.

But if you're still not sure about proceeding, you should think about it this way. Most of the 600,000 American business bankruptcies during the last decade, and many of the once-great institutions that have fallen far from their peaks, were on a path to eventual demise well before problems showed up in their financial statements. (Remember: Financial statements are *lagging* indicators.) So take the opportunity today to assess your organization's status against the nine principles. Reduce the risk that your organization will one day disappear from the landscape of modern business because of a failure to remain focused on the fundamentals. If you are reluctant to follow this path, there is only one alternative: Move out of the way so others can pursue the necessary changes.

A senior executive with a large U.S. company once told me how he passed the mantle to his successor. He prepared three envelopes for the newly appointed leader. The envelopes were labeled "#1 (open me first)," "#2 (open me second)," and "#3 (open me last)." At an appropriate occasion, he handed them to his successor with the following private instructions: "When things are going wrong in a big way, and you are having real trouble dealing with the problem, open envelope #1. The second time things are going wrong in a big way, open envelope #2. And when this happens a third time, open envelope #3." The contents of each envelope were as follows:

1. "When things go wrong, blame your predecessor."
2. "If things are still going wrong, reorganize."
3. "If things are still going wrong, prepare three envelopes."

17

READER EXERCISES ILLUSTRATING THE NINE PRINCIPLES

Are you confident that you have a good practical understanding of each of the nine principles and the entire Beat the Odds framework? Let's put it to the test. This chapter offers the reader some additional experience with the nine principles framework by providing real-life illustrations—and asks you to analyze each situation. Some of the exercises focus on negative examples (pending failures) and the balance of the exercises offer positive examples. A few include a mix of negative and positive dimensions.

You may see yourself or your organization in one or more of these situations. As you read each situation, keep in mind the pyramid of nine principles (see Figure 17.1). You will be challenged to identify which principles are at stake in each situation.

Several of the exercises also highlight the severe adverse consequences of failing to pay attention to one or more of the principles and can provide the motivation to make the personal commitment to change.

Following are scenarios from various types of companies. Please ponder the situation and the consequences before reading the analysis.

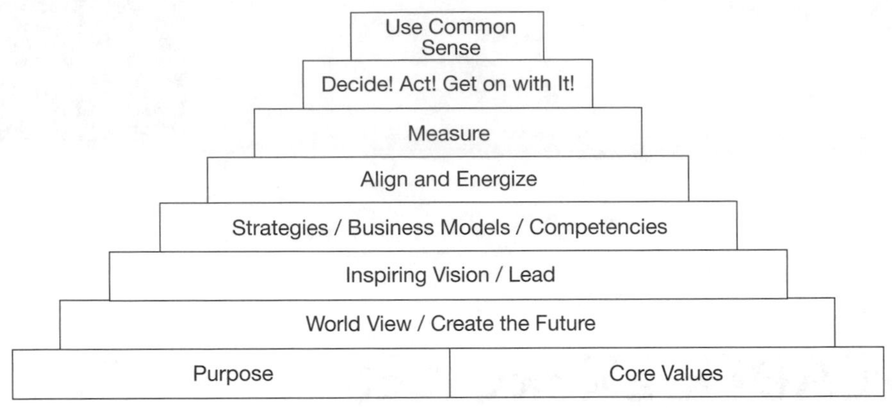

Figure 17.1 The pyramid of nine principles

ETHICS—UPHOLDING THE BASICS

Situation. At a Fortune 500 company, a senior manager falsifies his expense accounts and also accepts "gratuities" from a supplier. The manager is investigated, the facts are confirmed, and he is swiftly terminated from employment.

At almost the same time, at the same company, several lower-level business unit employees were determined to have had improper dealings with (and received significant personal benefits from) suppliers. They, too, are terminated for improprieties.

Consequences. Employees in this company saw—in these well-publicized situations—that there is no double standard when it comes to upholding the company's values and integrity. The senior manager and the business unit employees received similar treatment and consequences. This helped to foster a belief that no one enjoys special rules and consideration, and that senior management is serious about the values it espouses.

Before proceeding to the Analysis discussion, determine which principle or principles were at stake in this situation and where the company's management succeeded.

Analysis. This situation is an example of strong values in action, Principle 2 (Figure 17.2). Two points: First, permitting a double standard would have been very damaging; second, most managers would probably be relieved if they could handle situations like these through "retiring" the employee (if the

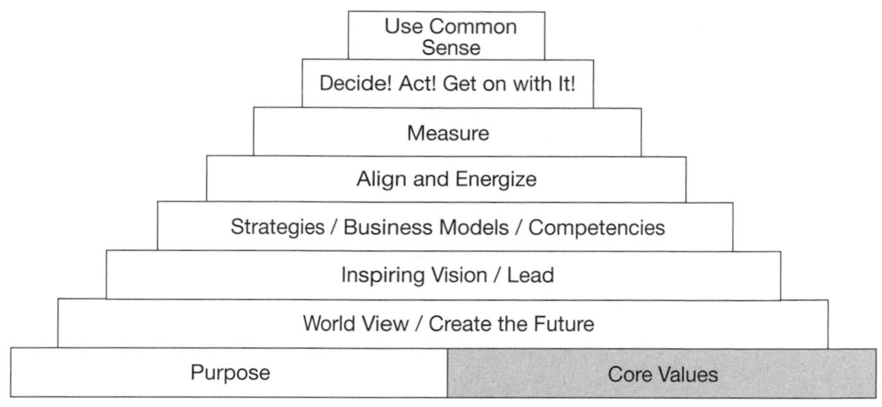

Figure 17.2

employee had enough years of service to be "retired"). This company had that option but chose not to use it, because it wanted to send a clear message to the entire organization.

The ability to portray a termination in a neutral or favorable light (i.e., a "retirement") is a tempting prescription for avoiding an honest reconciliation with an organization's values. Taking such a path, which this Fortune 500 company refused to do, can be very damaging to the company's values and thereby risks a continuation of the damaging behavior by others in the future. In addition, it can have ripple effects on the integrity of management in general, and on the commitment that management is trying to develop throughout the organization.

This company took the two bad situations and turned them into learning experiences for the entire organization. By doing so, it convincingly demonstrated its core values. There were no subsequent events of this nature for many years to come.

SIMULATIONS VERSUS THE REAL WORLD

Situation. Harry, a forty-something manager in a medium-sized company, enjoyed a comfortable career path in his functional "silo," Operations. He was competent and generally well liked. He accurately assessed the challenges in his larger department, including the inability of his boss, the aging COO, to deal with numerous personnel issues. He privately assured some of his coworkers that if one day he were running the department, he would not hesitate to correct the problems.

During assessments of his management potential, including simulations of real-world problems, Harry did well. He intellectually understood what needed to be done in the simulated situation, and he would take the necessary "actions," including dismissal of hypothetical problem managers.

Through a series of unplanned events, Harry on short notice was thrust into the actual position of chief operating officer for his company. He was suddenly faced with the opportunity to address the many issues his predecessor would not correct. The timing was critical, because the company was facing a crisis of confidence in company management.

Harry became paralyzed and took no action on the pressing problems of his department.

Consequences. Employees quickly became disenchanted with Harry, seeing him as a clone of his ineffective predecessor. The reputation of the company's CEO, who appointed Harry, was damaged. Harry himself became distressed and depressed, and in spite of private coaching from friends, he never was able to come to terms with his lack of action.

Before proceeding to the Analysis section, determine which principle or principles were at stake in this situation and where the company's management failed.

Analysis. Let's be clear about one thing: Harry is not at fault (other than accepting a job he was not qualified for). The real culprit is the system that allowed Harry to progress to this point in his career.

There are many Harrys out there, because many organizations fail on a key aspect of Principle 4—distinguishing between leadership and management in their promotion of key personnel (Figure 17.3).

As a minimum, this company needs to adopt a clear understanding and distinction between leadership and management. Furthermore, it needs to use multiple methods, including 360-degree leadership feedback, to identify the true leaders, and make succession decisions based on that information. Finally, when a mistake is made, corrective action needs to be taken, no matter how uncomfortable it may be. Failing to do so hurts the entire organization.

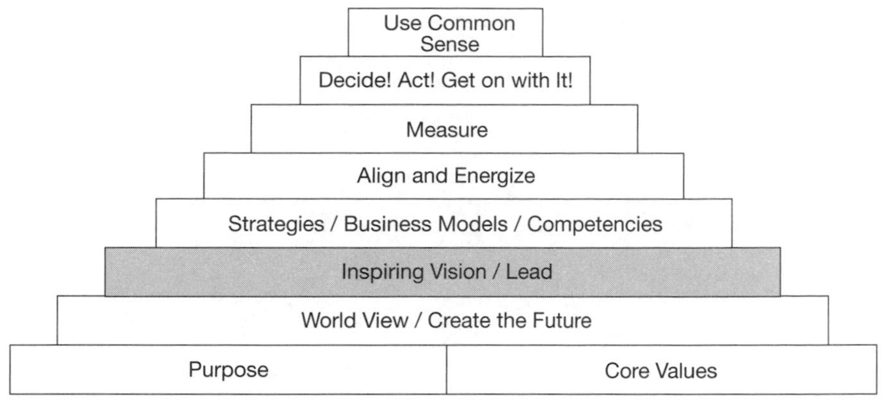

Figure 17.3

DAMN THE MARKET, FULL SPEED AHEAD

Situation. A U.S. manufacturer (Company A) was experiencing a significant challenge with one of its major product lines. This product had for several decades been a steady and significant contributor to corporate profits, but it was increasingly becoming a commodity as new, low-cost supply entered the market.

At the same time that Company A was evaluating what to do with its product strategy, two other companies (B and C) announced plans to enter the market by building new, very low-cost facilities targeted at this product category. They openly stated they would be the low-cost producers and, as a result, would be long-term players in this competitive market. Company A proceeded to enter an expensive bidding contest to acquire one of the other incumbent producers in this market (Company D), and it successfully acquired that company, thereby becoming an even larger, though still traditional and not low-cost, player in the market. Companies B and C were not dissuaded from their plans by Company A's acquisition (as Company A's management had hoped) and proceeded to build their new, low-cost facilities and establish new, lower pricing to attract customers.

Consequences. The result of Company A's actions was significant economic turmoil for Company A as the new competitors implemented their business models, demoralization of its employees (many of whom

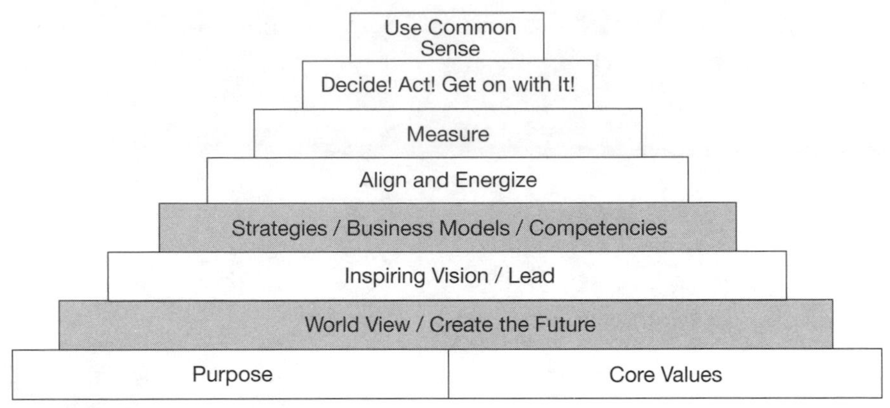

Figure 17.4

suspected that a huge strategy mistake had been made), and adverse impact on its stockholders.

Before proceeding to the Analysis discussion, determine which principle or principles were at stake in this situation and where Company A's management failed.

Analysis. This situation is an example of violating Principle 3: Create the Future, and also Principle 5: Develop the Right Strategies, Business Models, and Competencies (Figure 17.4).

Aristotle is credited with the quote: "He who the gods want to destroy, they will give 40 years of prosperity." Company A enjoyed its 40 years of prosperity and came to believe that its actions still determined market conditions.

In this particular product situation, it failed to candidly assess the likelihood that its new competitors would proceed with their plans regardless of Company A's actions. It also failed to recognize and deal with a fundamental business model shift that its new competitors were adopting, relying instead on trying to do more of the same thing (old business model). The outcome was inevitable.

In order to avoid repeating this costly mistake in other products/markets, this company needs to

- Become very serious about evaluating competitors' actions.
- Realize it is no longer able to affect other companies' plans.
- Seek out new business models.

- Given its diminished stature and financial condition, be open to alliances with other companies.

DO AS I SAY, NOT AS I DO

Situation: A brand-new CEO of a troubled company quickly went on the road to all company locations. His objective: to ensure that all employees fully understood the severity and urgency of the company's situation, and to enlist their active involvement in turning the ship around.

Among his themes were the following:

- The business environment is changing rapidly, and only companies that change faster than the environment have a chance to succeed (i.e., change is swirling all around us, and we have to get ahead of it).
- The company would be adopting a "performance ethic" that rewards successful change and results, and that has consequences for blocking change and not generating new and better results.

Within the first six months of his tenure, the new CEO made several high-level appointments that appeared to be in stark contrast to his fundamental themes. For example, he appointed as a senior officer a manager who was widely known to be a *resister* of change. He also appointed as a senior officer a manager who was a great talker on technical matters, but who was not known to have initiated any new ideas, nor achieved significant results, nor been willing to entertain taking business risks.

Consequences. The CEO's credibility was severely impacted by these and similar decisions. Employees became very cynical about the CEO's intentions, which was unfortunate because he was personally sincere; he just made flawed people and leadership selection decisions.

Before proceeding to the Analysis discussion, determine which principle or principles were at stake in this situation and where the CEO and his advisors failed.

Analysis. This situation represents a violation of Principle 4, because of the failure to draw a sharp distinction between leadership and management and the failure to select true leaders for several key positions. Arguably, it is also a violation of Principle 2, because the CEO introduced some key themes

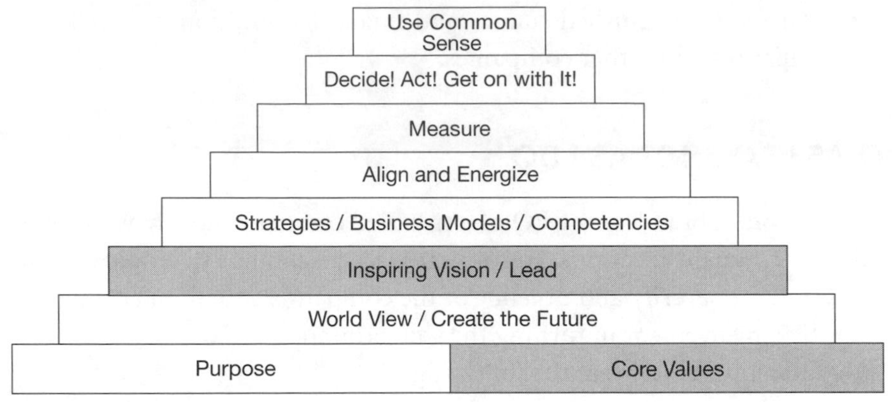

Figure 17.5

and values for the organization's success, then failed to personally act in a manner that reinforced those values (Figure 17.5).

The proper course of action, given the severe damage to the CEO's credibility, is the prompt reversal of those incorrect appointments. This is not a pleasant task, but it is made easier by one fact: The organization knows that mistakes were made, and would naturally expect the CEO to correct those mistakes and live up to the challenge he himself laid down. To prevent such mistakes in the future, this company should adopt 360-degree feedback on all key managers, to *measure* their leadership practices as one input to future decisions.

CAN YOU WIN IF YOU ARE PREDICTABLE?

Situation. A mature company with years of engineering and production heritage was adept at analyzing its own proposed capital projects. Extensive engineering, accounting, and purchasing input went into each project estimate. No stone was left unturned in the internal evaluation of project investment, contingencies, lead times, ramp-up schedules, and so on. The production and technical people knew which projects made sense, and had a well-defined 10-year "capital plan" showing all those wish list items.

The formal capital request write-up went through many revisions, to the point that the final executive summary was in many respects a work of art—carefully crafted to make the key selling points in a few pages. In all cases, a

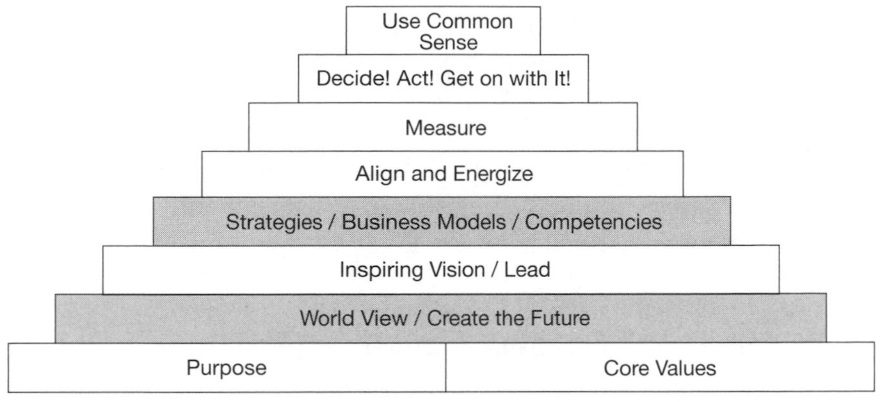

Figure 17.6

precisely calculated return on investment (ROI) was a prominent component of the write-up.

Unfortunately, the ROIs did not always come to pass. External factors seemed to regularly surprise this company, and its well-developed 10-year capital plan of projects began to bog down in unfavorable corporate economics. In addition, competitors seemed to regularly do inexplicable things—further upsetting forecasted project economics.

Before it was too late, this company's senior management took a critical look at what its underlying problems were and determined that it was too inwardly focused and also that its strategy process was too myopic.

Consequences. Just in time, this company successfully averted the strategic failure that it would inevitably have experienced. While not entirely out of the woods today, this company's employees and its external constituents have renewed confidence in its long-term outlook.

Before proceeding to the Analysis section, determine which principle or principles were at stake in this situation and where the company's management succeeded.

Analysis. In this case, the original underlying weakness was with Principle 3 (Create the Future). The company had significant strengths in engineering, procurement and accounting. But the company also was regularly surprised by developments in the marketplace, because of its inward focus and weakness in Principle 3. As a further consequence, it tended to pursue traditional strategies and projects (a weakness in Principle 5). (See Figure 17.6.)

To avoid failure, this company's top management successfully addressed the need to increase the attention it paid to the marketplace—especially to the potential game-changing behavior of competitors—and became more willing to consider nontraditional strategies, projects, and investments (creative application of Principle 5). An important part of making these changes in mind-set was the injection of fresh talent—from outside the industry—into the ranks of senior management.

ASKING THE RIGHT QUESTION IS IMPORTANT

Situation. A midsize company was struggling in its base business. It would occasionally have a "good year," but then it would have several difficult years in a row. As these cycles repeated, the company would shift its objectives from strategic objectives to very short-term, tactical objectives, and back again.

In this environment, the personal perspectives of the chief financial officer carried much weight. The CFO was very concerned about the appearance of the balance sheet. This concern translated into severe constraints on new investment activities and a preoccupation with trying to optimize results from some very old business models. He was also very concerned about cost structure, and this eventually became synonymous with head count reductions among the salaried staff, since this was an action that management could initiate on its own.

Consequences. Over a number of business cycles, the company implemented very aggressive efforts to manage spending and investing activities. It also effected very severe head count reductions among its salaried, nonunionized staff. In spite of these aggressive actions, the company saw its margins and its operating performance continuing to deteriorate—much to the consternation of all concerned. As that deterioration continued, renewed efforts at controlling spending and investing were initiated, and accelerated staff reductions were implemented. All of these actions did prevent the balance sheet from further deterioration, but the operating performance of the company continued to worsen, thereby aggravating the corporation's financial condition.

Before proceeding to the Analysis discussion, determine which principle or principles were at stake in this situation and where this company's management failed.

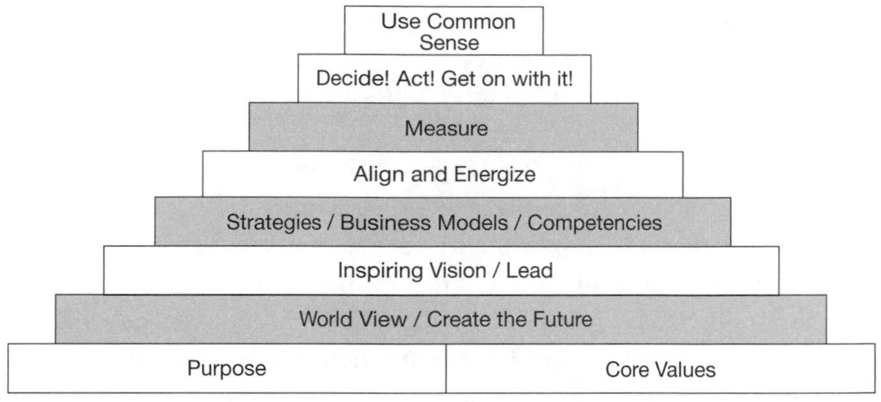

Figure 17.7

Analysis. Relating to our principles, there were several factors contributing to this company's difficulties. The narrow focus on the objectives of balance sheet appearance and head count reduction suggests a failure relating to Principle 7 (Measure Only What You Want to Achieve). But this was secondary to the primary failure: asking the right questions about what were the causes underlying the company's deterioration (Principle 3, Create the Future), combined with Principle 5, Develop the Right Strategies, Business Models, and Competencies (Figure 17.7).

In order to pull out of its decline, this company needs to

- Acknowledge the underlying and changing industry fundamentals that have been at the root of its long-term deterioration.
- Envision how it can succeed in this new world, by adopting new business models, by capitalizing on the strengths it still has, and by dealing with the weaknesses it has (possibly through alliances).

Nothing short of a shift in mind-set will spare this company from inevitable failure.

BECOMING GLOBAL THE WRONG WAY

Situation. An international company, with operations in seven countries, was experiencing performance problems. As one part of the solution, top management decided to become "more global."

Management consultants were brought in, and the company redesigned its organization in a radical manner. Historically, there was profit and loss (P & L) responsibility in each country, with a strong reporting relationship between the country organization and the worldwide headquarters. After the reorganization, there was no P & L responsibility in each country. P & L responsibility came together at the global CEO's office. In each country, there was functional (vertical) responsibility for sales and marketing, for operations, and for other functions. Each of these functions reported not to a country organization, but to a global functional office at headquarters. In addition, the in-country working relationship among these functions was not explicitly linked through local P & L performance.

Consequences. Organizational complexity worsened, and speed of decision making slowed down as most decisions that could have been made locally were now routed to "global headquarters."

Before proceeding to the Analysis section, determine which principle or principles were at stake in this situation and where the company's management failed.

Analysis. This well-intentioned reorganization, by ignoring several key principles, caused serious damage and loss of momentum in this company. With a definition of global that seemed to ignore regional and local market realities, Principle 3 (Create the Future) was overlooked. Also, Principles 6 (Align and Energize the Organization) and 7 (Measure Only What You Want to Achieve) were not addressed, which created misalignment, and—even worse—parts of the company were working at cross-purposes with each other (Figure 17.8).

This company needs to allow Principle 3 to play a prominent role in influencing the right organization structure. It must immediately work to simplify, standardize, and embed shared objectives across all parts of the organization. And it must align and energize the entire organization to work together.

12-MINUTE DRILL

Situation. An old-line manufacturer was experiencing numerous marketplace and internal challenges in its business. Over the course of two decades, its credit standing deteriorated continuously, and significantly, and it gave up

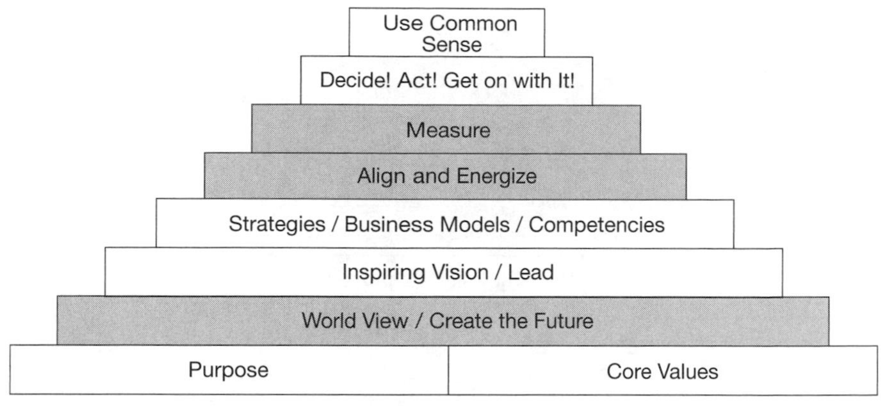

Figure 17.8

its dominant position in the industry to relatively young upstarts. It also found it increasingly difficult to retain its best young people, and even more difficult to attract new young people to the company.

As it evaluated the economic and industry trends, this company recognized that events seemed to be passing it by and that the world was changing at an even faster pace. In spite of this realization, management—top management in particular—seemed mired in policy debates, procedural formalities, personal agendas, and politics. Decision making seemed to be taking more time, not less time. In a world that was talking about "Internet time," this company's most senior executives could not huddle, quickly identify the issues, discuss the options, and execute. In an environment that demanded good "2-minute-drill" performance, this senior team seemed to be in a "12-minute" mode.

Consequences. The result of this inability to decide quickly and execute promptly included poor performance relative to more nimble competitors, and an increasingly concerned workforce. Eventually the workforce began to lose motivation and focus, and too many top-quality professionals began to look elsewhere for career satisfaction.

Before proceeding to the Analysis discussion, determine which principle or principles were at stake in this situation and where the company's senior team failed.

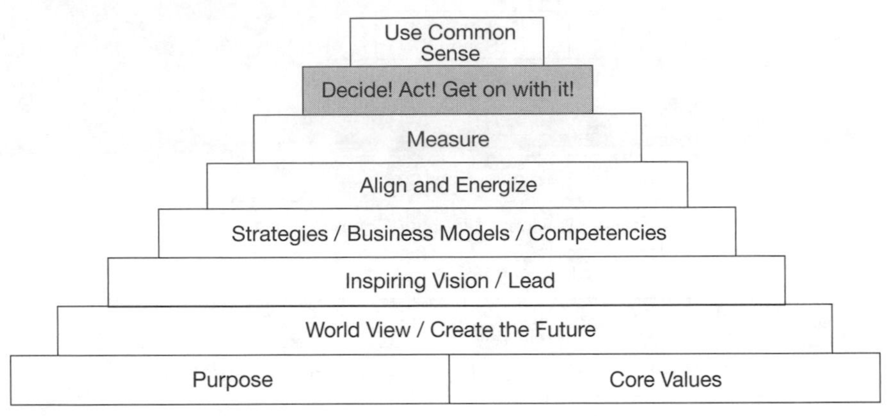

Figure 17.9

Analysis. This situation is symptomatic of a failure in Principle 8: Decide! Act! Get on with It! The question to ask, though, is why is Principle 8 failing? (See Figure 17.9.)

One possibility is that the individuals at the top are incompatible and are unable to work as a true team. A related possibility is that one or more of those individuals is dysfunctional, thereby contributing to the group itself being dysfunctional.

Another very real possibility: One or more of the underlying principles (i.e., 1 through 7) is in fact failing, and this is contributing to the failure of Principle 8. If an honest assessment of the top team is that it is not incompatible or dysfunctional, it is highly likely that the causative factor is a failure of one or more of the earlier principles.

This company—and this senior executive group—needs to look itself in the mirror and candidly assess what it sees. That process may well require anonymous feedback from the organization or the assistance of an unbiased third party. Additional thoughts about the process of gaining insights through a structured assessment process appear in Chapter 16 and in Appendix A.

When it comes to something as important as diagnosing your organization's issues and designing a relevant action plan, the bottom line is this: Don't guess, assess!

EPILOGUE: MAKING A DIFFERENCE STARTS HERE

The nine principles of Beat the Odds are the backbone of a strong management system for developing and sustaining a healthy company. Cynics might ask why that is so important. The answer, of course, goes well beyond the rewards for individuals—the future salary levels, health benefits, and promotion opportunities. Healthy companies drive a robust economy; they provide the bulk of the employment base in most communities, create wealth, deliver new products and services, and contribute tax dollars. Without healthy organizations, modern society will be less likely to achieve its full potential in almost every sense.

For both personal motives and society's broader needs, then, it becomes important that your own organization is successful—and that it continues to be so. Success is every manager's job and every manager's opportunity: The underlying premise of Beat the Odds is that you can influence the course of events and you can make a difference in your organization. The possibilities are limited only by what you are willing to try.

A valuable first step is to suggest or even to sponsor a Beat the Odds assessment of your organization. Even if you are not in a position to influence the entire enterprise, you surely will be able to influence the part you are responsible for or involved in. A practical way to begin is to utilize the assessment and diagnostic templates shown in Appendix A. The templates contain the core questions identified throughout the book. (Check for updates at www.BeatTheOddsBook.com or www.GreybeardAdvisors.com.)

Note that you don't need to build your own survey from scratch. At www.BeatTheOddsBook.com, you can choose a confidential, expanded Web-based version of the templates to speed up the assessment and diagnostic process. One advantage of using the Web-based version is that it allows my firm to compile diagnostic statistics across an even broader range of organizations and to further refine the templates.

One last request: I encourage readers to help extend the value of the Beat the Odds framework. It is particularly useful to gather fresh examples that point out the consequences when one or more of the nine principles are missing from an organization. It's also great to hear of examples in which an organization's declining performance was reversed by correcting deficiencies in one or more of the principles. So please send me your examples at www.BeatTheOddsBook.com. I look forward to hearing from you.

—Robert A. Rudzki

Appendix A

ASSESSMENT AND DIAGNOSIS TEMPLATES

To assist the reader in embarking on a successful assessment and diagnosis, as described in Part IV, this appendix provides assessment templates based on the nine-principles framework. The templates are composed of the core questions associated with each principle.

Templates of core questions are provided to obtain input from the following groups:

- Current top management
- Future leaders of the organization
- Employees
- External constituents (customers, suppliers)

Top–Down Self Assessment: Top Management

	Strongly Agree	Agree	Neither Agree nor Disagree	Disagree	Strongly Disagree
Principle 1					
Our organization's activities address one or more of our society's fundamental needs (i.e., we have a "purpose").					
Our organization has a clearly defined purpose.					
Our purpose is well understood by our employees.					
Our purpose is well understood by our external constituents (customers, suppliers).					
Our organization's purpose provides guidance to our employees.					
Top management regularly speaks about our purpose.					
We are true to our purpose.					
Principle 2					
Our core values are clearly defined.					
Our core values are easy to remember.					
Our core values are regularly communicated.					
Our core values are reinforced through daily actions.					
Our core values are authentic—they represent what we really care about, and how we conduct ourselves.					
Deviations from core values are quickly, decisively, and publicly dealt with.					

Top–Down Self Assessment: Top Management (Continued)

	Strongly Agree	Agree	Neither Agree nor Disagree	Disagree	Strongly Disagree
Our core values are passionately defended by management at all levels.					
Our core values apply equally to all employees at all levels (i.e., the consequences for deviation are the same regardless of level).					
Principle 3					
Our organization is externally focused.					
We are able to admit/confront the external reality of our business.					
We continuously monitor and assess developments that could affect our industry or our organization.					
We understand intimately how our customers are thinking and how their priorities are changing.					
We invest time to envision the future state of our industry.					
We invest time to imagine the possibilities for the future of our company.					
We are constantly on the lookout for new, nontraditional competitors who might surprise us.					
Principle 4					
Top management regularly articulates an inspiring vision of our organization to our employees.					

Top–Down Self Assessment: Top Management (Continued)

	Strongly Agree	Agree	Neither Agree nor Disagree	Disagree	Strongly Disagree
Our employees are excited about where our organization is heading.					
Our employees are willing to make a substantial personal and professional commitment to our inspiring vision.					
Our employees are truly committed to our organization's vision, rather than simply complying.					
Our organization understands the distinction between leadership and management.					
We have an appropriate balance in our organization between leadership talent and management talent.					
Management utilizes exciting objectives that engage and energize the organization.					
Our organization always utilizes 360-degree feedback to select and promote our future leaders.					
If we make a mistake selecting a leader, we are not afraid to correct that mistake in a reasonable period of time.					
Principle 5					
In our organization, strategy is focused primarily on the traditional planning activities of developing plans in relation to competition, and determining the allocation of resources (people, equipment, etc.).					

Top–Down Self Assessment: Top Management (Continued)

	Strongly Agree	Agree	Neither Agree nor Disagree	Disagree	Strongly Disagree
In our organization, considerable time is spent on how to "create the future," including understanding changing customer priorities, and designing how our business should be structured to ensure success ("business model").					
We spend considerable time and effort on innovation.					
We spend considerable time and effort identifying and developing the necessary competencies to succeed.					
Our organization believes that people are key assets.					
Our strategy development process is linked closely to our organization's purpose.					
Our strategy development process is linked closely to our core values.					
Our strategy development process is linked closely to our view of the world and our desired future.					
Our strategy development process is linked closely to our inspiring vision.					
Our business/business model is structured so that we can meet changing customer priorities in a profitable manner.					
We rely entirely on in-house competencies.					

Top–Down Self Assessment: Top Management (Continued)

	Strongly Agree	Agree	Neither Agree nor Disagree	Disagree	Strongly Disagree
Principle 6					
Management regularly communicates our organization's purpose to our employees.					
Management regularly communicates our core values to our employees.					
Management regularly communicates to our employees about the external realities of our business.					
Management regularly communicates our inspiring vision to our employees.					
Management regularly communicates our strategy to our employees.					
Our organization has simple structures that support what we are trying to accomplish.					
Our organization has simple processes that support what we are trying to accomplish.					
We have clear roles and responsibilities throughout the organization.					
We have well-understood reward and recognition systems.					
There are consequences for poor performance.					
There are consequences for behavior that is inconsistent with our core values.					
The consequences for management and nonmanagement are the same.					

Top–Down Self Assessment: Top Management (Continued)

	Strongly Agree	Agree	Neither Agree nor Disagree	Disagree	Strongly Disagree
Internal politics get in the way of making the right decisions.					
There is a high degree of personal intensity and commitment to the organization's objectives.					
Employees at all levels are willing to set aside personal agendas, egos, and personal preferences to do what is right for the organization's future.					
Our work environment is such that individuals are uncomfortable voicing their ideas or beliefs. As a result, if the organization starts to head down a path that individual members believe to be incorrect, no one is willing to say "this is crazy."					
Principle 7					
Our organization measures only a few, significant objectives.					
We measure mostly "leading indicators" (those things that might provide an early warning that problems are developing).					
We measure leading indicators relating to customers.					
We measure leading indicators relating to employees.					
We take appropriate action based on what we measure.					
What we measure is highly visible to all employees.					
What we measure is easily understood by all employees.					

Top–Down Self Assessment: Top Management (Continued)

	Strongly Agree	Agree	Neither Agree nor Disagree	Disagree	Strongly Disagree
Our employees are all linked to the same, few performance measures.					
Principle 8					
Our organization is "action-oriented."					
We focus on the results, not the procedures.					
We focus on doing the right things.					
We have clearly defined roles and responsibilities.					
Many of our leaders and managers regularly utilize "project plans" to communicate, coordinate, and manage toward timely results.					
We have streamlined, efficient, and repeatable processes.					
We make it easy for innovative ideas to succeed.					
Principle 9					
When faced with a procedural, political, or moral dilemma, leaders throughout our organization fall back on common sense to do what is right.					
Leaders in our organization are careful to properly define and describe the issues to be resolved.					

Top–Down Self Assessment: Top Management (Continued)

	Strongly Agree	Agree	Neither Agree nor Disagree	Disagree	Strongly Disagree
Leaders in our organization generally take the time to identify all possible solutions to an issue before making a decision.					
Leaders in our organization utilize a rigorous set of criteria to evaluate and select the best solution.					
There are regular occasions when the judgment of our leaders is called into question.					

Top–Down Self-Assessment: Future Leaders

	Strongly Agree	Agree	Neither Agree nor Disagree	Disagree	Strongly Disagree
Principle 1					
Our organization's activities address one or more of our society's fundamental needs (i.e., we have a "purpose").					
Our organization has a clearly defined purpose.					
Our purpose is well understood by our employees.					
Our purpose is well understood by our external constituents (customers, suppliers).					
Our organization's purpose provides guidance to our employees.					
Top management regularly speaks about our purpose.					
We are true to our purpose.					
Principle 2					
Our core values are clearly defined.					
Our core values are easy to remember.					
Our core values are regularly communicated.					
Our core values are reinforced through daily actions.					
Our core values are authentic—they represent what we really care about, and how we conduct ourselves.					

Top–Down Self-Assessment: Future Leaders (Continued)

	Strongly Agree	Agree	Neither Agree nor Disagree	Disagree	Strongly Disagree
Deviations from core values are quickly, decisively, and publicly dealt with.					
Our core values are passionately defended by management at all levels.					
Our core values apply equally to all employees at all levels (i.e., the consequences for deviation are the same regardless of level).					
Principle 3					
Our organization is externally focused.					
We are able to admit/confront the external reality of our business.					
We continuously monitor and assess developments which could affect our industry or our organization.					
We understand intimately how our customers are thinking, and how their priorities are changing.					
We invest time to envision the future state of our industry.					
We invest time to imagine the possibilities for the future of our company.					
We are constantly on the lookout for new, nontraditional competitors who might surprise us.					

Top–Down Self-Assessment: Future Leaders (Continued)

	Strongly Agree	Agree	Neither Agree nor Disagree	Disagree	Strongly Disagree
Principle 4					
Top management regularly articulates an inspiring vision of our organization to our employees.					
Our employees are excited about where our organization is heading.					
Our employees are willing to make a substantial personal and professional commitment to our inspiring vision.					
Our employees are truly committed to our organization's vision, rather than simply complying.					
Our organization understands the distinction between leadership and management.					
We have an appropriate balance in our organization between leadership talent and management talent.					
Management utilizes exciting objectives that engage and energize the organization.					
Our organization always utilizes 360-degree feedback to select and promote our future leaders.					
If we make a mistake selecting a leader, we are not afraid to correct that mistake in a reasonable period of time.					

Top–Down Self-Assessment: Future Leaders (Continued)

	Strongly Agree	Agree	Neither Agree nor Disagree	Disagree	Strongly Disagree
Principle 5					
In our organization, strategy is focused primarily on the traditional planning activities of developing plans in relation to competition, and determining the allocation of resources (people, equipment, etc.).					
In our organization, considerable time is spent on how to "create the future," including understanding changing customer priorities, and designing how our business should be structured to ensure success ("business model").					
We spend considerable time and effort on innovation.					
We spend considerable time and effort identifying and developing the necessary competencies to succeed.					
Our organization believes that people are key assets.					
Our strategy development process is linked closely to our organization's purpose.					
Our strategy development process is linked closely to our core values.					
Our strategy development process is linked closely to our view of the world and our desired future.					
Our strategy development process is linked closely to our inspiring vision.					

Top–Down Self-Assessment: Future Leaders (Continued)

	Strongly Agree	Agree	Neither Agree nor Disagree	Disagree	Strongly Disagree
Our business/business model is structured so that we can meet changing customer priorities in a profitable manner.					
We rely entirely on in-house competencies.					
Principle 6					
Management regularly communicates our organization's purpose to our employees.					
Management regularly communicates our core values to our employees.					
Management regularly communicates to our employees about the external realities of our business.					
Management regularly communicates our inspiring vision to our employees.					
Management regularly communicates our strategy to our employees.					
Our organization has simple structures that support what we are trying to accomplish.					
Our organization has simple processes that support what we are trying to accomplish.					
We have clear roles and responsibilities throughout the organization.					
We have well-understood reward and recognition systems.					

Top–Down Self-Assessment: Future Leaders (Continued)

	Strongly Agree	Agree	Neither Agree nor Disagree	Disagree	Strongly Disagree
There are consequences for poor performance.					
There are consequences for behavior that is inconsistent with our core values.					
The consequences for management and non-management are the same.					
Internal politics get in the way of making the right decisions.					
There is a high degree of personal intensity and commitment to the organization's objectives.					
Employees at all levels are willing to set aside personal agendas, egos, and personal preferences to do what is right for the organization's future.					
Our work environment is such that individuals are uncomfortable voicing their ideas or beliefs. As a result, if the organization starts to head down a path that individual members believe to be incorrect, no one is willing to say "this is crazy."					
Principle 7					
Our organization measures only a few, significant objectives.					
We measure mostly "leading indicators" (those things that might provide an early warning that problems are developing).					
We measure leading indicators relating to customers.					

Top–Down Self-Assessment: Future Leaders (Continued)

	Strongly Agree	Agree	Neither Agree nor Disagree	Disagree	Strongly Disagree
We measure leading indicators relating to employees.					
We take appropriate action based on what we measure.					
What we measure is highly visible to all employees.					
What we measure is easily understood by all employees.					
Our employees are all linked to the same, few performance measures.					
Principle 8					
Our organization is "action-oriented."					
We focus on the results, not the procedures.					
We focus on doing the right things.					
We have clearly defined roles and responsibilities.					
Many of our leaders and managers regularly utilize "project plans" to communicate, coordinate, and manage toward timely results.					
We have streamlined, efficient, and repeatable processes.					
We make it easy for innovative ideas to succeed.					

Top–Down Self-Assessment: Future Leaders (Continued)

	Strongly Agree	Agree	Neither Agree nor Disagree	Disagree	Strongly Disagree
Principle 9					
When faced with a procedural, political, or moral dilemma, leaders throughout our organization fall back on common sense to do what is right.					
Leaders in our organization are careful to properly define and describe the issues to be resolved.					
Leaders in our organization generally take the time to identify all possible solutions to an issue before making a decision.					
Leaders in our organization utilize a rigorous set of criteria to evaluate and select the best solution.					
There are regular occasions when the judgment of our leaders is called into question.					

Assessment: Employees

	Strongly Agree	Agree	Neither Agree nor Disagree	Disagree	Strongly Disagree
Principle 1					
Our organization's activities address one or more of our society's fundamental needs (i.e., we have a "purpose").					
Our organization has a clearly defined purpose.					
Our purpose is well understood by our employees.					
Our purpose is well understood by our external constituents (customers, suppliers).					
Our organization's purpose provides guidance to our employees.					
Top management regularly speaks about our organization's purpose.					
We are true to our purpose.					
Principle 2					
Our core values are clearly defined.					
Our core values are easy to remember.					
Our core values are regularly communicated.					
Our core values are reinforced through daily actions.					
Our core values are authentic—they represent what we really care about, and how we conduct ourselves.					
Deviations from core values are quickly, decisively, and publicly dealt with.					

Assessment: Employees (Continued)

	Strongly Agree	Agree	Neither Agree nor Disagree	Disagree	Strongly Disagree
Our core values are passionately defended by management at all levels.					
Our core values apply equally to all employees at all levels (i.e., the consequences for deviations are the same regardless of level).					
Principle 3					
Our organization is externally focused.					
We are able to admit/confront the external reality of our business.					
We continuously monitor and assess developments that could affect our industry or our organization.					
We understand intimately how our customers are thinking, and how their priorities are changing.					
We invest time to envision the future state of our industry.					
We invest time to imagine the possibilities for the future of our company.					
We are constantly on the lookout for new, nontraditional competitors who might surprise us.					
Principle 4					
Top management regularly articulates an inspiring vision of our organization to our employees.					

Assessment: Employees (Continued)

	Strongly Agree	Agree	Neither Agree nor Disagree	Disagree	Strongly Disagree
Middle management regularly articulates a consistent vision of our organization to our employees.					
Our employees are excited about where our organization is heading.					
Our employees are willing to make a substantial personal and professional commitment to our inspiring vision.					
Our employees are truly committed to our organization's vision, rather than simply complying.					
Our organization understands the distinction between leadership and management.					
We have an appropriate balance in our organization between leadership talent and management talent.					
Management utilizes exciting objectives that engage and energize the organization.					
Our organization always utilizes 360-degree feedback to select and promote our future leaders.					
If our organization makes a mistake selecting a leader, we are not afraid to correct that mistake in a reasonable period of time.					

Assessment: Employees (Continued)

	Strongly Agree	Agree	Neither Agree nor Disagree	Disagree	Strongly Disagree
Principle 5					
In our organization, strategy is focused primarily on the traditional planning activities of developing plans in relation to the competition, and on determining the allocation of resources (people, equipment, etc.).					
In our organization, considerable time is spent on how to "create the future," including understanding changing customer priorities, and designing how our business should be structured to ensure success ("business model").					
We spend considerable time and effort on innovation.					
We spend considerable time and effort identifying and developing the necessary competencies to succeed.					
Our organization believes that people are key assets.					
Our strategy development process is linked closely to our organization's purpose.					
Our strategy development process is linked closely to our core values.					
Our strategy development process is linked closely to our view of the world and our desired future.					

Assessment: Employees (Continued)

	Strongly Agree	Agree	Neither Agree nor Disagree	Disagree	Strongly Disagree
Our strategy development process is linked closely to our inspiring vision.					
Our business is structured so that we can meet changing customer priorities in a profitable manner.					
We rely entirely on in-house competencies.					
Principle 6					
Management regularly communicates our organization's purpose to our employees.					
Management regularly communicates our core values to our employees.					
Management regularly communicates to our employees about the external realities of our business.					
Management regularly communicates our inspiring vision to our employees.					
Management regularly communicates our strategy to our employees.					
Our organization has simple structures that support what we are trying to accomplish.					
Our organization has simple processes that support what we are trying to accomplish.					
We have clear roles and responsibilities throughout the organization.					

Assessment: Employees (Continued)

	Strongly Agree	Agree	Neither Agree nor Disagree	Disagree	Strongly Disagree
We have well-understood reward and recognition systems.					
There are consequences for poor performance					
There are consequences for behavior that is inconsistent with our core values.					
The consequences for management and nonmanagement are the same.					
Internal politics get in the way of making the right decisions.					
There is a high degree of personal intensity and commitment to the organization's objectives.					
Employees at all levels are willing to set aside personal agendas, egos, and personal preferences to do what is right for the organization's future.					
Our work environment is such that individuals are uncomfortable voicing their ideas or beliefs. As a result, if the organization starts to head down a path that individual members believe to be incorrect, no one is willing to say "this is crazy."					

Assessment: Employees (Continued)

	Strongly Agree	Agree	Neither Agree nor Disagree	Disagree	Strongly Disagree
Principle 7					
Our organization measures only a few, significant objectives.					
We measure mostly "leading indicators" (those things that might provide an early warning that problems are developing).					
We measure leading indicators relating to customers.					
We measure leading indicators relating to employees.					
We take appropriate action based on what we measure.					
What we measure is highly visible to all employees.					
What we measure is easily understood by all employees.					
Our employees are all linked to the same, few performance measures.					
Principle 8					
Our organization is "action-oriented."					
We focus on the results, not the procedures.					
We focus on doing the right things.					
We have clearly defined roles and responsibilities.					

Assessment: Employees (Continued)

	Strongly Agree	Agree	Neither Agree nor Disagree	Disagree	Strongly Disagree
Many of our leaders and managers regularly utilize "project plans" to communicate, coordinate, and manage toward timely results.					
We have streamlined, efficient and repeatable processes.					
We make it easy for innovative ideas to succeed.					
Principle 9					
When faced with a procedural, political, or moral dilemma, leaders throughout our organization fall back on common sense to do what is right.					
Leaders in our organization are careful to properly define and describe the issues to be resolved.					
Leaders in our organization generally take the time to identify all possible solutions to an issue before making a decision.					
Leaders in our organization utilize a rigorous set of criteria to evaluate and select the best solution.					
There are regular occasions when the judgment of our leaders is called into question.					

Assessment: External Constituents: Supplier Perspective

	Strongly Agree	Agree	Neither Agree nor Disagree	Disagree	Strongly Disagree
Principle 1					
This organization has a clearly defined purpose.					
Their purpose is understood by my organization.					
Their purpose is consistent with my organization's purpose.					
Principle 2					
This organization's core values are understood by my organization.					
Their core values are authentic—they represent what they really care about, and how they conduct themselves.					
Their core values are consistent with my organization's core values.					
This organization displays a high degree of integrity and honesty.					
Principle 3					
This organization is externally focused.					
They are able to admit/confront the external reality of their business.					
They continuously monitor and assess developments that could affect their industry or their organization.					

Assessment: External Constituents: Supplier Perspective (Continued)

	Strongly Agree	Agree	Neither Agree nor Disagree	Disagree	Strongly Disagree
Principle 4					
Their employees are excited about where their organization is heading.					
They regularly articulate an inspiring vision of their organization to their external partners (i.e., their customers and suppliers).					
As a supplier, I am excited about where their organization is heading.					
This organization makes a practice of recognizing accomplishments, including those from suppliers.					
Principle 5					
They spend considerable time and effort on innovation.					
They involve us, as a supplier, in their innovation process and objectives.					
In general, they regularly access the talents and competencies of their suppliers to do a better job themselves.					
Principle 6					
They regularly communicate their organization's purpose to customers and suppliers.					
They regularly communicate their core values to their customers and suppliers.					

Assessment: External Constituents: Supplier Perspective (Continued)

	Strongly Agree	Agree	Neither Agree nor Disagree	Disagree	Strongly Disagree
They regularly communicate to their suppliers about the external realities facing their organization.					
They regularly communicate their inspiring vision to their suppliers.					
They regularly communicate their strategy to their suppliers.					
It is clear to me how I (as a supplier) am expected to support their purpose, vision, and strategy.					
Employees at all levels are willing to set aside personal agendas, egos, and personal preferences to do what is right for their organization's future.					
Their work environment is such that individuals are uncomfortable voicing their ideas or beliefs. As a result, if their organization starts to head down a path that individual members believe to be incorrect, no one is willing to say "this is crazy."					
Principle 7					
They measure only a few, significant objectives.					
Suppliers have objectives that are linked to those same, few performance measures.					

Assessment: External Constituents: Supplier Perspective (Continued)

	Strongly Agree	Agree	Neither Agree nor Disagree	Disagree	Strongly Disagree
They express clearly their requirements and expectations of me as a supplier.					
Supplier performance measures are used appropriately to manage the customer/ supplier relationship toward mutually beneficial results.					
Principle 8					
Their organization is "action-oriented."					
They focus on the results, not the procedures.					
They have streamlined, efficient, and repeatable processes.					
They make it easy for innovative ideas to succeed.					
As a supplier, we know who to contact if we have a problem or request.					
The turnaround time on supplier requests is good.					
This organization does what it says it is going to do.					
Principle 9					
When faced with tough decisions, this organization tends to be swayed by internal political considerations.					

Assessment: External Constituents: Supplier Perspective (Continued)

	Strongly Agree	Agree	Neither Agree nor Disagree	Disagree	Strongly Disagree
There are regular occasions when the judgment of this organization's leaders is called into question.					

Open-Ended Questions for Suppliers:

Based on what I see with other customers' best practices, this company can improve itself by STARTING to:

____

____

____

____

Based on what I see with other customers' best practices, this company can improve itself by STOPPING to:

____

____

____

____

This company should definitely CONTINUE to:

____

____

____

____

Assessment: External Constituents: Customer Perspective

	Strongly Agree	Agree	Neither Agree nor Disagree	Disagree	Strongly Disagree
Principle 1					
This organization has a clearly defined purpose.					
Their purpose is understood by my organization.					
Their purpose is consistent with my organization's purpose.					
Principle 2					
This organization's core values are understood by my organization.					
Their core values are authentic—they represent what they really care about, and how they conduct themselves.					
Their core values are consistent with my organization's core values.					
This organization displays a high degree of integrity and honesty.					
Principle 3					
This organization is externally focused.					
They are able to admit/confront the external reality of their business.					
They continuously monitor and assess developments that could affect their industry or their organization.					

Assessment: External Constituents: Customer Perspective (Continued)

	Strongly Agree	Agree	Neither Agree nor Disagree	Disagree	Strongly Disagree
They understand how my needs, as a customer, are changing—and they try to stay ahead of the curve.					
Principle 4					
Their employees are excited about where their organization is heading.					
They regularly articulate an inspiring vision of their organization to their external partners (i.e., their customers and suppliers).					
As a customer, I am excited about where their organization is heading.					
This organization makes a practice of recognizing accomplishments, including those from their suppliers.					
Principle 5					
They spend considerable time and effort on innovation.					
They involve us, as a customer, in their innovation process and objectives.					
In general, they regularly offer access to the talents and competencies of their employees to assist us in our own innovation objectives.					
Principle 6					
They regularly communicate their organization's purpose to their customers.					

Assessment: External Constituents: Customer Perspective (Continued)

	Strongly Agree	Agree	Neither Agree nor Disagree	Disagree	Strongly Disagree
They regularly communicate their core values to their customers.					
They regularly communicate to their customers about the external realities facing their organization.					
They regularly communicate their inspiring vision to their customers.					
They regularly communicate their strategy to their customers.					
It is clear to me how I (as a customer) am expected to benefit from their purpose, vision, and strategy.					
Employees at all levels are willing to set aside personal agendas, egos, and personal preferences to do what is right for their organization's future.					
Their work environment is such that individuals are uncomfortable voicing their ideas or beliefs. As a result, if their organization starts to head down a path that individual members believe to be incorrect, no one is willing to say "this is crazy."					
Principle 7					
They measure only a few, significant objectives.					
Their objectives tend to be ones that are relevant to our own objectives as their customer.					

Assessment: External Constituents: Customer Perspective (Continued)

	Strongly Agree	Agree	Neither Agree nor Disagree	Disagree	Strongly Disagree
Supplier performance measures are used appropriately to manage the customer/ supplier relationship toward mutually beneficial results.					
Principle 8					
Their organization is "action-oriented."					
They focus on the results, not the procedures.					
They have streamlined, efficient, and repeatable processes.					
They make it easy for innovative ideas to surface and to succeed.					
As a customer, we know who to contact if we have a problem or request.					
The turnaround time on customer requests is good.					
This organization does what it says it is going to do.					
Principle 9					
When faced with tough decisions, this organization tends to be swayed by internal political considerations.					
As my supplier, they spend an appropriate amount of time at my operations learning about my needs, and making themselves available.					

Assessment: External Constituents: Customer Perspective (Continued)

	Strongly Agree	Agree	Neither Agree nor Disagree	Disagree	Strongly Disagree
They are not afraid to change a prior decision in order to do what is right.					
There are regular occasions when the judgment of this organization's leaders is called into question.					

Open-Ended Questions for Customers:

Based on what I see with other suppliers' best practices, this company can improve itself by STARTING to:

____

____

____

____

Based on what I see with other suppliers' best practices, this company can improve itself by STOPPING to:

____

____

____

____

This company should definitely CONTINUE to:

____

____

____

____

Appendix B

QUOTABLE QUOTES

Author's note: Here are great expressions and ideas that relate to the themes of this book. Many of these quotes have been submitted by colleagues from the business world. I hope you will not only enjoy these quotes but also use them constructively in your daily life. They are organized by principle.

PURPOSE

> *You cannot expect significant change unless you change something significant.*
>
> —***Center for Creative Leadership,*** Greensboro, North Carolina

> *You will become as small as your controlling desire; as great as your dominant aspiration.*
>
> —***James Allen***

> *There is great work to be done. The foundations of the new world must be laid by those who have the courage to change the old; by those whose arteries are still soft and clean, whose minds are still active, and hearts still generous.*
>
> —***Earl Warren***

You have to think about "big things" while you're doing small things, so that all the small things go in the right direction.

—Alvin Toffler

Anything less than a conscious commitment to the important is an unconscious commitment to the unimportant.

—Stephen Covey

Your goal should be just out of reach, but not out of sight.

—Denis Waitley

I thank God that I live in a country where dreams can come true, where failure sometimes is the first step to success and where success is only another form of failure if we forget what our priorities should be.

—Harry Lloyd

The choice of comfort is a paradox. Choosing to avoid the difficult is more comfortable in the short term; however, in the long term it results in discomfort. Most of us need to have tackled and conquered challenging tasks before we experience a sense of accomplishment and satisfaction.

—Ernie J. Zelinski, *The Joy of Thinking Big*

If the Creator had a purpose in equipping us with a neck, he surely meant us to stick it out.

—Arthur Koestler

You are not here merely to make a living. You are here in order to enable the world to live more amply, with greater vision, with a finer spirit of hope and achievement. You are here to enrich the world, and you impoverish yourself if you forget the errand.

—Woodrow Wilson on Definition of Purpose

CORE VALUES

It is easier to fight for one's principles than to live up to them.

—Alfred Adler

My basic principle is that you don't make decisions because they are easy; you don't make them because they are cheap; you don't make them because they're popular; you make them because they're right.

—Theodore Hesburgh, C.S.C.
Former president, University of Notre Dame

Of course the world is changing. It never stops—the technology, the pace, the players. What's far more interesting is what incites change. Every revolution, every school of philosophy, every movement worth joining, every defining enterprise starts the same way. Not with the grand or distant, but with something near and personal. It starts the same way. Every time.

—1997 IBM Annual Report

The reasonable man adapts himself to the world; the unreasonable one persists in trying to adapt the world to himself. Therefore, all progress depends on the unreasonable man.

—George Bernard Shaw

There is nothing wrong with change, if it is in the right direction.

—Winston Churchill

Leadership is basically a matter of how to be, not how to do it. Leaders need to lead by example, with clear, consistent messages, with values that are "moral compasses," and a sense of ethics that works full time.

—Frances Hesselbein

Know the difference between the principle of compromise and the compromise of principle.

—Author Unknown

A smile and good humor are signs that you dominate your fate.

—Stefan Garczyński, circa 1700

Who belittles sin, diminishes virtue.

—Jan Lemanski

The path of least resistance is what makes rivers run crooked.

—Elbert Hubbard

In order to be a leader, a man must have followers. And to have followers, a man must have their confidence. Hence, the supreme quality for a leader is unquestionably integrity. Without it, no real success is possible, no matter whether it is on a section gang, on a football field, in an army, or in an office. If a man's associates find him guilty of phoniness, if they find that he lacks forthright integrity, he will fail. His teachings and actions must square with each other. The first great need, therefore, is integrity and high purpose.

—Dwight D. Eisenhower

Nothing is politically right which is morally wrong.

—Thomas Jefferson

My grandfather once told me that there are two kinds of people: those who do the work and those who take the credit. He told me to try to be in the first group; there was less competition there.

—Indira Gandhi

CREATE THE FUTURE

The significant problems we face cannot be solved at the same level of thinking we were at when we created them.

—Albert Einstein

I am convinced that if the rate of change inside an institution is less than the rate of change outside, the end is in sight.

—John F. Welch, former GE chairman and CEO

If you can't imagine a better world, you can't change this one.

—Tad Williams

The greatest danger in times of turbulence is not the turbulence; it is to act with yesterday's logic.

—Peter Drucker

Creativity requires the freedom to consider "unthinkable" alternatives, to doubt the worth of cherished practices.

—John W. Gardner

It is not the strongest of the species that survives, nor the most intelligent, but rather the most responsive to change.

—Charles Darwin

Just because an idea is crazy doesn't mean it's wrong.

—Larry Soderblom, Jet Propulsion Lab scientist

When a distinguished but elderly scientist states that something is possible, he is almost certainly right. When he states that something is impossible, he is very probably wrong.

—Arthur C. Clarke

Nothing in life is to be feared. It is only to be understood.

—Marie Curie

Perhaps the greatest competitive challenge companies face is adjusting to—indeed, embracing—nonstop change . . . Companies will need to be in a never-ending state of transformation, perpetually creating fundamental, enduring change.

—David Ulrich, University of Michigan

He who the gods want to destroy, they will give 40 years of prosperity.

—Aristotle, 384–322 B.C.

Go as far as you can see and when you get there, you will always be able to see farther.

—Zig Ziglar

A hallmark of great companies is an ability to recognize the game has changed and to adapt.

—***Arthur Martinez,*** former CEO, Sears

If you resist change, you die. If you adapt to it, you survive. If you cause it, you lead.

—***Ray Noorda,*** former CEO, Novell

Imagination of what may be possible is more valuable than knowledge of what is.

—***Albert Einstein***

The difficulty lies not in the new ideas, but in escaping the old ones.

—***John Maynard Keynes***

The most effective way to cope with change is to help create it.

—***L. W. Lynett***

Change is the law of life, and those who look only to the past or present are certain to miss the future.

—***John F. Kennedy***

Things do change. The only question is that since things are deteriorating so quickly, will society and man's habits change quickly enough?

—***Isaac Asimov***

Those who cannot remember the past are condemned to repeat it.

—***George Santayana***

Today, however, we add the converse, to warn us and our successors against complacency and rigid thinking: If you remember the past too well, you will see no way that the future can ever be different.

—***Charles Sheffield***

Many businesses owe their success to their willingness to challenge prevailing assumptions and rules of their industry. Because most businesses don't have the presence of mind to challenge the status quo, a great deal of opportunity exists for the businesses and individuals who develop new methods by challenging the rules. If we look at any of today's highly successful businesses, we will see businesses that are risking, being different, and challenging the rules.

—**Ernie J. Zelinski,** The Joy of Thinking Big

Before everything else comes the need to see your customers clearly.

—**Kenichi Ohmae**

We must reverse a paradigm drummed into us from business school to the grave: "What worked in the past will work in the future."

—**Gary Hamel**

INSPIRING VISION/LEAD

A competitive world has two possibilities for you; you can lose, or, if you want to win, you can change.

—**Lester C. Thurow**

Leaders must challenge the process precisely because any system will unconsciously conspire to maintain the status quo and prevent change.

—**Kouzes & Posner,** The Leadership Challenge

One person with courage is a majority. —**Thomas Jefferson**

People can be divided into three groups:

Those who make things happen
Those who watch things happen
Those who wonder what happened

—**Author Unknown**

Everyone thinks of changing the world, but no one thinks of changing himself.

—Leo Tolstoy

We all leave footprints in the sand. The question is, will we be a big heel, or a great soul?

—Author Unknown

Faced with the choice between changing one's mind and proving that there is no need to change, almost everybody gets busy on the proof!

—Galbraith's Law

No leader can command or compel change. Change comes about when followers themselves desire it and seek it. Hence, the role of the leader is to enlist the participation of others as leaders of the effort. That is the sum and essence not only of leading change but also of good management in general.

—James O'Toole

Those with the courage to stick their heads above the crowd should beware: you become an easier target for people throwing stones.

—Author Unknown

There is nothing more difficult, more perilous to conduct, or more uncertain in its success than to take the lead in a new order of things. The innovator has for enemies all those who have done well under the old conditions, and lukewarm defenders in those who may do well under the new.

—Machiavelli's *The Prince*

You can let things happen, or you can make something happen.

—Author Unknown

First-rate people hire first-rate people; second-rate people hire third-rate people.

—Leo Rosten

A smooth sea never made a skillful mariner.

—English proverb

Treating people like numbers will prevent the company from meeting its numbers.

—Richard A. Moran, *Fear No Yellow Stickies*

A living thing is distinguished from a dead thing by the multiplicity of the changes at any moment taking place in it.

—Herbert Spencer

Pioneers get all the arrows, but they get the best campsites.

—Author Unknown

Do not fear the winds of adversity. Remember: a kite rises against the wind rather than with it.

—Author Unknown

Great spirits have always encountered violent opposition from mediocre minds.

—Albert Einstein

The ultimate measure of a man is not where he stands in moments of comfort and convenience, but where he stands at times of challenge and controversy.

—Martin Luther King, Jr.

Recognizing people who support the vision is a centerpiece to success. What gets recognized gets repeated.

—Lockheed Martin Utility Services

STRATEGY/BUSINESS MODEL/COMPETENCIES

Insanity is doing the same thing the same way and expecting different results.

—Author Unknown

The goal is to cause earthquakes . . . Never before has there been so much scope to rewrite the rules of the game.

—Gary Hamel

Strategy has to be subversive. If it's not challenging internal company rules or industry rules, it is not strategy.

—Gary Hamel

The universal flow of information puts a high premium on learning how to build the strategies and organizations capable of meeting the requirements of a borderless world.

—Kenichi Ohmae

Every organization—not just businesses—needs one core competence: innovation.

—Peter Drucker

Before everything else comes the need to see your customers clearly.

—Kenichi Ohmae

The best way to create wealth for employees and stockholders is to renew our commitment to developing and executing innovative strategies.

—Gary Hamel

There is only one boss. The customer. And he can fire everybody in the company from the chairman on down, simply by spending his money somewhere else.

—Sam Walton

I hated every minute of training, but I said, "Don't quit. Suffer now and live the rest of your life as a champion."

—Muhammad Ali

ALIGN AND ENERGIZE

Progress is a big word. But progress requires change, and change has its enemies.

—Robert F. Kennedy

There is no limit to what can be accomplished when no one cares who gets the credit.

—John Wooden

Nothing great was ever accomplished without enthusiasm.

—Ralph Waldo Emerson

Team spirit is what gives so many companies an edge over their competitors.

—George L. Clements

It is the greatest of all mistakes to do nothing because you can do only a little. Do what you can.

—Sydney Smith

You can't beat the competition unless you have internal alignment.

—Author Unknown

MEASURE

The measure you give will be the measure you get.

—New Testament, *Mark 4:24*

The measure of your quality as a public person, as a citizen, is the gap between what you do and what you say.

—Ramsey Clark

You get what you measure.

—Author Unknown

The measure of a master is his success in bringing all men round to his opinion 20 years later.

—Ralph Waldo Emerson

The saddest thing in the world is the murder of a beautiful theory by a gang of brutal facts.

—Author Unknown

Doing more things faster is no substitute for doing the right things.

—Stephen Covey

DECIDE! ACT! GET ON WITH IT!

The speed of the boss is the speed of the team.

—Lee Iacocca

The longer you wait, the deeper it gets.

—Author Unknown

Those who oppose change dissect the proposal to see
— if any conceivable problem might remain unsolved
— if any living being might not benefit and
— if any hypothetical harm can be imagined

—Author Unknown

The future does not belong to the big; it belongs to the agile.

—Percy Barnevik, former chairman, Asea Brown Boveri

We trained hard . . . but it seemed that every time we were beginning to form up into teams, we would be reorganized. I was to learn later in life that we tend to meet any new situation by reorganizing; and a wonderful method it can be for creating the illusion of progress while producing confusion, inefficiency and demoralization.

—**Petronius Arbiter,** Roman Navy, 210 B.C.

It's amazing what you can do when you don't know it can't be done.

—Author Unknown

The world hates change, yet it is the only thing that has brought progress.

—Charles F. Kettering

Even if you're on the right track, you'll get run over if you just sit there.

—Will Rogers

Opportunities are usually disguised as hard work, so most people don't recognize them.

—Ann Landers

How do you expect to win this race when you are walking along at your slow, slow pace?

—Aesop's Fables

COMMON SENSE

Not everything that is faced can be changed. But nothing can be changed until it is faced.

—James Baldwin

Wisdom too often never comes, and so one ought not to reject it simply because it comes late.

— ***Felix Frankfurter,*** U.S. Supreme Court Justice

An error doesn't become a mistake until you refuse to correct it.

—O. A. Battista

It's the same each time with progress. First they ignore you, then they say you're mad, then dangerous, then there's a pause and then you can't find anyone who disagrees with you.

—Tony Benn, British Labour politician

The resistance to change is very logical but not practical. You simply cannot improve unless you are willing to try something different. Change must be viewed as learning and learning is always positive. It's a matter of determining what you need to do and have the courage to give it a try.

—Mike Peterson, golf professional

When reasons are weak, attitudes stiffen.

—Stanislaw Jerzy Lec

Don't find fault. Find a remedy.

—Henry Ford

Let no one be ashamed to say yes today if yesterday he said no.
Or to say no today if yesterday he said yes. For that is life.
Never to have changed—what a pitiable thing of which to boast!

—Johann Wolfgang von Goethe

Have no fear of change as such and, on the other hand, no liking for it merely for its own sake.

—Robert Moses

Minds are like parachutes; they only function when they are open.

—Sir James Dewar

Failure lies not in falling down. Failure lies in not getting up.

—Traditional Chinese proverb

SOURCE NOTES

Author's Note: Much of the information in this book derives from personal experiences of the author and colleagues who contributed their experiences and their insights. Information is referenced below if it is derived from another source or, if in the opinion of the author, readers may want further description of the source.

ACKNOWLEDGMENTS

1. Kurzweil, Ray, and Terry Grossman. *Fantastic Voyage: Live Long Enough to Live Forever.* Emmaus, PA: Rodale Books, 2004.

CHAPTER 1

1. Dun & Bradstreet database information, confirmed in an e-mail from D & B to author in March 2005.
2. de Geus, Arie. *The Living Company.* Cambridge, MA: Harvard Business School Press, 2002.
3. Foster, Richard, and Susan Kaplan. *Creative Destruction: Why Companies That Are Built to Last Underperform the Market—And How to Successfully Transform Them.* New York: Currency Press, 2001.

4. Zook, Chris (Bain partner). *Profit from the Core.* Cambridge, MA: Harvard Business School Press, 2001; and Bain & Company Web site (www.bain.com).

CHAPTER 2

1. Robison, Peter. "Management Books Often Don't Work as Investment Guides." *Pittsburgh Post-Gazette.* April 8, 2004.

CHAPTER 3

1. Packard, David. Speech to a Hewlett-Packard in-house training class. March 8, 1960.
2. Gunther, Marc. "The Iger Sanction." *Fortune.* January 23, 2006.
3. La Monica, Paul. "Disney Buys Pixar." CNNMoney.com. January 24, 2006.
4. *Merck 2002 Annual Report.*
5. Medtronic, Inc. corporate Web site.
6. Respironics, Inc. corporate Web site.

CHAPTER 4

1. "Building a Brand on the Touchpoints That Count." *Mercer Management Journal* 17 (June 2004).
2. Johnson & Johnson's Credo is available at www.jnj.com/our_company/our_credo/index.htm.
3. Lublin, Joann S., and Mark Maremont. "Taking Tyco by the Tail." *Wall Street Journal.* August 6, 2003.
4. Pillmore, Eric M. "How We're Fixing Up Tyco." *Harvard Business Review.* December 2003.

CHAPTER 5

1. Useem, Jerry. "Another Boss Another Revolution." *Fortune.* April 5, 2004.
2. Lafley, A. G. "Answering Peter Drucker: On Defining What a Chief Executive Really Does." *Chief Executive Magazine.* April 2005.

3. Vogelstein, Fred. “Mighty Amazon.” *Fortune*. May 26, 2003.
4. Arndt, Michael. “How O’Neill Got Alcoa Shining.” *BusinessWeek*. February 5, 2001.

CHAPTER 6

1. Sherman, Len. CLO Symposium Keynote Presentation. Accenture. February 16, 2004.
2. Byrne, John A. “Chainsaw Al.” Excerpts from the book *Chainsaw: The Notorious Career of Al Dunlap in the Era of Profit-At-Any-Price*. *BusinessWeek*. October 18, 1999.
3. Prada, C. K. “C.K.’s Lessons for Executives.” Sidebar in “Business Prophet: How Strategy Guru C. K. Prahalad Is Changing the Way CEOs Think” by Pete Engardio. *BusinessWeek*. January 23, 2006.
4. Karnitschnig, Matthew. “For Siemens, Move into U.S. Causes Waves Back Home.” *Wall Street Journal*. September 8, 2003.
5. Boston, William, and Frederick Kempe. “Goal Is Game, Set, and Match.” (An interview with Heinrich von Pierer, president and CEO of Siemens AG.) *The Wall Street Journal*. February 2, 2001.
6. “Siemens Climbs Back.” *BusinessWeek*. June 5, 2000.
7. Bossidy, Larry, and Ram Charan. *Confronting Reality: Doing What Matters to Get Things Right*. New York: Crown Business, 2004.
8. Krzyzewski, Mike, and Donald T. Phillips. *Leading with the Heart*. New York: Warner Business Books, 2001.

CHAPTER 7

1. Schwartz, Peter. *The Art of the Long View*. New York: Doubleday, 1996.
2. Byrne, John A. “Chainsaw Al.” Excerpts from the book *Chainsaw: The Notorious Career of Al Dunlap in the Era of Profit-At-Any-Price*. *BusinessWeek*. October 18, 1999.
3. Brown, Roger. “How We Built a Strong Company in a Weak Industry.” *Harvard Business Review*. February 2001.
4. Boyle, Matthew. “Digital Deals Pit Xerox against Kodak.” *Fortune*. November 16, 2004.

CHAPTER 8

1. CRM Learning, L.P. Workshop materials from *Abilene Paradox, 2nd Edition.*
2. Bianco, Anthony, and Pamela L. Moore. "Downfall: The Inside Story of the Management Fiasco at Xerox." *BusinessWeek*. March 5, 2001.
3. Knowledge@Wharton. "The Cow in the Ditch: How Anne Mulcahy Rescued Xerox." Interview with Anne Mulcahy, Chairman and CEO of Xerox Corp. Published online at Knowledge@Wharton Web site. November 2005.
4. O'Reilly, Brian. "The Mechanic Who Fixed Continental." *Fortune*. December 20, 1999.
5 Serwer, Andy. "Hot Starbucks to Go." *Fortune.* January 26, 2004.
6. Towers Perrin Press Release. November 15, 2005.
7. Boselovic, Len "Excuse Me, Working Here." *Pittsburgh Post-Gazette*. December 5, 2005.

CHAPTER 9

1. Goldblatt, Henry. "Forty-Two Acquisitions and Counting: Cisco's Secrets." *Fortune*. November 8, 1999.
2. Thurm, Scott. "After the Boom: A Go-Go Giant of Internet Age, Cisco is Learning to Go Slow." *Wall Street Journal*. May 7, 2003.
3. Hackett Group presentation by Pierre Mitchell at The Conference Board eProcurement Conference. April 2005.
4. Harris, Jeanne G., and Thomas H. Davenport. *New Growth from Enterprise Systems: Achieving High Performance through Distinctive Capabilities.* New York: Accenture Institute for High Performance Business, 2006.
5. Sharman, Paul. "Value Based Management." *Focus Magazine* Web site. April 2006.
6. Danaher Web site (www.danaher.com).
7. Welch, David. "GM's Game Plan." *BusinessWeek*. February 10, 2003; Taylor, Alex III. "GM Gets Its Act Together. Finally." *Fortune*. April 5, 2004.

8. McIlroy, Peter. "Inside the Box: Robroy Learns Hard Lessons in Surviving a Century of Family-Run Business." *Pittsburgh Post-Gazette*. March 22, 2005.

CHAPTER 10

1. Useem, Michael, and Jerry Useem. "Great Escapes: Nine Decision-Making Pitfalls—and Nine Simple Devices to Beat Them." *Fortune*. June 27, 2005.
2. Tam, Pui-Wing. "An Elaborate Plan Forces H-P Union to Stay on Target." *Wall Street Journal*. April 28, 2003.
3. Humowitz, Carol. "Chiefs with the Skills of a COO Gain Favor as Celebrity CEOs Fade." *Wall Street Journal*. April 5, 2005.
4. Naik, Gautam. "Vasella Drives Stodgy Novartis into a New Era." *Wall Street Journal*. October 13, 2003.
5. Arner, Faith. "No Excuse Not to Succeed." *BusinessWeek*. May 10, 2004; Symonds, William C. "A Digital Warrior for Kodak." *BusinessWeek*. May 23, 2005.
6. Symonds, William C. "Kodak's Comeback: Still Undeveloped." *BusinessWeek* Online. January 31, 2006.

CHAPTER 11

1. Schultz, Ellen E., and Theo Francis. "Executives Get Pension Security While Plans for Workers Falter." *Wall Street Journal*. April 24, 2003.
2. Center for Science in the Public Interest (CSPI) letter dated November 6, 2003, to Mr. Timothy J. Muris, chairman, Federal Trade Commission. Available online at http://cspinet.org/new/pdf/letter_to_ftc.pdf.
3. Hymowitz, Carol. "In the Lead" column. *Wall Street Journal*. January 13, 2006.
4. Thurm, Scott. "Seldom-Used Executive Power: Reconsidering." *Wall Street Journal*. February 6, 2006.
5. Staff. "CEO Parker Forgoes Bonus . . . " *Pittsburgh Post-Gazette*. March 11, 2006.

CHAPTER 12

1. de Geus, Arie. *The Living Company*. Cambridge, MA: Harvard Business School Press, 2002.

CHAPTER 13

1. The case study in Chapter 13 was the result of first-hand interviews with the leadership team of Martin Guitar, plus the results of a Beat the Odds diagnostic assessment.

CHAPTER 14

1. The case study in Chapter 14 was the result of first-hand interviews with the leadership team of LANXESS, plus the results of a Beat the Odds diagnostic assessment.

CHAPTER 15

1. The case study in Chapter 15 was the result of first-hand interviews with the leadership team of ITT Industries, plus the results of a Beat the Odds diagnostic assessment.

CHAPTER 16

1. Editor's Note preceding "Letters to the Editor" section about Home Depot. *BusinessWeek*. March 27, 2006.
2. Ibid.

INDEX

A

Abilene Paradox, 72–73
Accenture, 47, 80
Accountability, 91, 140, 148–149
"Acquiring a world view," 37–38
Acquisitions, 40, 78, 107
  Compaq strategy, 89
  spree, 111, 112
Action-oriented culture, 87–95
Action plan, 156–157. *See also* Bias for action
  bottom up (other employees), 157
  external constituents, 157
  top down (future leaders), 156
  top down (senior executives), 156
  willingness to change and, 160
Adams, Scott, 4
Adelphia, 29
Agility, 128
AI (artificial intelligence), 104
Alcatel, 140
Alcoa, 40, 83
Aligning, energizing organization, 69–76
  at C.F. Martin, 117
  checklist, 75
  companies done well at, 73, 74–75
  different approaches to, 72
  litmus test for, 72
  for organizational health, success, 71
  "symptoms," well-aligned corporation, 71
Alliances, 62–63
Allied Signal/Honeywell, 52
Alternate management agendas, 20
Alternative energy, 36
Alternative solutions, 98–99
Amazon.com, 40, 64
American Airlines, 98
Anheuser-Busch, 123
Annual performance review, 50
Antarctic expedition, 46
Apollo landing, 46
Apple Computer, 36, 37, 39–40
Araskog, Rand, 140
Artificial intelligence (AI), 104
Assessment templates, 179–213
  Assessment: Employees, 196–203
  Assessment: External Constituents: Customer Perspective, 209–213
  Assessment: External Constituents: Supplier Perspective, 204–208
  Top-Down Self-Assessment: Future Leaders, 188–195
  Top-Down Self-Assessment: Top Management, 180–187
Asset-driven approach, 128

B

Bain & Company, 4

Bakken, Earl, 22
Balanced Scorecard, 79
Balance sheet, 118, 172–173
Bankruptcy, 3, 160–161. *See also* Chapter 11 bankruptcy protection
Bargaining power, 57–58
Baseline assessment, 159
BASF, 134
Bayer, 10
Bayer Chemicals, 126–127, 128–129, 130
Bayer Group, 126
"Bell" companies, 40–41
Benchmarking, 148
Best Managed Companies in America, 139
Best practices, 148
Bethlehem Steel
  bankruptcy of, 3, 19
  cost-cutting corporate strategy, 57
  efficiency-effectiveness data, 66, 67
  Enron and, 29
  history, 18
  as premier corporation, 10
  purpose and, 20
  strategy and, 58
  vision statement, 46
Bethune, Gordon, 52–53, 73, 74
Bezos, Jeff, 40
BHAG (Big Hairy Audacious Goal), 50
Bias for action, 87–95. *See also* Action plan
  checklist, 93–94
  companies done well at, 92–93
Big-box hardware vendor, 65
Big Hairy Audacious Goal (BHAG), 50
"Big picture" information, 45
"Black belts," 141
"Blockers of progress," 70
"Blue-skying," 36
Boak, Dick, 116
Boardroom, 29–30
Bonuses, 93, 131–132
Bossidy, Larry, 52
Boston University, 113
BP (British Petroleum), 36, 37, 39–40
Brand, 28–29
  extensions, 60
  identity, 144
"Breakout sessions," 160
Breakthrough change, 50
Breen, Edward D., 32, 70
Bright Horizons Family Solutions, 64
British Petroleum (BP), 36, 37, 39–40
Broadband market, 41
Built to Last (Collins and Porras), 9, 50
Bush, George Herbert, 139
Business development group, 36
Business-intelligence "dashboards," 80
Business model. *See also* Principle 5
  checklist, 65–66
  companies done well at, 63–65
  description of, 60
  discrete, 67
  life cycle of, 60
  shift, 167–169
  strategy and, 63
Business process innovation, 66, 67–68
BusinessWeek, 40, 160
Buyout master, 140

C

Cable TV, 39–40
Call center, 100
Capital Cities/ABC, 20
Capital projects, 170–172
Captive mind-set, 37, 42
Carnegie, Andrew, 75
Carnegie Mellon University, 38
Carp, Daniel, 93
Case study exercises. *See* Reader exercises
Cash management, 129
Categories of objectives, 80
Center for Creative Leadership, 120

Center for Science in the Public Interest (CSPI), 98
CEO. *See* Chief executive officer
C.F. Martin & Co. *See* Martin Guitar
CFO (chief financial officer), 172
"Chainsaw Al," 48–49, 59
Change
  creating, 49
  receptiveness to, 50
  resistance to, 70, 169
  willingness to, 160
Channel management, 121
Chapter 11 bankruptcy protection. *See also* Bankruptcy
  at Bethlehem Steel, 19, 57
  at Kmart, 48
Charan, Ram, 52
"Chart wars," 44, 88
Chemicals industry. *See* LANXESS Corporation
Chemical Week, 133
Chief Executive, 38
Chief executive officer (CEO)
  credibility, 169–170
  leader selection by, 51
  leadership and, 46–47
  purpose and, 23, 25
Chief financial officer (CFO), 172
Chief learning officer (CLO), 47
Chief operating officer (COO), 23, 25
Chief procurement officer (CPO), 51
China, 36–37, 134, 135
Chrysler Corporation, 63, 70
Ciba-Geigy, 93
Cisco Systems, 78
Clean technologies, 36
Clinton, Bill, 139
CLO (chief learning officer), 47
Collins, Jim, 50
Comcast, 39–41
Command and control, 160
Common sense, 97–101
  checklist, 100–101
  companies done well at, 99–100
Communication
  formal, 130
  internal, 130
  of results, Principles 1 to 5, 70–71
  structured feedback, 11
  of vision, 44–45
  weekly status report, 93
Compaq, 89
Compensation
  executive, 32
  packages, 93
  structure, 132
Competencies, 61–63. *See also* Principle 5
  checklist, 65–66
  companies done well at, 63–65
  key, at Respironics, 24
  leveraging available, 64
Competing for the Future (Prahalad), 50
Competitive advantage, 37
Competitors
  competencies and, 61
  game-changing behavior of, 172
  in-industry, 58
  inward emphasis by, 37
  more nimble, 174–176
  nontraditional, 18–19, 40, 149
"Confident, executive image," 100
Confronting Reality (Bossidy & Charan), 52
Conglomerates, 112, 126, 140
Consumer, 20
Consumer broadband market, 41
Consumer-electronics, 38–39
"Content-based purpose," 138
Continental Airlines, 52–53, 73, 74
Conventional approach, 37, 38
COO (chief operating officer), 23, 25
Cooperative problem solving, 113
Core business processes, 81
Core initiatives, 78
Core leadership traits, 45
Core practices, Respironics, 24

Core purpose, 21
Core values, 27–33
authenticity of, 33
companies done well at, 31–32
description of, 28
drafting, 33
questions about, 32
typical, 28
"Corporate anorexia," 78
Corporate audit, 32
Corporate competency, 61–63
Corporate culture
action-oriented, 89
avoiding debate, 88
at C.F. Martin, 121, 122
encouraging debate, 99
"hidden values," 30–31
at LANXESS Corp., 135
measurements and, 83
reinvigorating itself, 90
superficially "polite," 88
Corporate direction. *See* Vision
Corporate embarrassments, 20
Corporate ombudsman, 32
Corporate reorganization. *See* Restructuring
Corporate scandals, 101
Corporate social responsibility (CSR), 19
Corporate strategy. *See* Strategy
Corporate-wide initiative, 78
Cost
control, 37, 129
-cutting, 37, 59, 65, 135
employee as, 28
internal, 37
low-cost regions, 147
reduction, corporate strategy, 57
CPO (chief procurement officer), 51
Cross-company engineering, 150
Cross-company mandate, 147
Cross-functional mandate, 147
Cross-purposes, working at, 174
Cross-training, 120, 121
Crum, Scott, 138, 139, 145
CSPI (Center for Science in the Public Interest), 98
CSR (corporate social responsibility), 19
Culture. *See* Corporate culture
Current reality, 38–39
Customer
alienation of, 75
bargaining power of, 58
negative feedback, 160
priorities, 38, 61
relationship continuum, 29
satisfaction, 79
target customer, 59
template for assessment, 209–213
"touch-point chain," 29

D

Daimler, 70
DaimlerChrysler, 70
Danaher, 81, 146
Danaher Business System (DBS), 81, 82
Data-driven decision-making, 80
DBS (Danaher Business System), 81, 82
Dearth, Randy, 44, 56, 126, 129, 130, 132, 136
Decision making. *See also* Bias for action
changing prior decision, 100
crisp, disciplined, 88–89
slow, 175
two different approaches, 99
Defense sector, 140, 142
de Geus, Arie, 103–104
Dell, 60
Diagnosis templates. *See* Assessment templates
Diagnostic process, 33
Digital broadband service, 41
Digital photography, 42, 88
Digital products and services, 65

Dilbert comic strip, 4, 45
Disaster assistance, 131, 139
Discrete business model, 67
Disney. *See* Walt Disney Co., The
Disruptive innovations, 67
Dot-com bubble, 58
Downsizing, 78. *See also* Restructuring
Drucker, Peter F., 4, 37
Duke University, 54
Dunlap, Al, 48–49, 59

E

Early adopters of change, 50
Earnings before interest, tax, and deductions (EBITDA), 128, 129, 133, 135
Earnings per share (EPS), 80, 81
Eastman Kodak, 42, 88, 93
EBITDA (earnings before interest, tax, and deductions), 128, 129, 133, 135
e-business, 40
Eco-initiatives, 37
"Ecomagination," 36
Economic trends, 175
Effectiveness, 67, 78
Efficiency, 67, 78–79
Eisner, Michael, 20–21
Emerson Electric, 64–65
Employee. *See also* Compensation; Head count reduction
- benefits, 136
- dissatisfied, 75, 79
- diversity and inclusion, 145
- feedback, 74, 157
- "retiring," 164-165
- roles and responsibilities, 91, 103–104
- staffing, 78
- template for assessment, 196–203
- untapped performance potential, 76

"Enablers," 71
End user, 20
Energizing. *See* Aligning, energizing organization
Engen, Travis, 140
"Engineered for life" tagline, 144
Engineering and manufacturing company, 138
Enron, 29, 31
Enterprise resource planning (ERP), 120–121
Entrepreneurs, 36
Environment, 36
EPS (earnings per share), 80, 81
ERP (enterprise resource planning), 120–121
ESL Investments, Inc., 48
Ethical conduct, 32, 164–165
Evangelize about vision, 44
Executive
- compensation, 32, 100
- recruiters, 46–47

Executive management. *See* Senior management
Exercise center, 136
"Exit interviews," 157
External constituents, 44, 157
External facilitator, 160
External factor, 42
External focus, 41
External market, 111

F

Family legacy, 113
Family-run firms, 109, 123
"Fast-food" business, 75
Federal prosecution, 31
FedEx, 60
Film-based photography, 93
Financial management, 133
Financial statement, 161
Fiorina, Carly, 89–90
"Firefighters," 90
"Five Forces" framework, 57–58

Fluid technology company. *See* ITT Corporation
Forbes, 139, 149
Ford, William, 57
Ford Motor Company
  strategy, 57
  vision statement, 46
For-profit organizations, 76
Fortune, 5, 74, 78, 149
Fortune 500, 5, 10, 47, 51, 164–165
Foundation principles, 103, 104. *See also* Nine principles; Principle
Franchise, 20, 64, 74
Frankfurt Stock Exchange, 128
Fresh thinking, 42
FTE (full-time equivalent), 66
Full-time equivalent (FTE), 66
Functional excellence, 144
Functional "silo," 165
Future, creation of, 35–42

G

Gap analysis, 155, 160
Gates, Bill, 60
GE. *See* General Electric
Geneen, Harold, 140
General Electric (GE)
  chairman, 36–37
  customer satisfaction, 79
  future, creation of own, 39–40
  shareholder returns, 139
  strategy and, 63
  vision statement, 46
General Motors (GM), 3, 83
George Washington University, 72
Gerber, 22
Giuliano, Lou, 140–141, 145
Global businesses, 38, 173–174
Global workforce strategy, 146
GM (General Motors), 3, 83
Goodyear, 58–59
Governance chief, 32
Grasso, Dick, 98
Great Depression, 112
Guitars. *See* Martin Guitar
Gym, 136

H

Hackett Group, 78
Harvey, Dr. Jerry, 72
Head count reductions, 66, 78, 172–173
Head of corporate audit, 32
Healthy organization, 105, 155–161, 177
Heitman, Dr. Axel C., 127–128, 129, 134
Hewlett-Packard (HP), 19–20, 89–90
"Hidden values," 30
Hill, Nick, 148
High-tech bubble, 78
Home Depot, 160
Honeywell, 52
HP (Hewlett-Packard), 19–20, 89–90
"Hub-and-spoke" system design, 53
Humanitarian assistance, 131
Human resource department, 54, 120. *See also* Employee

I

IBM, 65
Iger, Bob, 21
Imagineering unit, Disney, 35–36
Immelt, Jeff, 36–37
Improvements, 83
Incentive system, 32, 131–132
India, 134
Individual. *See* Employee; Senior management
Industrial engineers, 113
Industrial manufacturer. *See* ITT Corporation
Industry trends, 175
Innovation. *See also* Reinvention
  corporate strategy and, 67
  cost-cutting and, 66
  at LANXESS Corp., 133–134
  reluctance to adopt, 88
In Search of Excellence, 9

Inspiring vision. *See also* Principle 4; Vision
 articulating, 45–47, 51
 checklist, 53
 failing to articulate, 44
Internal complexity, 94
Internal costs, 37
Internal facilitator, 160
International Steel Group, 42
Internet, 40, 60
"Intrapreneurs," 36
Inventory management, 118
iPod handhelds, 36
ITT Corporation, 137–151
 acquisitions, 140, 142
 "Best Managed" citation, 149
 Defense Electronics and Services, 142, 143
 divestitures, 142
 "flight manual" at, 148–149
 Fluid Technology, 142, 143, 150
 future plans, 150–151
 improvement priorities, 145
 ITT management system (IMS), 141–142, 146
 leadership, emphasis on, 145–148
 look inside of, 142–144
 "Most Admired" ranking, 149
 Motion & Flow Control, 143
 outsiders looking at, 149–150
 products and services, 138, 139
 push to "premier," 144–145
 strategy and, 63
 strength areas, pyramid, 149
 three-way split of company, 140
 value-based management at, 81

J
J&J (Johnson & Johnson), 31, 99–100
Japan, 121
Jobs, Steve, 21
Johnson & Johnson (J&J), 31, 99–100
Joint ventures, 62–63

K
Katzenberg, Jeffrey, 20
Kennedy, President John F., 46
Key competencies, Respironics, 24
KFC, 98
"Killer re's," 92
Kmart, 48
Knowledge base, 122
Kodak, 42, 88, 93
Kouzes, James M., 49
Kozlowski, Dennis, 31–32
Kraft Foods, 60
Krzyzewski, Mike, 54

L
Labor union, 37, 111
Lafley, A. G., 38, 98
Lagging indicators, 79, 81, 161
Lambert, Edward S., 48
LANXESS Corporation, 44, 125–136
 Beat the Odds insights, 132
 brand-new business, 126–127
 CEO of, 56
 clear structures at, 131
 corporate culture, 135
 CPO of, 125
 fast decision making, 127–129
 future plans, 134–136
 getting down to business, 129–139
 global presence, 128, 129
 incentives, 131–132
 "management by walking around," 44
 metrics, focused, 132
 "NewCo" spin-off, 127–128
 progress to date, 132–134
 responsibilities, defined, 131
 value redefined at, 130–132, 134
LANXESS Foundation, The, 131
Leaders, 148–149
Leadership
 "bullying" style of, 49
 change and, 49

development model, 146
feedback on behavior, 50
five key practices, 49
future leaders, 156, 188–195
at ITT Corporation, 145–148
management and, 47, 48
not just for CEOs, 46–47
poor performers, 53
traits, 45
up-and-coming leaders, 132
Leadership Challenge, The (Kouzes and Posner), 49
Leading indicators, 79, 81
Leading with the Heart (Krzyzewski), 54
"Leakage," 107
Lean manufacturing, 68
Lean production, 147
Legacy constraints, 36, 57
Levi Strauss, 123
"Little black books," 109, 110
Living Company, The (de Geus), 103
Living entity analogy, 103–105
L.L. Bean, 100
Lombardi, Keith, 115, 117, 118, 119, 120, 121
Long-term health of corporation, 155–161
Long view, 99
Loranger, Steve, 137–140, 141–142, 146–147, 148–149
Lost business, 61
Low-cost regions, 147
Lowe's, 22, 60
LTV Steel, 42
Lunar landing, 46

M

Management. *See also* Senior management
actions aligned with words, 45
alternate agendas of, 20
consultants, 113
controls, 113
discipline, legacy of, 140–142
"high potential" managers, 120
integrity of, 164–165
labor unions and, 37
leadership and, 47, 48
"Management by walking around," 44
"Management system," 81, 107
Management tool kit. *See* ITT Corporation
Manufacturing
operations, 114
work processes, 113
Maquiladora, 118
Marketing tool, 77
Market intelligence, 39
Marketplace strategy, Amazon.com, 40
"Market positioning," 57
Market share, 119, 122
Martin, C. F. III, 112, 113
Martin, C. F. Jr., 111–112
Martin, Christian ("Chris") IV, 111, 113–115, 117–118, 120
Martin, Christian Frederick, 111
Martin, Frank Henry, 112
Martin, Frank Herbert, 111, 112–113
Martin Guitar, 109–123
acquisition run, 111, 112
core values at, 115, 122
corporate culture, 121, 122
dancehall disco effects on, 111
"Dreadnought" model, 112
famous Martin owners, 109, 116
financial measures, 119–120
focus on premium guitars, 113
future plans, 121–123
improvements, acceleration of, 118–119
leadership at, 117, 120, 122
"limited edition" guitars, 114, 115–116
management processes at, 110
operations management, 120–121
organization structure, 121

product range expansion, 114
progress to date, 119–121
strength areas, pyramid, 119
workforce management, 120
X-bracing system, 112
Martin, Thomas, 144, 148
Materials management, 118
MBA case studies, 64–65
McCormick, Christopher, 100
McIlroy, Peter, 83–84
Measurement, 77–85
"business level," 81
checklist, 84
companies done well at, 82–84
"diagnostic," 81
focus and, 78
lagging indicators, 79
leading indicators, 79
of performance, 71
"process level," 81
Medtronic, 22–23
Mentoring program, 132
Mercer Management Consulting, 29
Mercer Management Journal, 29
Merck, 21–22
Merger
hi-tech, 89
Kmart/Sears, 48
opportunities, 36
Metrics. *See also* Measurements
financial, 81
hierarchy of, 80
"super," 84
Mexican production facility, 118, 121
Micromanagement, 20
Microsoft Corporation, 60
Military defense, 140, 142
Minnich, George, 147, 150
Mission, not-for-profits, 76
Momentum
building, 92, 150
loss of, 174
"Most Admired Companies," 5, 149
Mulcahy, Anne, 57, 65, 73
Multi-industry companies, 144
Musical instruments. *See* Martin Guitar
Music Trades, 119

N

Negative surprises, 37
Nelson, Willie, 116
Net-promoter scores, 79
Networking, 62–63
New business processes, 66, 67
"New economy," 40
New England Journal of Medicine, 22
New-market strategies, 37
New product design, 36, 37, 60, 66
New York Stock Exchange (NYSE), 98, 107
Nine principles. *See also* Principle; Reader exercises
breakdown within each of, 5–6
framework for, 12–14, 157
introduction to, 11–12
living organisms and, 105
not to be cherry-picked, 157
pyramid of, 14, 164
Noncore operations, 133
Nontraditional competitors, 18–19, 40, 149
Nontraditional strategies, projects, 172
Not-for-profit organizations, 76
Novartis AG, 93
NYSE (New York Stock Exchange), 98, 107

O

Objectives
categories of, 80
narrow focus on, 173
purpose and, 19
Office lottery pools, 82
O'Neill, Tom, 125–126, 130, 131
Online mall, 40
Online research services, 159

Operational excellence, 92, 147–148
Operations excellence chief, 151
Opportunity
  China and, 37
  seizing, 38
Organization
  chart, 74
  complexity of, 94, 174
  design, 74
  implications for, 103–105
  as living entity, 103–105
Organizational culture. *See* Corporate culture
Organizational success, 14
Outsourcing
  materials and parts, 147
  services, 126
  tactical work elements, 62
Outward Bound course, 115
Ovitz, Michael, 20
Ownership, 135

P

Packard, David, 19–20
Palo Alto Research Center (PARC), 67
P&L responsibility, 174
"Paralysis by analysis," 88
PARC (Palo Alto Research Center), 67
Parker, W. Douglas, 100
Pella, 60
Pensions and health care, 57
Perez, Antonio, 93
Performance measurement. *See* Measurement
Performance problems, 74
Performance-related bonuses, 93
Petronius Arbiter, 87–88
PFE (Program for Executives), 38–39
Pharmaceutical industry, 93
Phone companies, 40–41
Photocopying technology, 48
Pittsburgh Post-Gazette, 134
Pixar Studios, 21
Planning cycles, 118, 120
Point of sale, 28
Polymers. *See* LANXESS Corporation
Porras, Jerry I., 50
Porter, Michael, 57
Posner, Barry Z., 49
Prahalad, C.K., 50
"Price before volume" strategy, 135
Principle. *See also* Foundation principles
  1, 17–25
  2, 27–33
  3, 35–42
  4, 43–54
  5, 55–68
  6, 69–76
  7, 77–85
  8, 87–95
  9, 97–101
Print advertising campaign, 121
Processes, repeatable, 92
Procter & Gamble, 22, 38, 99
Procurement
  components of, 62
  head count targets, 66
Product
  complexity, 118
  families, 121
  innovations, 67
  line, 129, 167
  strategy, 167–169
Production
  cycle time, 122
  workflow, 113
Productivity improvement, 83
Product quality levels, 114
Profiles of success. *See* Success profiles
Profit-sharing plan, 100, 115
Program for Executives (PFE), 38–39
"Program offices," 67
"Project workplan" tool, 90, 91–92
Public confidence, 29
Pumps. *See* ITT Corporation

Purpose. *See also* Principle 1
companies done well at, 21–23
core purpose, 21
defined, 19
must never change, 20
purpose of, 138
Pyramid of principles, 14, 164

Q

Quality levels, 114
Quotes
on alignment, 225–226
on bias for action, 226–227
on business model, 224–225
on common sense, 228–229
on competencies, 224–225
on core values, 217–218
on creating the future, 219–221
on energizing, 225–226
on inspiring vision, 222–224
on leadership, 222–224
on measurement, 226
on purpose, 215–216
on strategy, 224–225

R

R&D department, 36
Radio-frequency identification (RFID), 120
Reader exercises, 163–176
12-minute drill, 174–176
asking the right question, 172–173
becoming global the wrong way, 173–174
can you win if you're predictable?, 170–172
damn the market, full speed ahead, 167–169
do as I say, not as I do, 169–170
ethics—upholding the basics, 164–165
simulations vs. real world, 165–167
Recognition systems, 71
Recommended approach, 37, 38
Reengineering team, 27
Reinvention, 144–145
Relative roles, 104
Reorganization. *See* Restructuring
Repeatable processes, 92
Repeat business, 61
"Resource allocation," 57
Respironics, 23, 24
Restructuring, 38, 87. *See also* Downsizing
at LANXESS Corp., 129, 133, 135
root problem and, 74
of sales force, 73
Retailers, 48
Retiree pensions, 57, 98
Return on invested capital (ROIC), 79, 80, 81, 148
Return on investment (ROI), 171
Reward systems, 71
Risk management, 94, 135
Robroy Industries, 83–84
ROI (return on investment), 171
ROIC (return on invested capital), 79, 80, 81, 148
Roles and responsibilities, 91, 103–104
Root-cause analysis, 95
Root problem
measurements and, 85
performance problems and, 74
Ross, Wilbur, 42
Royal Dutch/Shell, 3, 57, 103

S

Safety, improvement, 83
Sales force restructuring, 73
Samsung, 38–39
Sarbanes-Oxley, 31
Scenario planning, 150
"Scenarios," 57
Schultz, Howard, 74
Sears, 48
Self-awareness, 122, 137

Self-critical nature, 149–150
Self-sustaining organizations, 38
Selloff, product line, 129
Senior education officer, 47
Senior management. *See also* Management
  360-degree feedback, 50, 51, 53–54, 79
  action plan, 156
  confidence in ability of, 76
  core values and, 28, 33
  ethics, 164–165
  firefights and, 90
  fresh talent, 172
  new business processes and, 67
  passing the mantle, 161
  retreat, LANXESS Corp., 130
  role, foundation principles, 103, 104
  slow to make decisions, 174–176
  template, self assessment, 180–187
  vision and, 44
Services platform, 65
"70 percent solution," 87–88
Severance package, 20
Shackleton, Sir Ernest, 46
Shareholders, 100
Sherman, Len, 47
Short-term pressures, 20
Siemens, 52
"Silo," 165
Simulations, 165–167
Six Sigma, 52, 68, 147. *See also* Value-based Six Sigma
"Skip-level interviews," 54
Social responsibility, 19
Societal needs
  corporate purpose and, 18, 19
  growth and, 25
Sony, vision statement, 46
Sourcing, 147
South Korea, 38
Southwest Airlines, 31, 77
Spin-off, 126, 127
Starbucks Coffee, 74–75
Stockholder value
  business model and, 60
  purpose and, 19, 20
  value-based management and, 81
Stock options, 74, 93
Stock price, 32, 133
Strategic competencies, 61–63
Strategic objectives, 81, 172
Strategic sourcing, 67–68
Strategic vision. *See* Vision
Strategy. *See also* Principle 5
  another dimension to, 59
  business model and, 63
  checklist, 65–66
  companies done well at, 63–65
  cost reduction as, 57
  development, 56, 57–58, 60
  innovation and, 66–67
  one-year plan, 113
  organizational capabilities and, 56
  "price before volume," 135
  tactical elements and, 56
  top-line growth, 57
"Strategy du jour," 46
Strengths, weaknesses, opportunities, and threats (SWOT) analysis, 57
Structured feedback, 121
Succession planning, 50, 121, 122
Success profiles, 107. *See also* ITT Corporation; LANXESS Corporation; Martin Guitar
Sunbeam, 48–49, 59
"Super metrics," 84
Supplier
  bargaining power of, 58
  end users and, 20
  strategy, 59
Supply chain metrics, 79
Survey, 157–159
  advice for conducting, 159
  introduction of, 158, 159
  for major constituencies, 157–158
SWOT analysis (strengths, weaknesses, opportunities, and threats), 57

T

Tactical activities, 66
Tactical competencies, 61–63
Tactical objectives, 172
"Take This Job, Please (TTJP)" index, 82
Target, 48
Target customers, 59
Taylor, Frederick Winslow, 79
Telecommunications products business, 140
Templates. *See* Assessment templates
Tenges, Dennis, 116
Thatcher, Margaret, 99
Theory X management style, 112–113
Theory Y collaborative management style, 113
"Think time," 63
"Think week," 60
Thoman, G. Richard, 73
Threat
  China and, 37
  of new entrants, 57–58
  of substitute products/services, 58
360-degree feedback, 50, 51, 53–54, 79, 166, 170
T-Mobile USA, 100
Top management. *See* Senior management
Total Quality movement, 79
Towers Perrin, 76
"Town hall" meetings, 130, 132
Transactional activities, 66
Trends, 175
Troubled company, 169–170
Trust, 28–29, 54
TTJP ("Take This Job, Please") index, 82
Tyco International, 31–32, 70
Tylenol tampering, 99–100

U

United Steelworkers of America, 42
University of Chicago, 118
USAID, 139
U.S. Airways, 100
U.S. economy, 135
User groups, 121
U.S. Marine Corps, 87
U.S. steel industry, 42
Utility company, 30

V

Value-based goal deployment (VBGD), 148
Value-based leadership development (VBLD), 146–147
Value-based management (VBM), 81, 140, 144, 148
Value-based Six Sigma (VBSS), 140–141. *See also* Six Sigma
"Value centers," 142
"Value investing," 58
Value system
  internal culture and, 30
  at LANXESS Corp., 130–132, 134
Vasella, Dr. Dan, 93
VBGD (value-based goal deployment), 148
VBLD (value-based leadership development), 146–147
VBM (Value-based management), 81, 140, 144, 148
VBSS (Value-based Six Sigma), 140–141. *See also* Six Sigma
Violin Makers Guild, 111
Vioxx, 22
Vision. *See also* Inspiring vision; Principle 4
  articulating, 45, 48, 50, 51
  channels for, variety of, 45
  communication of, 44–45
  companies done well at, 52–53
  enthusiasm for, 44
  examples, 24, 46
"Visioning," 36
von Pierer, Heinrich, 52

W

Waggoner, Richard, 83
Wall Street, 48, 150. *See also* Stockholder value
Wall Street Journal, 89, 90
Wal-Mart, 48
Walt Disney Co., The, 20–21, 35–36
Waste, 78
Web site
  for this book, 178
  core values and, 29
  Greybeard Advisors, 178
  vision and, 44–45
Weekly status report, 92
Welch, Jack, 52
Wells, Frank, 20
Wharton School, The, 58
"Whistle-blower" hot lines, 32
"Whiteboarding," 36
Williamson, John, 150, 151
Worker-management animosity, 116–117
Workforce alignment, 45
Workforce strategy, 146
Workplan, 90, 91–92
World-class companies
  efficiency and, 78
  measurements and, 83
  "program offices" at, 67
WorldCom, 29, 31, 140
World War II, 112
Worldwide market share, 119

X

Xerox Corporation, 48, 57, 65, 67, 73
Xpress internal magazine, 130

Y

Yun, Jong-Yong, 39

Z

Zetsche, Dieter, 70
Zildjian, 123